Great Men in
the Second World War

Great Men in the Second World War

The Rise and Fall of the Big Three

Paul Dukes

Bloomsbury Academic
An imprint of Bloomsbury Publishing Plc

B L O O M S B U R Y
LONDON · OXFORD · NEW YORK · NEW DELHI · SYDNEY

Bloomsbury Academic

An imprint of Bloomsbury Publishing Plc

50 Bedford Square	1385 Broadway
London	New York
WC1B 3DP	NY 10018
UK	USA

www.bloomsbury.com

BLOOMSBURY and the Diana logo are trademarks of Bloomsbury Publishing Plc

First published 2017

© Paul Dukes, 2017

Paul Dukes has asserted his right under the Copyright, Designs and Patents Act, 1988, to be identified as Author of this work.

British Library Cataloguing-in-Publication Data
A catalogue record for this book is available from the British Library.

ISBNs:	HB:	978-1-4742-6808-0
	ePDF:	978-1-4742-6810-3
	eBook:	978-1-4742-6809-7

Library of Congress Cataloging-in-Publication Data
Names: Dukes, Paul, 1934- author.
Title: "Great men" in the Second World War : the rise and fall of the big three / Paul Dukes.
Description: London : Bloomsbury Academic, 2017.
Identifiers: LCCN 2016046315 | ISBN 9781474268080 (hardback) | ISBN 9781474268097 (epub)
Subjects: LCSH: World War, 1939-1945–Diplomatic history. | Churchill, Winston, 1874-1965. | Roosevelt, Franklin D. (Franklin Delano), 1882-1945. | Stalin, Joseph, 1878-1953. | Truman, Harry S., 1884-1972. | Attlee, C. R. (Clement Richard), 1883-1967. | BISAC: HISTORY / Military / World War II. | HISTORY / Modern / 20th Century.
Classification: LCC D748 .D84 2017 | DDC 940.53/320922–dc23
LC record available at https://lccn.loc.gov/2016046315

Cover Images: © (top) Paul Popper/Popperfoto/Getty Images, (middle) Mondadori Portfolio/ Getty Images, (bottom) Keystone-France/Gamma-Keystone/Getty Images

Typeset by Integra Software Services Pvt. Ltd.
Printed and bound in Great Britain

To find out more about our authors and books visit www.bloomsbury.com.
Here you will find extracts, author interviews, details of forthcoming events and the option to sign up for our newsletters.

To Joseph, Ike, Francesca and Samuel

Contents

Preface

In 2014, on the title page of *The History Manifesto* (published by Cambridge University Press and available online), Jo Guldi and David Armitage announced 'a call to arms to historians' in which they posed the question: 'Why is history – especially long-term history – so essential to understanding the multiple pasts which give rise to our conflicted present?' As part of their answer, they made more than thirty references to the long-term approach known as the *longue durée*, described in 1946 by Fernand Braudel but much evolved since. In their estimation (p. 90):

> The new *longue durée* has emerged within a very different ecosystem of intellectual alternatives. It possesses a dynamism and flexibility earlier versions did not have. It has a new relationship to the abounding sources of big data available in our time.... As a result of this increased reserve of evidence, the new *longue durée* also has greater critical potential.

Here is an aspiration that is stimulating indeed, if difficult to realize.

In its original sense, I myself adopted the Braudelian approach in *The Last Great Game: USA versus USSR: Events, Conjunctures, Structures* (reprinted by Bloomsbury in 2016). Now, bearing *The History Manifesto* of Guldi and Armitage in mind, I attempt to adopt at least some of their updated *longue durée* while recognizing that much of it, including big data, is not easily applied to the focus of my attention, the role of the individual in history.

Firmly believing that, while all individuals are unique, they can be understood only in comparison with others, I have chosen for this present study not one but five individuals, each in his turn one of the leaders of the three great victorious powers in the Second World War. The identity of the Big Three changed significantly during the last months of the conflict. Roosevelt died in April 1945 and was succeeded by Truman. Churchill lost to Attlee in the election of July. Stalin alone provided individual continuity throughout the conferences of the Big Three, and immediately beyond. These changes added a further dimension to the discussion at the Potsdam Conference in particular, when continued use of the term 'Big Three' became somewhat problematic. Soon afterwards, the use of the atomic bomb at Hiroshima and Nagasaki began to dwarf mankind but gave an awesome responsibility to some individuals, particularly Truman.

It is unlikely that any of the successive members of the Big Three would have agreed with Braudel's reduction of the significance of the individual in the broad sweep of the *longue durée*, for their outlooks were all formed in the late nineteenth century when the terms 'Great Men' and 'Great Powers' were in general use – see Wikipedia for helpful working definitions. Both terms have been applied to the Big Three in the Second World War; indeed, the people and the places often appear synonymous, with the consequence of a certain ambiguity. Hence, the questions arise, to what extent did the leaders exert their own influence, and to what extent could they be considered to be simply the spokesmen for their countries? How significant was it that Truman and Attlee had less colourful personalities than Roosevelt and Churchill? Further questions concern their morality and their responsibility: should they be judged by historians as good or bad, not guilty or guilty, with Stalin alone falling into the second category?

The formation of the Big Three stemmed from the necessity to sink their differences in order to win the Second World War. Their break-up began with two major developments: the emergence of irreconcilable differences between the United States and the UK on the one hand and the USSR on the other with the onset of the Cold War; and the confirmation of the comparative weakness of the UK at the beginning of the end of empire. From the start of this dual process, then, the three great powers were being replaced by two superpowers (or, to be more accurate, one superpower, the United States, with the other future superpower, the Soviet Union, way behind). The book ends with a general discussion of the role of great men in the Second World War.

We shall examine the part played by individuals in the rise and fall of the Big Three largely through the records of their conferences at Tehran, Yalta (Crimea) and Potsdam (Berlin) with some subsidiary attention to descriptions of other meetings. These records have many biases and omissions, no doubt, but are the best we have. In order to promote objectivity, the Soviet, American and British accounts are taken in turn as the points of departure for discussion of the Tehran, Yalta and Potsdam conferences, respectively, significant disagreements between the three accounts being noted where they occur. In pursuance of the main aim, nearly all the references in the chapters dealing with the three conferences, two to six, are taken from the records and other contemporary sources. I have tried to take a fresh look at these texts, to describe and comment on what three men said to each other in a series of meetings towards the end of the Second World War, especially when they were all together but also when there were just two of them. In this manner, I hope to catch many of the nuances in the relationship bringing the global conflict to an end, never forgetting that millions of men and women were involved in it in an active or passive manner. Recognizing that objectivity is elusive, that my direct observation may well be different to yours, I nevertheless hope to throw at least some light on the role of Great Men as representatives of Great Powers, and to illustrate the manner in which the men and the powers are sometimes difficult to distinguish. Since many of the relevant documents are readily available with an increasing number online, you may judge the accuracy of my version or indeed produce your own alternative.

An insistent word on what the book is not. It does not pretend to be a potted history of the Second World War, omitting for the most part subjects which received little or no mention in the conversations of the Big Three. However, a certain amount of commentary is provided, normally at the beginning or the end of the chapters in order to provide some context for the Great Men's relationship, always bearing in mind Braudel's low estimate of the importance of the role of the individual.

Of the great men as individuals, Roosevelt and Stalin left no memoirs, and Attlee's are laconic to an extreme degree. Truman's are fairly full, but Churchill wrote by far the most: as he himself joked, he attempted to capture history by writing it – we must be careful not to let him succeed. To take a major example, towards the end of his influential six-volume work on the Second World War, there is little about the later stages of the Potsdam Conference, although they were of considerable significance for the outcome of the global conflict, especially in Asia and the Pacific, to which Churchill gave minor attention in general. He himself wrote: 'The closing scenes of the war against Japan took place after I left office, and I record them only briefly' (Volume 6, p. 558). Because events in Asia and the Pacific are less familiar but at least as momentous as those in Europe and the Atlantic, I give them more attention towards the end of the book, always remembering that this was indeed a *world* war.

While my primary aim has been to get back to the texts, I have made some use of the Big Three's own writings, as well as memoirs and diaries written by their associates, and the rich historiography on the subject, especially in the languages spoken by the Big Three, English and Russian. There has been a vast amount of description and analysis of the negotiations of the Big Three, much of it of high quality. Of the works listed in the Select Bibliography, those by Edmonds, Feis and Fenby (coincidentally together) consider this theme most closely, but their approach differs from mine in at least two ways: they say more about the rise than the fall of the Big Three; and they discuss the role of individuals in general less than their embodiment in the Big Three. I have added some brief remarks on Further Study. Footnotes are given, but more as the obligation of the author than as a necessity for the reader.

More than forty years of teaching has made me increasingly aware of 'generation parallax', the apparent difference in the significance of a historical period when viewed from a different chronological angle. Born fifteen years or so after the conclusion of the First World War, I have always found it remote. My own point of view has been formed to a considerable extent by my experience of the Second World War and after. Some of my early years were spent on the periphery of the London Blitz. I saw Churchill in the Victory Parade in London in 1945, saw and heard Attlee at a dinner in Cambridge in 1951, saw and heard Truman at the tenth anniversary of the United Nations in San Francisco (where I nearly literally bumped into Stalin's right-hand man Molotov) in 1955. While you yourselves can see and hear all of them, including Roosevelt and Stalin, on YouTube (if a picture is, as is often said, worth a thousand words, how many words is a moving, talking picture worth?), I am bound to recognize how unfamiliar some of the topics considered in the book must be to people born several decades after it came to an end, even if the Second World War as a whole maintains widespread interest. I have therefore put some explanatory information in square brackets while recommending Wikipedia (which, used with care, is a most useful aid) as a supplement. Generations following the Second World War became involved with mine in the Cold War, strong echoes of which may still be detected today. But the greatest problem facing recent generations is ecological, not how to win a world war but how to save the planet. Therefore, we all need to bear in mind the historic present as we contemplate the past.

While absolving all of the following relatives, friends and colleagues from any responsibility for the finished product, I am grateful to those who have read and commented on earlier drafts in full or in part: Cathryn, Daniel, Ruth and Bernard Dukes from family; Michael Dey, Murray Frame, John Kent and Geoffrey Roberts among friends. I owe a particular debt to the members of an informal Far East discussion group: Wang Li, Yamazaki Mikine and Kim Seung Young, and, as ever, derive great benefit as well as pleasure from my association with members of the History Department and other colleagues at the University of Aberdeen. Acknowledgement for sympathetic efficiency is due to associates of Bloomsbury and for informed advice to a series of anonymous reviewers. Most of all, I thank my wife Cathryn, as before, for many readings, much discussion and constant support.

Paul Dukes

King's College, Old Aberdeen, 30 September 2016

Introduction: Great Men and Great Powers

Introduction

Many people are familiar with Lord Acton's dictum: 'Power tends to corrupt and absolute power corrupts absolutely.' However, rather fewer are acquainted with what comes before and after. Acton precedes his famous pronouncement with another: 'Historic responsibility has to make up for the want of legal responsibility.' Similarly, Geoffrey Roberts has observed of one notorious individual:

> History can be a kind of court. The prosecution wants us to condemn Stalin outright for his crimes or his inadequate leadership. But as jurors it is our duty to review all the evidence, including that for the defence, and to see the whole picture. This may not make it easy to arrive at a verdict but it will enhance our historical understanding and equip us with the knowledge that could enable us to do better in the future. History *can* make us wiser, if we allow it to.

Acton was more comprehensive in his condemnation, supplementing his dictum thus: 'Great men are nearly always bad men.'[1] For the most part, the great men to be discussed in this book are not thought of as bad men. There is indeed one outstanding exception, J. V. Stalin, whom few would want to defend as good in view of the part that he played in the deaths of millions of Soviet citizens in the 1920s and 1930s. He has also been widely blamed for the disastrous manner in which the Soviet Union was attacked in 1941, ignoring all words of warning, and for the size of the losses sustained by the USSR during the war, owing to his further errors. Other members of the Big Three too have had ups and downs in evaluation, even been the objects of severe criticism, but none of them has received as much condemnation as Stalin. Following Roberts, I shall attempt here to assess Stalin and other members of the Big Three and the power they wielded as part of the 'whole picture'.

For this purpose, I shall make special use of the *longue durée* as suggested by Fernand Braudel, who in 1946 proposed an approach to history along three paths. The first consisted of the structure, 'The Role of Environment', which was 'almost timeless history – in which all change is slow, a history of constant repetition, ever-recurring cycles', with a heavy emphasis on human contact with 'the inanimate': land, sea and climate, communications and cities. The second path, conjunctures involving 'Collective Destinies and General Trends', concerned economic systems, states, civilizations and forms of war. The third, to which I shall pay special attention, is entitled 'Events, Politics and People', which Braudel described as 'surface disturbances, crests of foam that the tides of history carry on their strong backs' – 'the most exciting of all, the richest in human interest, and also the most dangerous'. He continued:

> We must learn to distrust this history with its still burning passions, as it was felt, described, and lived by contemporaries whose lives were as short and short-sighted as ours .... Resounding events are often only momentary outbursts, surface manifestations of these large movements and explicable only in terms of them.[2]

In 1946, when Braudel published these words, less than a year had elapsed since the end of the Second World War, most of which he had spent in a prisoner of war camp while the Big Three were trying to bring the global conflict to an end. This experience, remote from libraries and archives, had no doubt given him ample opportunity for reflection about the nature of his craft. While his work clearly indicated that he was thinking more of the sixteenth century than the twentieth, his wise words have remained of great influence in recent years. Nevertheless, we must be fully aware that, seventy years on, much has happened since 1946 to modify Braudel's original observations, especially concerning 'The Role of the Environment', no longer consisting of 'almost timeless history ... in which all change is slow'. Even in 1945, the atomic bombs used at Hiroshima and Nagasaki were much more than 'momentary outbursts'.

But I shall begin with a discussion of the role of the individual in the nineteenth century, when all members of the Big Three were born. If Lord Acton acted as counsel for the prosecution of great men, so to speak, in 1887, Thomas Carlyle had boldly made the case for their defence forty years or so before him:

> Universal History, the history of what man has accomplished in this world, is at bottom the History of the Great Men who have worked here. They were the leaders of men, these great ones; the modellers, patterns, and in a wide sense creators, of whatsoever the general mass of men contrived to do or attain; all things that we see standing accomplished in the world are properly the outer material result, the practical realisation and embodiment, or Thoughts that dwelt in the Great Men sent into the world.

More succinctly, Carlyle declared 'No great man lives in vain. The History of the world is but the Biography of great men.' The final example given by him was a mournful exile on the island of St Helena, his early promise unfulfilled – 'poor Napoleon: a great implement too soon wasted, till it was useless: our last Great Man!'[3]

As 'great implement', Napoleon would be the embodiment of the nation-state as promoted by the French Revolution, but he would also come to represent authoritarian government. In whichever role, he remains a byword for an outstanding individual even today.

Napoleon as the converse of the great man appears in the discussion of the role of the individual in history at the end of Leo Tolstoy's epic novel *War and Peace* written in the 1860s. Having considered at some length the French invasion of Russia in 1812, in particular the conduct of the battle of Borodino by Napoleon and his opponent Kutuzov, he asserts that, while Napoleon tries to alter the tide of history, Kutuzov goes along with it.

In a philosophical Epilogue, Tolstoy declares that 'History has for its subject the life of nations and humanity'. In ancient times, either a Divinity or a hero guided by a Divinity led the nations, 'or, in its highest flights, the welfare and civilization of humanity in general, by which is usually meant the people inhabiting a small, north-western corner of a large continent'. Even after the French Revolution, the view persisted that '(1) nations are guided by individuals, and (2) there exists a certain goal towards which the nations and humanity are moving'. The campaign of 1812 was still seen as 'the result of Napoleon's will', to which the will of the people had been transferred, particularly by those united for joint action in an army.

But for Tolstoy, (1) 'Power is the relation of a given person to other persons, in which the more this person expresses opinions, theories and justifications of the collective action the less is his participation in that action'; and (2) 'The movement of nations is caused not by power, nor by individual activity, nor even by a combination of the two, as historians have supposed, but by the activity of *all* [Tolstoy's italics] those who participate in the event, and who will always combine in such a way that those who take the largest direct share in the event assume the least responsibility and *vice versa*.'

To be sure, while natural scientists could not explain such phenomena as the interaction of heat and electricity or of atoms, Tolstoy averred, historians could not be expected to explain human behaviour, especially since the problem of free will was present in every stage of history, juxtaposed with that of necessity. Yet, 'our impression or free will and necessity is gradually diminished or increased according to the degree of connexion with the external world, the greater or lesser degree of remoteness in time and the degree of dependence on causes which we see in the phenomenon of a man's life that we examine'.

Commenting on his own points, Tolstoy asserted: (1) There is no freedom in space. We are where we are. (2) There is no freedom in time. Once an action has been taken, no other is possible, and this becomes clearer the more time progresses. (3) We can never reach a conception of complete free will nor of complete necessity. However, 'Free will is for history only an expression connoting what we do not know about the laws of human life'. As in other sciences, the more we know about these laws, Tolstoy insisted, the more free will is diminished. In the case of the advances made by Copernicus and Newton, 'it was necessary to surmount the sensation of an unreal immobility in space and to recognize a motion we did not feel'. In the study of history 'it is similarly necessary to renounce a freedom that does not exist and to recognize a dependence of which we are not personally conscious'.[4]

Napoleon I was a great man for Carlyle in 1840, and the converse for Tolstoy in the 1860s. His nephew, Napoleon III, was the butt of Karl Marx's scorn following the revolution of 1848 as he claimed to show 'how the class struggle in France created circumstances and relationships that made it possible for a grotesque mediocrity to play a hero's part'. After observing that Napoleon I and III illustrated how history repeats itself, first as tragedy, then as farce, Marx went on to declare: 'Men make their own history, but they do not make it just as they please; they do not make it under circumstances chosen by themselves, but under circumstances directly found, given and transmitted from the past. The tradition of all the dead generations weighs like a nightmare on the brain of the living.'[5]

Fifty years after 1848, in the wake of Marx, G.V. Plekhanov wrote:

A great man is great not because his personal qualities give individual features to great historical events, but because he possesses qualities which make him most capable of serving the great social needs of his time, needs which arose as a result of general and political causes. Carlyle, in his well-known book on heroes and hero-worship, calls great men *beginners*. This is a very apt description. A great man is precisely a beginner because he sees *further* than others, and desires things *more strongly* than others [Plekhanov's italics]. He solves the scientific problems brought up by the preceding process of intellectual development of society; he points to the new social needs created by the preceding development of social relationships; he takes the initiative in satisfying these needs. He is a hero. But he is not a hero in the sense that he can stop, or change, the natural course of things, but in the sense that his activities are the conscious and free expression of this inevitable and unconscious course. Herein lies all his significance; herein lies his whole power. But this significance is colossal, and the power is terrible.[6]

A little later than Plekhanov, Max Weber, one of the founders of modern sociology, gave an alternative view. As David Beetham puts it, for Weber the leader 'is an individualist; the source of his actions lies in himself, in his own personal convictions, and not in his following or associates'. In Weber's own words, 'It is not the politically passive "mass" which produces the leader, but the political leader who recruits a following and wins the mass through "demagogy"'. This is so 'under even the most democratic arrangements', especially if the leader is 'charismatic', that is knowing only 'inner determination and inner constraint'. Whereas Marx sought to overthrow capitalism through the action of a class-aware proletariat, Weber aimed to show that the proletariat could be integrated within the capitalist system under a strong leader.[7]

We will return to the problem of the evaluation of the individual leader as discussed during and after the Second World War at the end of the book. Before then, our approach to our subject will be as follows. The rest of this chapter concentrates on the context of the formation of the Big Three, the early lives of the individuals concerned accompanied by the development of their countries, the 'Great Powers'. It goes as far as the years of the Second World War up to the eve of the first Big Three conference at Tehran, taking account of some bilateral meetings. Chapters 2–6 trace the development of the Big Three through the conferences at Tehran, Yalta and Potsdam, as well as other significant meetings involving just two of them or their representatives. With a minimum of comment and context, confined primarily to the conclusion of each chapter, the main aim here is to set out fairly and squarely, if concisely and without too much repetition, what the great men said to each other as the great powers fought to bring the world war to an end in Europe and in Asia as their relationship developed. Chapter 7 focuses on the dual process of the victory over Japan and the fall of the Big Three accompanied by the emergence of the Big Two, the United States and USSR, as superpowers while the British Empire was in evident decline. Chapter 8 evaluates the roles of the leaders of the two superpowers, Stalin, Roosevelt and Truman in the arrival of the Cold War, then the parts played by Churchill and Attlee in the process of the end of empire. It concludes with an assessment of the place of individuals in history in general, giving particular attention to arguments on this subject put forward in the twentieth century, especially from 1941 onwards, before a final consideration of the great men in the Second World War in particular.

At the beginning of the Second World War, the individuals who were to become the Big Three were far from friends. And this was not just because the trio had never met. Their views clashed on a variety of questions concerning war and peace and economic, social and cultural policy. They would disagree seriously about the year in which the Second World War began. For the USSR and the United States, it would be 1941, for the UK alone 1939. There was even a problem about what to call each other. Personally, Stalin was unhappy when he was told that Churchill and Roosevelt talked of him as 'Uncle Joe'. Of the two titles he assumed during the war, he expressed a preference for 'Marshal' over 'Generalissimo'.

Moreover, as far as the Big Three as countries was concerned, the inaccurate terms 'America', 'England' and 'Russia' were all used frequently, before the war, during and after it. As should have been better known, or more normally recognized, the Big Three consisted of the United States of America, the United Kingdom of Great Britain and Northern Ireland and the Union of Soviet Socialist Republics. Cumbersome though these titles may have been, it should not have been difficult to refer consistently to the United States, the UK and the USSR.

Like most other confusions, this one can be resolved through history. To put the point simply, while England dominated the UK, the United States towered over the Americas and Russia was by far the major republic in the USSR. However, as with many questions in history, the simple answer is not enough; far better, then, to spell it out at greater length, always bearing in mind the Braudelian *longue durée*, contrasting 'collective destinies and general trends' including states and societies with the 'surface disturbances' of events, politics and people. These will be discussed more fully in Chapters 7 and 8. For now, a convenient point of departure is Paul Kennedy's observation: 'the historical record suggests that there is a very clear connection *in the long run* between an individual Great Power's economic rise and fall and its growth and decline as an important military power (or world empire).'[8]

Let us look first at the second half of the nineteenth century, when the term 'Great Power' was already in full use and many of the circumstances affecting in particular the Big Three as great powers either arose or began to take on new shape. This same period of history is all the more appropriate since it included the birth and early life of the Big Three as individuals, including the original trio, Churchill, Stalin and Roosevelt, and the two replacements, Truman and Attlee.

So let us first take these men in the chronological order of their birth, beginning with the years leading up to the outbreak of the First World War in 1914. Winston Leonard Spencer Churchill was born at Blenheim Palace near Oxford on 30 November 1874. He was the son of Lord Randolph Churchill, a leading Conservative politician, and grandson of the seventh Duke of Marlborough. His mother was the American Jennie Jerome. He learned about the British Empire at Harrow school and trained to fight for it at Sandhurst military college. From 1895, he wielded the pen as well as the sword, first in

Cuba, then in India and Sudan. Having already written for newspapers and published books, Churchill resigned his commission to become a full-time journalist in South Africa during the Boer War which broke out in 1899. He was captured and then escaped. In 1900, he first became a Conservative MP, but switched to the Liberals four years later ostensibly over the issue of free trade. He was appointed Under-Secretary for Colonies in 1905, President of the Board of Trade in 1908, Home Secretary in 1910 and First Lord of the Admiralty in 1911. Meanwhile, in 1908, he had married Clementine Hozier, and, according to his own account, lived happily ever after.

Stalin was born Iosif Vissarionovich Djugashvili in a hut in Gori, a small town in Georgia, then part of the Russian Empire, on 6 December 1878 (not 21 December 1879 that became his official birthday).[9] His father, Vissarion, was a cobbler; his mother, Ekaterina, a washerwoman. Allegedly, Vissarion was a drunkard who beat his son and wife savagely. Ekaterina managed to get 'Soso' (the first of several pseudonyms) into the Church School at Gori in 1888, and he won a scholarship to the Seminary in Tbilisi, the capital, in 1894. He was expelled in 1899 because of his interest in Marxism and then joined the Russian Social Democratic Workers' Party. He became 'Koba', a professional revolutionary, and soon incurred the first of several terms of imprisonment. He was active in the Revolution of 1905 and first met Lenin, who dubbed him the 'wonderful Georgian'. A visit to London for a party congress in 1906 was followed by periods of exile in Siberia. Before the outbreak of the First World War, possibly in deliberate assonance with Lenin ('man of the River Lena'), he had become Stalin ('man of steel').

Franklin Delano Roosevelt was born on 30 January 1882 at Hyde Park, New York. He was the son of James Roosevelt, a wealthy landowner, and Sara Delano, also from the upper crust of American society. He attended Groton school before Harvard University where he edited the student newspaper *The Crimson*. He then studied at the Columbia University School of Law, and qualified for the New York bar. In 1905, he married his fifth cousin once removed, Eleanor Roosevelt, a formidable woman in her own right. Entering politics as a Democrat, he was elected to the New York Senate in 1910.

Clement Richard Attlee was born on 3 January 1883 in Putney, London. He was the son of Henry Attlee, a prominent solicitor, and Ellen. He went to Haileybury School and Oxford University before training as a lawyer and being called to the bar in 1905. He became manager of Haileybury House boys' club in the East End of London in 1907 and joined the Independent Labour Party in 1908. In 1913, he was appointed lecturer in social administration at the London School of Economics.

Harry S.[10] Truman was born on 8 May 1884 in the small town of Lamar, Missouri. His father, John Anderson Truman, was a farmer, his mother, Martha Ellen Young, the daughter of a farmer. The family left the farm in 1890 for the town of Independence, where Harry achieved academic success at school despite his poor eyesight. In 1903, soon after his father's bankruptcy, he became a bank clerk, at first in Independence, then in Kansas City, attempting other occupations before returning to work on his mother's family farm. He retained an optimistic faith in progress even after several business failures.

Similar observations about faith in progress might be made about other individual members of the Big Three, since they were all creatures of the largely optimistic nineteenth century. However, the twentieth century was already in the making, all of the Great Men being brought up in a key period of Great Powers, 1865–96, which historian Walter LaFeber has characterized as 'Laying the Foundations for "Superpowerdom"'.[11] These were the years in which the United States rapidly developed its agriculture and industry, after the North's victory in the Civil War while rounding out its frontiers and finally subduing the Native Americans. The United States purchased Alaska from the Russians in 1867 and annexed Hawaii before Japan or any other nation could do so in 1898. In 1898, too, the United States forcefully removed Spain from Cuba, Puerto Rico and the Philippines. By the end of the century, it was exerting considerable influence over the northern and southern continents of the Western Hemisphere, while increasing it in the Pacific region and Asia. In China, 'America' pursued the Open Door policy of free competition in the face of other powers striving to carve out spheres of influence for themselves. These included the British and Russian empires.

The British Empire was the most powerful that the world had ever seen, occupying well over 11 million square miles of territory with a population of more than 400 million. In 1876, Queen Victoria became Empress of India and the 'little woman' continued to be an imposing figurehead for dominions and colonies until her death in 1901. But a major challenge to British power was made by the Boers in South Africa in 1899, peace coming in 1902. In the same year in the Far East, Great Britain sought to protect its interests in Hong Kong and elsewhere through alliance with Japan. In the Far East as well as Central Asia and the Middle East, a great threat had appeared in the shape of the Russian Empire. However, the British finally made an accommodation with Russia in 1907 following entente with another old enemy, France, in 1904. The threat now appeared to come from the German Empire, expanding by leaps and bounds since its formal foundation in 1871, and often referred to as 'Prussia', its core element, like 'England' in relation to Great Britain.

After the Crimean War of 1854–6 had shown up Russian backwardness in comparison with its major adversaries, the UK and France, the emancipation of the serfs and other reforms encouraged a considerable degree of social and economic progress until a dreadful reversal in war with Japan from 1904 to 1905. Before that, over several centuries, successive tsarist regimes were assimilating Ukraine, the Baltic provinces and Finland while sharing Poland with Prussia and Austria; taking over the Transcaucasian states and reducing the power of Turkey in the Middle East; consolidating control in Siberia, reaching into Central Asia and the Far East. The foundations for later 'superpowerdom' were less certain in the Russian case than in the American, however, even if progress was considerable before the trauma of regime change. For in 1905, the position of Tsar Nicholas II was under threat already from the First Russian Revolution. Further progress ensued, but entry into the First World War in 1914 further weakened the tsar's position and then undermined it.

After Nicholas II abdicated in the Second Revolution of February 1917, Stalin rose to greater prominence as Lenin and Trotsky led the movement towards the Third Revolution in October 1917. The price of victory was heavy, however, not only in millions of deaths and vast amounts of destruction in Soviet Russia itself during the ensuing Civil War and Allied Intervention, but also in the loss of important parts of the former empire such as Poland, the Baltic states and Finland. Meanwhile, in the Treaty of Versailles of 1919 and others emanating from the Paris Peace Conference, the first Big Three, Lloyd George, Clemenceau and Woodrow Wilson, determined the post-war shape of Europe and much of the wider world, the surviving British and French empires joining the United States in the determination of the fate of those that had fallen, especially the Austrian, German, Russian and Turkish, with the aim of forestalling any threat from a power excluded from the conference, Soviet Russia. The American President Woodrow Wilson set out a plan for the maintenance of peace in the League of Nations, but his own country rejected it and others could not make it a success. His successor, Warren G. Harding, hosted the Washington Conference of 1921–2 on the Limitation of Armament and on Pacific and Far Eastern Questions, reducing the influence of other empires, the British and Japanese in particular, while maintaining the Open Door in China. But again, the negotiating powers could not establish lasting stability.

For further information on the Big Three as individuals, let us turn to the *Encyclopaedia Britannica*, whose position as the leading reference work in English had been established not only by contributions from a wide range of experts but also by the high status of its dedicatees. The multi-volume Eleventh Edition of 1910–11 had been published by the Cambridge University Press with a dedication by permission to 'His Majesty George the Fifth, King of the United Kingdom of Great Britain and Ireland and of the British Dominions beyond the seas, Emperor of India' on the one hand and 'William Howard Taft, President of the United States of America' on the other. The Twelfth Edition of 1921–2, adding three supplementary volumes, was dedicated to George V as before and the American president, now Warren Gamaliel Harding, newly designated 'The Two Heads of the English-Speaking Peoples', and published by *Encyclopaedia Britannica* in London and New York.

The dedication and publication details of three further supplementary volumes comprising the Thirteenth Edition of 1926 remained the same, except for the replacement of Harding by Calvin Coolidge as American president. However, the editor J. L. Garvin declared that, given fifteen years of violence leading to 'a universal revolution in human affairs and the human mind', it was now 'almost unquestionably right to depart from the principle of Olympian judgment practised by the *Encyclopaedia Britannica* at long leisure in more stable times'.[12] Let us look at how the 'universal revolution' had affected the members of the Big Three in and beyond the pages of the authoritative reference work, bearing in mind the importance still attributed to the role of 'Great Men' in the history of 'Great Powers' in the years before the outbreak of the Second World War.

The entry on Winston Leonard Spencer Churchill summarizes his political and military activity in the Great War before observing that the Liberal Prime Minister Lloyd George 'disliked his Russian policy and the expensive campaigns conducted against the Bolshevists under his inspiration'. It includes information on his defeat as an independent anti-Socialist candidate in Westminster in 1924 before switching parties again to become a Conservative MP and Chancellor of the Exchequer. Joseph Stalin has his own entry as, after Lenin's death in 1924, 'the most influential member of the Communist party and general secretary of the central committee of the Communist party', but there is no entry on Franklin Roosevelt (who had made a brief appearance in the Twelfth Edition as Assistant Secretary of the Navy), Harry Truman or Clement Attlee, all of whom still had to make their distinctive mark in the leading reference work of the early twentieth century.

During the First World War, Major Attlee was on active service in the Turkish Dardanelles at Gallipoli in the campaign originated by Churchill, then in Mesopotamia and France, while Captain Truman served in France exclusively. Subsequently, during the interwar years, they both pursued political careers. In 1920, Attlee became first Labour Mayor of Stepney and in 1922, Labour MP for Limehouse. In 1921, he married Violet Millar, who was a great support throughout his career. After holding junior ministerial posts in Ramsay Macdonald's administration, he became leader of the much reduced Labour Party in 1935. After demobilization, Truman came home to Independence, Missouri, wooing and winning Elizabeth (Bess) Wallace in 1919. After several business failures, including a partnership in a haberdashery in Kansas City which soon went bankrupt, he was drawn into local politics as a cog in the corrupt 'machine' run by 'Boss' Tom Pendergast, demonstrating energy and talent while keeping a no doubt troubled conscience to himself. In 1934, he was elected Democratic Senator for Missouri and went off to Washington with the advice from his patron Tom Pendergast: 'Work hard, keep your mouth shut, and answer your mail.'[13] As yet, he had shown little interest in international affairs.

To turn to the original Big Three, Churchill as Chancellor of the Exchequer from 1924 to 1929 returned Great Britain to the Gold Standard in 1925, a move that made a considerable contribution to the ensuing economic slump. In 1926, he was a resolute opponent of the General Strike, thus alienating himself even further from the socialist left. His opposition to Indian independence widened the gulf between him and the leadership of the Conservative Party. He lived off his pen meanwhile, completing a biography of his ancestor *Marlborough*, the victor at the great battle of Blenheim in 1704, while arguing in favour of rearmament before becoming First Lord of the Admiralty for the second time with the outbreak of war on 3 September 1939.

Soon after being stricken by polio in 1921, Franklin D. Roosevelt began to show a remarkable resilience and optimism that carried him through the governorship of New York before securing the Democratic nomination for president and going on to defeat the incumbent Republican President Herbert Hoover in 1932. Urging his fellow Americans to realize that there was nothing to fear but fear itself, he brought in the first measures of the New Deal to help the United States emerge from the Great Depression. The aim was to save the domestic economy before giving any attention to the international situation, but as the 1930s wore on, the realization grew that the United States could not escape involvement in the new world crisis. Making sure that the Americas were secure through what he called his 'good neighbor' policy, Roosevelt strove in vain to restrain expanding powers elsewhere, especially Japan, through 'quarantine' and embargo. The actual entry into war was sudden with the Japanese attack on Pearl Harbor, Hawaii, on 7 December 1941.

Having made a summary appearance in the *Encyclopaedia Britannica* in 1926, J. V. Stalin was to dominate the *Great Soviet Encyclopaedia*, begun in the same year. Not only was he to be specially featured in volume 52, following Lenin and Leninism in volume 36 and Marx and Marxism in volume 38, but his influence was evident throughout. Indeed, the official Soviet ideology, 'Marxism-Leninism', was in fact to a large extent 'Stalinism'. In a sense, Stalin was the Napoleon of the Russian Revolution, becoming the embodiment of the Soviet state as he established his own dictatorship. In 1932, he himself gave a traditional Marxist answer to a question about the role of individuals in history, emphasizing that they must be aware of the conditions in which they operated. Beyond that, Peter the Great was 'but a drop in the sea, whereas Lenin was a whole ocean'. He himself was just a pupil of Lenin's and the aim of his life was to be a worthy pupil, he insisted, while decisions were made in the Soviet Union in a collegial rather than individual manner.[14] In fact, the circumstance that Stalin came as near to becoming a god as an atheistic culture would allow makes it difficult to assess his role as individual beyond the further circumstance that he is normally viewed in the West as a devil, a subject to which we will return in our concluding chapter. In the shorter run, the suicide in 1932 of his wife Nadezhda Alliluyeva, whom had married in 1919, appears to have affected him deeply.

If Roosevelt's initial aim in the 1930s had been to save capitalism in the United States, Stalin's had been to build socialism in the USSR. In 1931, he made a famous speech declaring: 'To slacken the tempo would mean falling behind.' Stalin went on to give an account of 'the continual beatings' old Russia suffered 'because of her backwardness'. Soviet Russia must strive mightily to resist 'the jungle law of capitalism'. His speech concluded: 'We are fifty or a hundred years behind the advanced countries. We must make good this distance in ten years. Either we do it, or we shall go under.'[15] In Stalin's view, the situation demanded the forced pace of Five Year Plans and the ruthless purge of those deemed to be wreckers and dissidents. Ten years was indeed all that the Soviet Union was given, for on 22 June 1941, Nazi Germany launched a ferocious offensive. Even before that, there had been heavy fighting in the Far East in 1938 and 1939 as the Red Army repelled probing attacks by the Japanese. And to protect its western flank, after the failure of talks with the UK and France in the wake of their appeasement of Nazi Germany, the Soviet Union partitioned Eastern Europe with Germany by the Pact of 23 August 1939. This Pact helped to prompt the declaration of war by the UK and France on Germany on 3 September after its invasion of Poland. Later, in his *History of the Second World War*, Churchill wrote that, if Soviet policy was cold-blooded, 'it was also at the moment realistic in a high degree'.[16] Again to protect its western flank, the Soviet Union engaged in the Winter War with Finland from November 1939 to March 1940. This move was widely regarded elsewhere as an act of aggression by a big power on a small one.

The future superpowers entered the Second World War after surprise attacks, both of which have been subjects of great controversy, Stalin and Roosevelt both being blamed for negligence in the face of several warnings about the impending catastrophes. Most analysts would shrink from taking the comparison further, however, given Stalin's record as the leader ultimately responsible for the death of millions. Some, without apologizing for Stalin, would argue that even he needs to be seen in his full context which includes not only pressing domestic circumstances but also the increasingly difficult international situation in which heavy emphasis was given to the significance of other dictators such as Hitler, Mussolini and Tojo.

The rise of the Big Three

On 3 September 1939, the UK and France declared war on Germany. Of course, some would say that it did not become a world war until the entry of the USSR and USA in 1941, others that it had already begun with the Spanish Civil War of 1936–9 in which both Fascist Italy and Nazi Germany intervened in spite of the advocacy by the UK and France of a policy of 'non-intervention'. There is indeed a case for saying that the global conflict began with the Japanese invasion of Manchuria in 1931, soon intensified by the creation of the puppet state of Manchukuo early in 1932, leading towards an invasion of China in 1937 and the clash with the Soviet Union in the border regions in 1938 and 1939. Far Eastern developments were of considerable concern to the British and French empires as well as to the United States, although no direct threat was immediately perceived, and priority was given to Europe.

In the early months of 1940, when there was a lull in European hostilities, there was as yet no Big Three, not even a dual relationship between the UK and United States. On 21 January 1940, *The New York Times* wrote that 'a feeling of intense irritation with Britain, which, it is feared, is spreading in the United States ... has developed in official quarters here over the adamant British attitude towards joint problems'. These included what appeared to Americans to be high-handed British behaviour at sea and restrictions on American imports into Great Britain.[17] British feelings of isolation increased especially with the collapse of France in the early summer of 1940. But Free French forces were able to assemble in Britain under the leadership of Charles de Gaulle, while a puppet government was installed at Vichy. Churchill, who had become prime minister in May, looked for support to his mother's country, the United States, and sought to overcome misunderstandings.

On 11 September 1939, Churchill had received the following communication from President Roosevelt:

> It is because you and I occupied similar positions in the [First] World War that I want you to know how glad I am that you are back again in the Admiralty. Your problems are, I realise, complicated by new factors, but the essential is not very different. What I want you and the Prime Minister to know is that I shall at all times welcome it if you will keep me in touch personally with anything you want me to know about.

Thus began one of the most remarkable correspondences of the Second World War, continued through to Roosevelt's death in April 1945. Churchill later recalled that he had met Roosevelt only once in the First World War, and 'had been struck by his magnificent presence in all his youth and strength'. Unfortunately, nevertheless, he seems not to have paid much attention at the time to Roosevelt, who in return found him aloof.[18]

Now that he was the prime minister, Churchill developed his friendship with the American president, first of all by correspondence, the prime minister insisting that, although approved by a 'select circle' of advisers, communications with the president should be both personal and private. Churchill wrote later: 'My relations with the President gradually became so close that the chief business between our two countries was virtually conducted by these personal interchanges between him and me. In this way our perfect understanding was gained.'[19] Although the understanding was to become less than perfect, at first two was indeed company. As we shall see later, the Big Three was something of a crowd.

While Roosevelt urged Stalin to align the USSR with the Western powers, relations were not helped by the announcement in April 1941 of a neutrality pact between the Soviet Union and Japan to add to the agreements they both had with Nazi Germany. Then, after the German invasion of the Soviet Union on 22 June 1941, the prognosis was no better. As Walter LaFeber tells us, the US State Department soon issued a statement condemning the Soviet policy on religion and asserting that 'communistic dictatorship' was as intolerable as 'Nazi dictatorship'. Nevertheless, since Germany was the greater threat, the Soviet Union should receive help. Senator Harry S. Truman spoke for many of his fellow Americans in his statement: 'If we see that Germany is winning we should help Russia and if Russia is winning then we ought to help Germany and that way let them kill as many as possible, although I don't want to see Hitler victorious under any circumstances.' LaFeber comments:

> Possessing drastically different views of how the world should be organized, unable to cooperate during the 1930s against Nazi and Japanese aggression, and nearly full-fledged enemies between 1939 and 1941, the United States and the Soviet Union finally became partners because of a shotgun marriage forced upon them by World War II.[20]

No doubt, before the Nazi invasion, Stalin's views were the mirror image of Truman's to the extent that he hoped that the war would be confined to the West, that Hitler and his enemies would weaken each other while the Soviet Union continued to build up its strength. This hope was dashed by the sudden fall of France in the summer of 1940. Meanwhile, Churchill was attempting to come to terms with his deep-set antipathy towards the communist regime while worried that some American aid might be diverted from Great Britain to the Soviet Union. At the same time, aware of what Gabriel Gorodetsky calls 'the gradual dependence of British policy-making on the Americans', Churchill vigorously asserted the needs of his side in what was already becoming a triangular relationship if not yet the Big Three.[21]

An early opportunity for him to make his case was his meeting with Roosevelt in August 1941: appropriately for two former naval persons, this was at sea off Newfoundland. After the national anthems, there ensued Divine Service, with a spirited rendition by the two leaders and the sailors of their two countries of 'Onward, Christian Soldiers'. The most public testimony of later discussions was embodied in the joint declaration made on 12 August 1941. The 'Atlantic Charter', as it became known, set out eight broad principles for the establishment of human rights and a lasting peace after the destruction of Nazi tyranny. The reservation made by the two countries for 'due respect for their existing obligations' was considered by Churchill a sufficient guarantee of the UK's imperial responsibilities. However, whatever formulations were agreed, the unequal nature of the 'special relationship' could not be easily disguised. What became known as 'Lend-Lease' and 'destroyers for bases' agreements contained elements not only of American generosity to a beleaguered ally but also of hard-nosed promotion of American self-interest.

A pointer towards later Big Three meetings was constituted by a joint message to Stalin, suggesting a high-level meeting in Moscow to discuss how support could most expeditiously be continued for the Soviet Union's 'brave and steadfast resistance' to Hitlerism. To some extent, the way had been prepared in London and Moscow by Roosevelt's special adviser Harry Hopkins in 1940 and 1941 and British Foreign Minister Anthony Eden in Moscow in December 1941, among others.

After the attack on Pearl Harbor earlier that month, which had been followed by the bombing of Hong Kong and Singapore, Churchill proposed a visit to Roosevelt now that the two were 'in the same boat'. A guest at the White House after a somewhat hazardous sea voyage, Churchill joined Roosevelt in detailed discussions about the further prosecution of the war across the Atlantic and the Pacific, agreeing again on the primacy of the former.

Churchill made a speech to Congress with emphasis on the need for collaboration between the UK and USA before moving on to Ottawa where he addressed the Canadian Parliament. Back in Washington, DC, on 1 January 1942 he signed the United Nations Pact founded on the Atlantic Charter with Roosevelt, the Soviet ambassador Maxim Litvinov and T. Soong representing China. More than twenty other nations also joined in the Pact, including India at Roosevelt's insistence and Churchill's grudging acceptance. Churchill was also unhappy at any hint from Roosevelt that, free from a difficult past relationship with the Soviet Union, the president might be a better negotiator with Stalin than the prime minister. After a short rest in Florida, where he experienced some slight heart problems, Churchill returned to London from Bermuda in a 'flying boat' or seaplane.

In June 1942, soon after the Soviet Foreign Minister Molotov had been in Washington, DC, arguing the case for an early opening of a second, Western Front in Europe, Churchill flew over the Atlantic again for more bilateral talks between the British and American leaders at Hyde Park, the president's country house, and managed to stall on the issue of the Second Front. More positive on this issue, Roosevelt also confirmed that US troops would soon be involved in North Africa. The news from the Pacific was encouraging, but not so good from the Soviet Union, to which the Western Allies were finding it difficult to send supplies, especially round Norway's North Cape where convoys were suffering grievous losses. For the sake of later collaboration between the Big

Three as well as strategic imperatives, it was considered advisable to maintain concentration on Europe. There was some discussion of collaboration on 'Tube Alloys', the code name for the atomic bomb project, still to be kept secret from the Soviet Union.

Then, in August 1942, Churchill flew again for another 'summit' meeting, on this occasion via Cairo and Tehran to Moscow. Churchill requested that Averell Harriman accompany him for the sake of togetherness, unaware that the president would instruct his representative to sound out the possibilities for a face-to-face meeting between the American and Soviet leaders. The first hours of the talks were difficult, focused as they were on the Second Front. Stalin said that he could not understand the difficulties involved in attacking France across the Channel in 1942, asking why the Western Allies were so afraid of the Germans. If you did not take risks, you could not win the war, he argued, and the only way to test the quality of your troops was to blood them in battle. The two leaders were in closer agreement about the importance of bombing Germany before Churchill went on to present the arguments for an attack on France from the Mediterranean. In order to make his ideas clearer, Churchill showed a picture that he had drawn of a crocodile, indicating to Stalin the advantages of attacking him through the soft belly as well as via the hard snout. A large globe proved to be a second visual aid. It could hardly have escaped Stalin's notice that the promise of action in the Mediterranean, as well as of further aid through the Persian Gulf, would also protect British imperial interests.

On the morning of 13 August, there was another difficult meeting, Stalin again accusing the Western Allies of fear in face of the Germans, and of breaking promises, too. He insisted that, since they had control of the air, they could make a landing on the Cherbourg peninsula. Churchill explained again the difficulty of crossing the Channel. He also said that Stalin's approach to the talks had been less than comradely, that Great Britain had fought alone for a year and then had done as much as it could in aid of Russia, while the Americans were 'very good in applauding the valiant deeds done by others'. Victory would be assured if the three great nations maintained their alliance. More temperate discussion followed of various Soviet and Western weapons, about the defence of the Caucasus and about plans for US aircraft to fly over Siberia. But Stalin commented that 'Wars are not won with plans.' He gave

Churchill and Harriman an *aide-mémoire* arguing that a Second Front could have been opened in 1942 because Germany's best forces had been transferred to the Eastern Front.

Also on 13 August, Churchill discussed with Molotov the problem of France. When the People's Commissar for Foreign Affairs warned of the danger of pushing the puppet Vichy government into active support of Germany, Churchill responded that 'the British fought with France for three hundred years, at the time of Louis XIV, Napoleon, etc.' But, riposted Molotov, Great Britain and France were allies in the twentieth century. Churchill went on to observe that they had been allies in the nineteenth century, too, in the Crimean War. Allies against Russia?, Molotov asked. Yes, said Churchill, but that was tsarist Russia. Molotov commented: there was no other Russia then. Here was an early anticipation of the historical allusions that were to be made frequently in meetings of the Big Three.

At a state banquet on the evening of 14 August, Churchill confessed to being very active in the intervention that had followed the Russian Revolution. Stalin had said, 'all that is in the past, and the past belongs to God'. Put out by seemingly endless mutually congratulatory toasts among the Russians, however, on the way back to his lodgings in a *dacha*, Churchill 'was like a bull maddened by the pricks of the picadors' and threatened to return home. He thought that Stalin had spoken to him as 'a representative of the greatest empire that had ever existed in the world' in a manner completely inadmissible. Fortunately, things took a turn for the better on the evening of 15 August, when the two leaders were able to establish a more personal rapport. Drawn into an informal dinner in Stalin's modest Kremlin apartment after high-level military conversations during the day, Churchill found himself bound to defend the record of the Arctic convoys and of the British navy in general, arguing that 'Russia is a land animal, the British are sea animals'. The two leaders considered one of Churchill's pet plans for a British landing in Norway, which could free the North Cape and ease the path of the convoys. When conversation switched to more historical military matters, in particular to some of the individuals concerned, Churchill referred to the 'genius' of his ancestor Marlborough, but Stalin gave his opinion that 'Britain had an even more talented general Wellington, who defeated Napoleon'. While they were waiting for the final bland communiqué on a 'just war of liberation' through to 'the complete destruction of Hitlerism and any similar tyranny' to be brought, the two leaders discussed the policy of collective farms. Stalin asserted that it had been a terrible necessity to plough the land with tractors in order to overcome the problem of famine, and that only collective farms with workshops could carry out such a policy. Stalin also provided what he obviously thought was light relief by making merciless fun of Molotov.[22]

In the following months of 1942, the British and the Americans were worried about the possibility of Soviet collapse on the Eastern Front, widely recognized as the key to the outcome of the war in Europe, while still in disagreement about the nature of the Second Front to the west. And there was no significant progress in North Africa or the Far East. But then early in November, the US Navy inflicted huge losses on the Japanese fleet at Guadalcanal, the British army won a victory at El Alamein, the US army landed in North Africa and the Red Army began an encirclement of the enemy at Stalingrad.

Confident that these engagements marked the end of the beginning, Churchill tried without success to get Roosevelt to come to London for further talks. But he did manage to persuade the president to come to Casablanca in Morocco in January 1943 for another bilateral meeting, even though Roosevelt was anxious to involve Stalin in a three-way conference, writing to Churchill: 'I do not want to give Stalin the impression that we are settling everything between ourselves before we meet him. ... I think that you and I understand each other so well that prior conferences between us are unnecessary'. Roosevelt was also thinking of a Big Four adding Chiang Kai-Shek to the group.

At Casablanca, there were several staff discussions that the two leaders did not attend, but they were both more than ready to consider matters of grand strategy. Once again, the cross-Channel Second Front was put off. There was some bilateral discussion of American daylight bombing, which, it was believed, would reduce the number of battlefield losses, undermine German and boost Soviet morale. There were also some difficult conversations with General Charles de Gaulle, who was more than anxious that the French interest should be represented until the *patrie* could be liberated. The two English-speaking leaders confirmed the policy of 'unconditional surrender', which could act as another reassurance to Stalin as well as discouraging him from a separate peace with Hitler. After the completion of the formal business, there was a photo call including de Gaulle and a short break for Churchill and Roosevelt at Marrakesh including a jovial sing-song.[23]

Now that the beginning was past, Roosevelt's thoughts began to turn towards the end, and afterwards, too. He held regular meetings about post-war problems, with some emphasis on the embryonic Big Three relationship, anxious to avoid the appearance of the UK and USA working against the USSR, but also concerned that the British Empire might become a rival in international influence to the United States. He insisted that he was not a Wilsonian idealist and would avoid the binding commitments of the League of Nations. But he also came to believe that a Big Four including China would have to wield 'police powers' in the United Nations, putting muscle into the Atlantic Charter.

Meanwhile Churchill was in favour of a 'United States of Europe' that would include the Soviet Union while keeping Germany disarmed. He also sought an Anglo-American condominium to avoid the 'measureless disaster' that would ensue 'if Russian barbarism overlaid the culture and independence of the ancient States of Europe'. He opposed the elevation of China as a world power, fearing that it would lead to 'a faggot [client] vote on the side of the United States in any attempt to liquidate the overseas British Empire'. For his part, Stalin wanted to consolidate Soviet interests in Eastern Europe, for example by promoting a government in Poland that was more friendly than the government in exile in London. He was as yet showing little open interest in the Far East.[24]

There was some American anxiety that Churchill's Mediterranean strategy might revive old anxieties about Anglo-Russian rivalry in Southeastern Europe and the Middle East and thus help to persuade Stalin to make a separate peace with Hitler. In May 1943, the prime minister flew to Washington to reinforce the case for attacking Nazi Germany via the 'soft underbelly' of Europe. Roosevelt insisted on the necessity on the need for a Second Front across the Channel and extracted an agreement from Churchill on a target date of March 1944 for what was now called Operation Overlord. There was also some discussion of Southeast Asia, and of continued collaboration on the development of the atomic bomb. Keen to allay Soviet suspicions about delay in the opening of the Second Front, Roosevelt made overtures for a face-to-face meeting with the Soviet leader, lying to Churchill that the initiative had come from Stalin himself. As the Western Allies pushed through Sicily and the Red Army moved forward after the greatest tank battle in history at Kursk, Churchill pressed for a further summit meeting, including Stalin if possible.

From 12 to 14 August 1943, Churchill and Roosevelt renewed their friendship at the president's family home, Hyde Park, before travelling on to Quebec for a further conference. They agreed to send another suggestion to Stalin for a triangular meeting but also to withhold from him any information about progress on the atomic bomb. Strategic emphasis remained on Europe, in particular preparations for Operation Overlord. Churchill still wanted to concentrate on the Mediterranean as Italy was about to be invaded. Any suggestion from Stalin that he should be involved in discussions about post-war policy in Italy was to be rejected, he considered. Further attention was also given to the strategy to be employed in the Far East. Control of the seas was agreed as a priority but the question of attack from the air stimulated considerable divergence of opinion. Should it best be via China or the Pacific? Underneath, the problem concerned Britain's fair share in the war against Japan following defeat of Germany. Mountbatten's appointment as Chief of Combined Operations in Southeast Asia was a reassurance. As Churchill reported to Deputy Prime Minister Attlee and the War Cabinet on 25 August, 'The black spot at the present time is the increasing bearishness of Soviet Russia. ... Stalin has of course studiously ignored our offer to make a further long and hazardous journey in order to bring about a tripartite meeting'.[25] Indeed, Western relations with the Soviet Union worsened in August 1943 as Stalin recalled Ambassador Litvinov from Washington and Ambassador Maisky from London under suspicion of being too sympathetic to the policies of their hosts. However, the way forward was made smoother by a conference of the foreign ministers in Moscow from late October to early November.

In spite of further problems, agreement was finally reached on a first conference of the Big Three at Tehran in Persia (Iran), with a preliminary meeting at Cairo, Egypt, in late November. But the Soviet representatives withdrew from this meeting when they learned that the Chinese leader Chiang Kai-shek had also been invited. En route to Cairo in November 1943, Churchill wrote a paper describing recent operations in the Mediterranean, including the Italian surrender in September. Churchill argued that further operations in Italy were being hampered not only by continued German resistance there but also by preparations for Overlord before concluding that 'It is certainly an odd way of helping the Russians, to slow down the fight in the only theatre where anything can be done for three months'. Before formal meetings, Churchill and Roosevelt both met Chiang Kai-shek and his wife, who was a great charmer. But Chiang did not like Churchill and was suspicious of Roosevelt, while all three leaders had different priorities: Roosevelt was most interested in the Pacific, Churchill in Europe and the Empire, Chiang in the Asiatic mainland. These varying viewpoints emerged in the formal sessions when there was no substantial agreement on strategy, although a Cairo Declaration drawn up at American instigation called for the unconditional surrender of the Japanese and the return of all the territories seized by them. Churchill took an early opportunity to reiterate his concerns for the Mediterranean as well as his full support for Overlord, before the Americans presented the British with a memorandum advocating the appointment of a supreme commander of the operations of the United Nations (as the Allied forces were now called) against Germany in both the Mediterranean and the Atlantic. In the response to the British Chiefs of Staff on the same day, a comparison was made with the command of Marshal Foch in the First World War that was limited to the Western and Italian fronts, excluding Salonika, Palestine and Mesopotamia. The British memorandum asserted: 'There must be some limit to the responsibilities which Allied Governments can delegate to a single soldier, and the sphere now proposed seems to exceed these limits considerably.' Churchill remained under the impression that an American would lead Overlord while a Briton would command the Mediterranean.

On Thanksgiving Day, 25 November, the president invited Churchill and his daughter for 'a family affair', including the traditional dinner. Churchill wrote later: 'This jolly evening and the spectacle of the President carving up the turkeys stand out in mind among the most agreeable features of the halt at Cairo.' He went on to observe that at last 'The difficulties of the American Constitution, Roosevelt's health, and Stalin's obduracy' were swept away along with the difficulties of travel 'by the inexorable need of a triple meeting, and the failure of every other alternative but a flight to Tehran'.[26]

Keeping to our resolve to concentrate on what happened and what was said with the minimum of comment, let us nevertheless make a brief interim observation. On the eve of Tehran, the relationship between Great Britain and the United States that had started out so well was already under a strain that the goodwill of a Thanksgiving Dinner could not disguise. As we have just seen, concerns arising from the imperial heritage in general and the First World War in particular were operating on British minds. From the American perspective, with the transatlantic distance leading towards a single view of Europe and its global context, higher command should reside with the greater power. A constant focus for disagreement was the forthcoming Second Front, with British emphasis on the Mediterranean and American on the Channel. Of course, the United States was also profoundly concerned with the Pacific theatre of war. Soviet attitudes towards world problems, Asian as well as European, were about to be discovered at Tehran, but there was already some evidence during the preliminaries that Stalin and his entourage were prepared at least to engage with the arguments of their Western Allies, themselves ready enough to let bygones be bygones. Clearly, however, the Soviet side was conscious of the Russian imperial heritage in Europe, and of the loss of Warsaw and a considerable slice of Poland as well as the Baltic states and Finland after the First World War, while not forgetting the reversals in Asia during the Russo-Japanese War of 1904–5. It is difficult to say when that term the Big Three was first used for the UK, USA and USSR and their leaders, but the concept certainly achieved full realization at Tehran.

Tehran: 'Friends in Fact, in Spirit and in Purpose'

Tehran

After Churchill and Roosevelt had arrived safely after flights of six hours or so from Cairo to Tehran, Soviet Foreign Minister V. M. Molotov talked of a plot to assassinate one or more of the Big Three. Roosevelt was persuaded to move from the comparatively remote American Legation to the heavily guarded Soviet Embassy which was very close to the British Embassy. Thus, Churchill could easily walk to what in his estimation 'might be said to be for the time being the centre of the world'.[1]

Roosevelt was soon able to exercise his preference for personal diplomacy in a previously aborted first meeting with Stalin on 28 November 1943. Roosevelt began by saying 'I am glad to see you. I have tried for a long time to bring this about.' Stalin acknowledged blame for the delay, explaining that he had been preoccupied by military matters. Roosevelt then asked Stalin about the situation on the Eastern European Front. Roosevelt said that he would like to divert thirty to forty German divisions from this front, but that it would be difficult to keep an American force numbering about two million 3,000 miles away from the United States. Stalin said that he understood this. Turning to the post-war period, Roosevelt said that he would like to discuss later the manner in which the British and American merchant fleets, both of them by then much too big, might be distributed in such a way that the Soviet Union would be able to commence the development of commercial shipping. Stalin approved of Roosevelt's intention to let other Allies have some merchant ships, and felt bound to add that 'after the war Russia will be a big market for the United States'. At the same time, Roosevelt observed, 'the Americans will need great quantities of raw materials'. That was why he thought that 'there will be close trade ties between our countries'. Stalin agreed, adding that 'if the Americans will deliver equipment to us, we shall be able to deliver to them raw materials'.

Roosevelt told Stalin that he had held interesting conversations with Chiang Kai-shek. He had not wanted to involve the Chinese leader in meetings such as the present one, but believed that the Chinese were satisfied with the decisions taken at them. Stalin said that Chiang Kai-shek's troops were not fighting well against the Japanese, but this was the fault of their leaders. Roosevelt informed Stalin that the Americans were sending the Chinese equipment for thirty divisions, with the same amount to follow later.

Stalin then asked about recent disturbances in Lebanon, and who was to blame for them. Roosevelt put the blame on the French who had great influence there and who had arrested the president and his cabinet. Roosevelt said that Stalin would not have liked de Gaulle if he had met him. Roosevelt also expressed the opinion that 'the French are a good people but they need absolutely new leaders not over 40 years old, who have not held any posts in the former French Government.' Stalin agreed with this, going on to observe that 'some leading strata in France want to be cleverer than all the Allies and intend to deceive the Allies. They apparently expect the Allies to present them France ready-made, and do not wish to fight on the side of the Allies but prefer to collaborate with the Germans'. Roosevelt went on to say that Churchill was of the opinion that France would be fully reborn after the war to become a great power, but he himself did not think so, adding that 'The French will have to work a great deal before France really becomes a Great Power'.

Stalin responded by doubting that the Allies would shed blood to liberate Indochina in order for the French to bring back their colonial regime. The Japanese had boosted the idea of independence in Burma and Thailand, and something similar might be done in Indochina. The events in Lebanon were also showing the way forward. He believed that Churchill was in favour of a freer regime in Lebanon, and so the same could be introduced into Indochina. Roosevelt said that he concurred completely. He had been pleased to discover that Chiang Kai-shek did not want Indochina while believing that its people were not yet ready for self-government. Certainly, the people were worse off than at the beginning of French domination, a hundred years previously. Meanwhile, the Americans had prepared the people of the Philippines for fulfilment of the promise of self-government. Indochina should be assigned to three or four trustees so that its people too could be made ready for self-government in thirty years or so.

Roosevelt considered that 'the same is true of the other colonies', but he believed that Churchill would be less than enthusiastic about such a proposal through fear of the same principle being applied to his own colonies. When Secretary of State Cordell Hull had visited Moscow recently, he had taken with him a document prepared by Roosevelt himself on an International Commission for the Colonies which would in a completely open manner inspect the situation in colonies all over the world with a view to its improvement. Stalin thought that requests and complaints could be handled by a commission such as that being proposed by Roosevelt. The president went on to warn Stalin not to mention India to Churchill, who did not want to consider how to solve the problem there until after the war, and the marshal agreed that it was 'Churchill's sore spot'. However, Roosevelt continued, Great Britain would have to do something with India, and he wanted to talk sometime to Stalin about this question, going on to observe that 'the parliamentary system of government was unsuitable for India' and something like the Soviet system might be more appropriate, beginning from below rather than above. Stalin commented that to begin from below was to follow the path of revolution. Roosevelt went on to say: 'People standing aside from the question of India could solve it better than people directly concerned with this question.' Stalin commented that 'people not concerned with India can naturally take a more objective view of things'.[2] According to the Soviet version but not the American, Stalin asked Roosevelt what was meant by 'unconditional surrender', since the idea was considered insulting by the enemy and intensified their efforts. According to the Soviet account, Roosevelt gave no answer to the question, but talked of the days of his youth in Germany.[3]

At the first plenary meeting later on 28 November 1943, Roosevelt claimed the privilege of speaking first as the youngest head of government present and went on to assure the members of the new family gathered at the conference that they were there with one purpose, to win the war as soon as possible. They would all speak in a friendly, open and candid manner, but would not make public what they said. Their three nations would draw closer to create the basis for the close cooperation of future generations. Roosevelt then asked Churchill to say something about the importance of the meeting and its meaning for humanity.

The prime minister declared that theirs was 'the greatest concentration of world forces that ever existed in the history of mankind'. Together, they could reduce the length of the war, win it and assure the future of mankind. Asked by Roosevelt if he would like to say anything, Stalin observed that they were being pampered by history, who had given them great forces and opportunities. The marshal continued: 'I hope that we shall do everything at this conference to make due use, within the framework of our co-operation, of the power and authority that our peoples have vested in us.'

Roosevelt then gave a review of the war from the American point of view. He referred to the war in the Pacific where US forces numbering more than one million bore the brunt, while keeping China in the war on the mainland with the aid of British forces in Burma led by Lord Mountbatten. He turned to what he called 'the most important theater of war – Europe' and the question of greatest concern to the Soviet Union, the crossing of that 'disagreeable body of water' known as the English Channel. Plans had been considered for the previous year and a half but no precise date had yet been set because of inadequate tonnage of shipping. The intention was to launch the expedition by about 1 May 1944, but there would have to be coordination with operations in the Mediterranean which might delay it for two or three months. The Western Allies would welcome the advice of their Soviet friends on how they could best relieve pressure on the Eastern Front.

Agreeing in principle with what Roosevelt had said, Churchill pointed out that 'the British had every reason to be thankful that the English Channel was such a disagreeable body of water'. Welcoming the progress being made against Japan, Stalin regretted that Soviet forces could not yet make a contribution as they were preparing a large-scale offensive to follow up their unexpected successes of August and September against the forces of Germany and their Finnish, Hungarian and Romanian satellites. Acknowledging the significance of bringing freedom of navigation to the Mediterranean, Stalin recalled the crossing of the Alps by Marshal Suvorov in 1799. He went on to say that operations to the south of that mountain range would not help operations against the Germans, although an attack could be made from the Balkans at the heart of Germany if Turkey would open up the way. However, Germany's weakest spot was France. Difficult though it would be, a strike across the Channel would be of greatest use.

Churchill responded by saying that such an attack codenamed Operation Overlord was already being prepared, and he could give much information to indicate why it had not been carried out in 1943. Forces in the Mediterranean Sea and the Indian Ocean were also being deployed to advance the common cause, and the entry into the war of Turkey if achieved could enable direct contact to be made between the Western Allies and Russia without the difficulties faced by the convoys to her northern ports. Roosevelt thought there might be some mutual advantage to a landing in the Adriatic to support Tito's partisan activity in Yugoslavia while the thrust into Italy would be scaled down after Rome had been taken. Stalin considered that 'it would be better to make Overlord the basis of all operations in 1944' with support from a further landing in the south of France. In the Soviet experience, an attack on the enemy from two sides had proved a great success. He doubted that Turkey would join in the war. Roosevelt added that if he were in the position of the Turkish president, he would ask for terms that could only result in harm to Overlord. Churchill suggested that diversionary operations in Yugoslavia might be helpful, also commenting that Christmas was a poor season for turkeys in England. When this facetious remark was explained to Stalin, the Soviet marshal expressed his regret that he was not an Englishman. Churchill also observed: 'We all have feelings of friendship for each other, but we naturally have differences. We need time and patience.' Stalin said: 'That's right.'[4]

On the evening of 28 November, Roosevelt was the host at a Big Three dinner. He agreed to a considerable extent with Stalin's observations that France had lost the right to keep her empire and that 'the entire French ruling class was rotten to the core'. Churchill intervened to observe that Great Britain wanted no additional territory but that the Big Three plus China would share the responsibility for world peace and, therefore, some strategic points should be under their control. In discussion about the future of Germany, Roosevelt wanted the very word *Reich* to be eliminated, while Stalin thought that militarism must go too, through control, disarmament and even dismemberment. Stalin also insisted that 'the Baltic States had by an expression of the will of the people voted to join the Soviet Union and that this question was not therefore one for discussion'. At that point, Roosevelt and Churchill kept their disagreement with Stalin to themselves.

Roosevelt announced his interest 'in the possibility of a sovereignty fashioned in a collective body such as the United Nations; a concept which had never been developed in past history'. After he retired, Churchill and Stalin continued the conversation on German disarmament, the marshal disagreeing with the prime minister about making a distinction between the leaders and the people. The two of them concurred, however, about Poland's western frontier moving westwards, Churchill making the analogy with the drill movement 'left close' and illustrating the point with three matches representing Germany, Poland and the Soviet Union.[5]

Stalin and Roosevelt met together again in the afternoon of 29 November. Roosevelt began by lending Stalin a report on Tito, and giving him a memorandum on Soviet bases being made available to American bombers for attacks on Germany in conjunction with operations from air bases in the UK, and other memoranda with proposals for the same facility in the Soviet Far East and for naval operations in the north-western region of the Pacific. All these matters should be kept top secret, he added. Roosevelt also wanted to discuss with Stalin the shape of the post-war world settlement, including China in a proposal for a Four Power Declaration. A future United Nations should not be like the League of Nations, but would consist of from thirty-five to fifty nations making recommendations on non-military matters. It should meet in different places like the assembly of twenty-one American republics. Stalin asked if the new organization would be centred on Europe or the world, and who would comprise its executive body. Roosevelt replied that it would be on a world scale, while its Executive Committee would consist of the Four Powers, plus two countries from Europe and one each from South America, the Middle East, Asia and the British Dominions. After some discussion of the remit of the new organization, Stalin asked if a Police Committee would have coercive power. In reply, Roosevelt gave an example drawn from pre-war history. In 1935, when Italy launched its surprise attack on Abyssinia, he had asked Britain and France to close the Suez Canal, but they had referred the matter to the League of Nations, thus allowing Italy to continue its aggression.

In such a case, the proposed Police Committee consisting of four countries would be able to close the Suez Canal quickly.

After further elaboration from Roosevelt, Stalin wondered if it might not be better to have two organizations, one for Europe and the other for the Far East or for the world. Roosevelt replied that this idea was not far from Churchill's, except that the prime minister had proposed three organizations, one for Europe, another for the Far East and a third for the Americas. However, Roosevelt continued, the fact that the United States would not be a member of the European organization would make it even more difficult to send American troops to Europe than it had been in 1941, when without the Japanese attack on Pearl Harbor (followed by the German declaration of war on the United States), Congress would not have agreed to such a proposal. Stalin asked if it would be necessary for American troops to be sent to Europe if a world organization such as that proposed by Roosevelt were created. Roosevelt replied that it would not be necessary in the event of any future aggression in Europe. Britain and Russia would have to send their troops while the United States would make available planes and ships. Two kinds of force could be used in the face of a threat of aggression or revolution: the first quarantine to prevent the fire spreading; the second, an ultimatum followed by bombardment or occupation in the event of non-compliance.

Stalin went on to say that at the previous evening's dinner after the president's departure he had talked with Churchill about keeping the peace in the future. The prime minister had not taken a serious view of the problem, considering that Germany would not be able to recover for some time. But Stalin thought that this could happen in fifteen or twenty years. He looked back at what had happened in history. In 1914, Germany had continued its aggression begun forty-two years before in 1870–1 (in the Franco-Prussian War). In 1939, twenty-one years later, Germany had struck again. The time necessary for revival was being reduced. Moreover, the Germans would be able to overcome any restrictions placed upon them. Both Germany and Japan could be deterred in the future only if the organization that was to be created were given the power to occupy the points of greatest strategic significance. Roosevelt said that he was in full agreement, and considered that the two of them had made great progress in their talks, too.[6]

The second plenary meeting of the heads of government in the afternoon of 29 November was preceded by the presentation of a ceremonial sword to Stalin by Churchill on behalf of George VI and his people to 'the steel-hearted citizens of Stalingrad (an event which may still be viewed online)'. This was followed by a report on the morning's military meeting concerning Operation Overlord, Yugoslavia and Turkey. Stalin asked who carried 'the moral and military responsibility for the preparation and execution of Operation Overlord'? Without such a person, there would be only talk. Churchill said that the British government had already declared itself ready to accept an American commander-in-chief for Overlord since the United States would deploy the greater forces. But a British commander-in-chief would be more appropriate for the Mediterranean since British forces formed the majority there. He thought that Roosevelt would agree that the question of the command of Overlord would be settled in a fortnight.

Churchill next expressed his concern at the quantity and difficulty of the problems facing them all at this 'unique' conference on which millions of people had placed their hopes. He went on to a detailed consideration of operations in the Mediterranean, in progress in Italy, in prospect in southern France. He thought that there might be some advantage to combined raids in the Balkans, where 'we have neither interests nor ambitions' but there was the possibility of keeping busy some of the forces of Germany and her satellites. Pressure should be exerted on Turkey to enter the war with a warning that her rights in the Bosporus and the Dardanelles might be affected otherwise. Roosevelt observed that he considered dates to be very important, and that Overlord should be begun early in May or with some postponement if other operations were being carried out in the Mediterranean. Any action in the Balkans should not be allowed to delay Overlord. When Stalin sought a specific date for Overlord, Churchill said that it could not be given, and that operations in the Mediterranean should not be interrupted since the forces there should not be kept idle and passive. Ignoring the interjection of Stalin that it looked as if he were suggesting that the Russians wanted the British to be idle, Churchill went on to give further detailed attention to the Mediterranean.

Stalin asked how long they were all going to stay in Tehran; Roosevelt answered that he was ready to stay there as long as Stalin, and Churchill expressed his readiness to stay as long as necessary. After some discussion of the activities of French forces in the Mediterranean, Roosevelt suggested that the question might be referred to the military committee, and Churchill agreed. Refuting the need for such a committee, Stalin insisted again that the date and the command of Overlord and any need for further operations in the south of France must be decided in order that Soviet attacks could be prepared accordingly. Three or four days had previously been agreed for the conference, and the Russians would have to leave Tehran by 2 December. When Roosevelt insisted that he wanted no delay in Overlord, but Churchill stressed the importance of operations in the Mediterranean, and suggested that the military committee could deal with these small differences, Stalin declared: 'We can solve these problems ourselves, because we have more rights than the military committee. If I may permit myself an incautious question, I should like to know whether the British believe in Operation Overlord or simply speak of it to reassure the Russians.' Roosevelt with Churchill's support suggested that the committee should meet the following morning, after which they and Marshal Stalin could then consider all questions at luncheon.[7]

At dinner on 29 November, Stalin made several digs at Churchill, at one point saying that Russians might be simple but they were not blind and could see what was in front of their eyes. Evidently, the marshal was far from happy at the prime minister's attitude to both Overlord and Germany. To stop the revival of Germany and its launch of yet another war, he proposed that 50,000, even 100,000, senior German officers should be executed and that the victorious Allies should keep such a firm grip on the world's most important strategic points that Germany could be immediately stopped if she moved as much as a muscle. A similar policy should be adopted towards Japan. While Roosevelt said that 49,000 or more German officers should be executed, Churchill objected strongly to the cold-blooded killing for political purposes of soldiers fighting for their country. Regarding strategic points around Germany and Japan, Roosevelt said that they should be held in trusteeship. Churchill said that Britain wanted no more territory or bases, but would not give up what she already had without a struggle, mentioning Singapore and Hong Kong in particular. In due course, some of her Empire might be released, but this would be done by Britain herself according to her own moral principles. Stalin suggested that the British Empire deserved expansion, especially around Gibraltar, and that Britain and the United States might introduce friendly governments in both Spain and Portugal. He gave an evasive answer to Churchill about Soviet territorial interests.[8]

In the early afternoon of 30 November, Stalin met Churchill for a conversation lasting about one hour. The British prime minister beginning by observing that he himself was half-American via his mother. Stalin interjected that he had already heard this. Churchill went on to observe that he was very fond of the Americans and completely loyal to them. Nothing that he said should be taken as an indication of a wish to do the Americans down, but some things were best said privately. Firstly, he wanted the marshal to know that there were up to three or four times more British forces than American in the Mediterranean. That was why he was so interested in this theatre of operations, and wanted to protect 'this great British army' from idleness. A choice was therefore necessary between continuance of these operations and the launch of Operation Overlord. Moreover, the Americans wanted the British to undertake a landing in the Bay of Bengal in March 1944. This involved another difficult choice. Already both American and British divisions had been withdrawn from the Mediterranean as the Americans insisted on keeping to the date fixed for Overlord. This explained the slow progress in Italy. As for Overlord, Churchill had first expected that the British would appoint a commander for the trans-Channel crossing, but he had accepted Roosevelt's suggestion made at Quebec that the Americans would appoint the commander for Overlord where they would have greater numbers, and the British for the Mediterranean where they had numerical superiority.

Stalin asked Churchill if Eisenhower would lose command in the Mediterranean to the British. Replying in the affirmative, Churchill added that the delay in making the appointment for Overlord was caused by high-level domestic considerations in the United States, but he hoped that the question might be resolved before the end of the conference. There was also a further difficulty arising from a shortage of landing craft. As soon as Stalin made his historic statement about joining in the war against Japan, which was a sensitive and important question for the Americans, as was for China, Churchill was confident that they would find enough landing craft either in the Mediterranean or in the Pacific.

Churchill wanted to assure Stalin that he was not neglecting Overlord, and that a formidable British force would be assembled consisting of 'the best British troops' and including 'battle-wise divisions transferred from the Mediterranean'. The transfer was being facilitated by the heavy toll taken of enemy submarines. Churchill also favoured a landing in the South of France to be coordinated with Overlord and carried out by some forces from Italy while others held the front. The prime minister went on to give further details of operations in Italy, including 'a miniature Stalingrad' near the mouth of the River Tiber.

Invited by Churchill to ask questions, Stalin said that the Red Army was counting on Overlord. He was apprehensive that if it did not occur in May, deterioration in the weather would then make it impossible. If Overlord were not undertaken, this would lead to 'great disappointment', 'bad feelings' and 'a very bad feeling of isolation' and so he would like to know so that he could forestall such reactions. Churchill assured Stalin that the landing would take place successfully provided the Allied forces maintained numerical superiority and the Germans were unable to bring thirty or forty divisions over to France. He was less apprehensive about the landing itself than about what would ensue thirty to forty days further on. Stalin went on to assert that as soon as they knew that the landing in the north of France was to take place in May or June, the Russians would prepare not one but several attacks. Spring was the most appropriate time because the troops could usually make use of a breathing space in March and April to have a rest. The attacks would stop any transfer of troops to France by the Germans, who were in fact transferring troops to the Eastern Front as it fell back towards German borders where there was no channel or sea. Stalin asked again for the date of Overlord. Churchill said that he could not provide an answer to this question which they were to discuss at luncheon. He concluded the meeting by giving Stalin a map concerning the situation in Yugoslavia that Stalin might wish to compare with his own information.

At the ensuing Big Three luncheon, Roosevelt gave Stalin 'a good piece of news'. Operation Overlord had been agreed for May 1944 with an auxiliary operation taking place in the south of France, the size of which would depend on the number of available landing craft. Churchill pointed out that the exact timing of Overlord would depend on the phase of the moon. Stalin said that he was not asking for the precise date, but commented that one or two weeks in May would be necessary to complete the operation. Roosevelt reported that according to available information the period from 15 to 20 May would be most appropriate for Overlord. Stalin informed his allies that the Russians would have ready 'a strong blow at the Germans' to coincide with their landings in France, and Roosevelt thought this would be most welcome since it would stop the enemy from effecting any transfer of troops from East to West. Churchill went on to talk of some of the British preparations for Overlord including what was to become known as PLUTO (Pipe Line Under The Ocean), a special means of delivering fuel via the bed of the Channel. Stalin gave this news a warm reception.

Asked by Churchill about the proposals for the Far East made at Cairo, Stalin said that China should be made to fight for the restoration of her former territories. After Stalin conceded that the Soviet Union's vast territories had probably saved her from defeat, Churchill commented that such a vast land deserved access to warm water ports. Stalin raised the question of navigation through the Turkish straits in a preliminary manner, referring to previous restrictions. Churchill disavowed such objections, although he did not want to discuss the subject at the present time when it was desirable that Turkey enter the war. But he added the hope that Russian naval and merchant fleets would both be seen on seas and oceans throughout the world. When Stalin observed that this had not been the view of Lord Curzon, British foreign secretary during the First World War, Churchill conceded that he could not disagree. But Stalin went on to say that Russia was different too at that time.

Switching the subject to the Baltic, Roosevelt put forward the idea of making the cities of the medieval Hanseatic League into a free zone with an internationally guaranteed freedom of passage through the Kiel Canal. Stalin approved of this idea, but then reverted to the question of the Far East, which Churchill welcomed. When the marshal went on to say that Vladivostok was not always an ice-free port, and the Japanese dominated the nearby straits, Roosevelt suggested an internationally guaranteed port at Dairen might well be agreeable to the Chinese. Churchill repeated that Russia must have warm-water ports. He also considered it important that the nations that governed the world after the war should have no territorial or other ambitions. Hungry and ambitious nations were dangerous. There was some discussion about how the Big Three might bring their talks to an end in conjunction with their foreign ministers.[9]

The third plenary meeting of the Conference of the heads of government took place in the later afternoon of 30 November. After Stalin was informed again that Overlord would be started in May with a supporting operation in Southern France, Churchill said that the joint British and American staffs would consult with Stalin on the coordination of these attacks so that the enemy might be struck simultaneously on both sides. Stalin undertook again to order a large offensive in May to stop enemy forces being transferred from the Eastern to the Western Front. Roosevelt assured Stalin that a commander-in-chief would be appointed in a few days after he and Churchill returned to Cairo where detailed planning would continue.

Churchill suggested that attention should now be turned from military to political questions. Stalin agreed to stay another day if necessary. Roosevelt went on to say that the staffs could give a draft of the communiqué. When Stalin asked if this would be the part relating to military operations, Churchill replied: 'Of course. The communiqué must be brief and mystifying.' Stalin added: 'But without any mysticism.' Churchill believed that the enemy would soon learn of the impending attack because of the necessary large-scale preparations, although attention would be given to ways of achieving camouflage.

Agreeing that such an operation could not be 'hidden in a sack', Stalin described how the Soviet forces had made considerable use of dummy tanks and planes and of mock airfields while attacks were prepared quietly at night with radio silence where the offensive was planned. Churchill commented: 'Sometimes truth has to be safeguarded with the aid of untruth.'[10]

On 30 November a dinner was hosted by Churchill to celebrate his sixty-ninth birthday, and many toasts were exchanged by the Big Three. When Churchill suggested that the marshal deserved inclusion among the leading figures of Russian history with the title of 'Stalin the Great', the marshal responded that it was easy to be a great leader in Russia, but the real heroes were the people, fighting heroically. Even cowards could become heroes, especially if the alternative for them was to be killed. Churchill praised Roosevelt's courage and action that had averted revolution in 1933. Stalin praised the productive capacity of the United States, turning out under the great leadership of the president twice as many planes as the Soviet Union and Great Britain between them, and delivering many of them to the Soviet

Union. Claiming the last word, Roosevelt declared 'as we leave this historic gathering, we can see in the sky, for the first time, that traditional symbol of hope, the rainbow'.[11]

On 1 December, there was a sitting during luncheon. First, the question was discussed of how much support Turkey should receive from Great Britain and the United States if it entered the war and how its entry should fit in to the overall strategy. Roosevelt said that he would have to exercise care in making any promises because of commitments elsewhere. Stalin agreed that Turkey should allow the Allied air forces to make use of her territory. Churchill brought up the possibility of bringing in landing facilities from the Indian or Pacific Ocean. Roosevelt emphasized the huge distance from the Mediterranean to the Pacific, adding that as the US forces moved northwards towards Japan, they needed landing facilities there. During discussion of joint air operations, Churchill said that in order to expel the German air force from the Greek islands, 'we are prepared to pay with one of our planes for every destroyed German plane'. He agreed that the Turks must be given materiel aid but said that they must also be told that if they did not join in the war against Germany they would not be invited to the peace conference. Roosevelt wanted the Dardanelles to be made open for the commerce and fleets of the world whether or not Turkey entered the war. Again, the focus switched to the Baltic, in particular to Finland. Stalin proposed to guarantee Finland's independence, but wanted to shift the 1939 frontier to protect Soviet security and to impose reparations for damage brought about in the war of 1939–40. Churchill appeared to accept this proposal as long as Finland was not weakened further, but Roosevelt was not so accommodating, while hoping for an anti-German government in Finland.[12]

In the afternoon, the president came to see the marshal on a matter of internal American politics. He explained that, because of the importance of the votes of six to seven million American citizens of Polish descent, he could not immediately take part in any resolution of the question of the post-war Polish frontiers. As far as the Baltic Republics of Lithuania, Latvia and Estonia were concerned, he joked that he would not go to war with the Soviet Union when it reoccupied them, but he hoped that some day they could be accorded the right of self-determination. Stalin responded that such a question had never been raised when these republics were part of tsarist Russia at an earlier time of alliance with the United States and Great Britain during the First World War, and he could not understand why it was being brought up now. The will of the people could be expressed through the Soviet constitution. When Roosevelt said that it would be of help to him personally if Stalin would say something publicly about future elections, the marshal replied that there would be many opportunities for such expressions of the popular will. There ensued some discussion of post-war world organization, and of secret talks concerning air bases in the Far East.[13]

A further roundtable meeting ensued in the early evening of 1 December. Roosevelt said that he would like some discussion on the questions of Poland and Germany. Stalin added the question of the communiqué, which Roosevelt said was being prepared. Molotov then brought up the question of the transfer to the Soviet Union of a share of Italy's navy and merchant fleet, Stalin adding preferably to the Black Sea, but to the North Sea if Turkey did not enter the war. Roosevelt and Churchill agreed that these ships would be delivered by January 1945 – Churchill adding that he would like British ships and submarines to help the Russian navy in the Black Sea if Turkey stretched her neutrality in the event of being afraid to join in the war.

Roosevelt then introduced the question of Poland, expressing the hope that the Soviet government would be able to restore relations and renew talks with the *émigré* Polish government. Stalin replied: 'The agents of the Polish Government, who are in Poland, are connected with the Germans. They are killing partisans. You cannot imagine what they are doing there.' Churchill said that Poland was 'a big issue.' He understood the historical difference between the Russian and British attitudes towards Poland, particularly in view of Britain's pre-war weakness and France's abandonment of her Munich guarantees. Nevertheless, Great Britain had entered the war because it had given Poland a guarantee. Churchill also accepted that the borders of Germany, Poland and the Soviet Union must all be moved to the west to protect the Soviet Union's security.

Stalin said that the Soviet Union was in favour of the revival and strengthening of its neighbour Poland, but had broken off relations with the *émigré* government in London (on 25 April 1943) because it had 'joined Hitler in slandering the Soviet Union'. However, Stalin continued, he would be ready to talk to it again if its agents in Poland broke their ties to the Germans and gave support to the Polish partisans. He also considered that there should be a reversion to the 1939 eastern frontier, which would mean that the Ukrainian and Belarusian republics would both regain lands that were rightfully theirs.

Roosevelt introduced the topic of the partition of Germany, Churchill immediately observing that he was in favour of this in general and in particular of it in Prussia, 'the root of evil', with Bavaria and other provinces also being separated from Germany. Roosevelt agreed that Prussia should be weakened as it was made independent. There should be other independent states as well as two regions, one centred on Kiel and Hamburg, the other on the Ruhr and the Saar, to be administered by the United Nations or internationally. Churchill commented 'You have said a mouthful', going on to repeat that Prussia should be strictly isolated and then to suggest that southern German provinces could be included in a federation of the Danube basin whose peoples had not been a cause of war. Stalin considered that, if there were to be partition of Germany, no new associations of states needed to be brought in. He wanted to consider Roosevelt's ideas for weakening Germany. He assured Churchill that it was not only the Prussians who fought doggedly, although Soviet soldiers readily accepted the surrender of Austrians. In his view, Austria and Hungary needed to be kept separate, and there was no necessity for a Danubian federation. Agreeing with Stalin, Roosevelt said: 'Fifty years ago there was a difference but now all German soldiers are alike.' However, he went on to add: 'It is true that this does not apply to the Prussian officers.' Churchill expressed his concern that if Germany were not partitioned into combinations of provinces, then at some point German unification would ensue. Stalin said that there was no way of making such unification impossible. Asked by Churchill if he preferred a divided Europe, Stalin replied: 'Europe has nothing to do with it', adding that the division of Germany into independent states needed further discussion.

Churchill returned to the question of Poland, which seemed to him 'to be more urgent because the Poles can make a great deal of noise'. He proposed that the heart of the Polish state and people 'must be situated between the so-called Curzon Line and the line of the Oder River', although further study would be needed. Stalin said that the Russians had no ice-free ports on the Baltic and therefore wanted to acquire them in the shape of Königsberg and

Memel along with a hinterland in East Prussia, 'particularly since these are age-old Slav lands'. He would accept Churchill's formula if Churchill accepted this transfer. Churchill replied: 'This is a very interesting proposal which I will make a point of studying.'[14]

After Tehran

The conclusion of the war in Europe constituted the main theme of the Communiqué on the Conference of the heads of government of the Allied Countries, the USSR, the United States and Great Britain, signed on 1 December 1943. However, the theme was presented in a broad manner only, talking of plans to destroy German forces along with 'complete agreement as to the scope and timing of the operations to be undertaken from the East, West and South'. The communiqué asserted: 'No power on earth can prevent our destroying the German armies by land, their U-boats by sea, and their war plants from the air.' Moreover, declared Roosevelt, Stalin and Churchill, 'We recognise fully the supreme responsibility resting upon us and all the United Nations to make a peace which will command the good will of the overwhelming mass of the peoples of the world and banish the scourge and terror of war for many generations.' The three statesmen looked with confidence 'to the day when all peoples of the world may live free lives, untouched by tyranny, and according to their various desires and their own consciences'. They concluded: 'We came here with hope and determination. We leave here, friends in fact, in spirit and in purpose.' There was also a specific Declaration regarding the host nation Iran, but no mention of the Far East.[15]

Indeed, the communiqué was uncommunicative. So that 'all peoples of the world' might 'free lives', as it said, what Churchill had called at the first plenary meeting 'the greatest concentration of world forces that ever existed in the history of mankind' would have to be turned on Japan as well as Germany. Most of the Big Three's discussion at the Tehran Conference concerned Eastern Europe and the Second Front in particular and this is reflected in the record of the conference. With the advance of the Red Army beyond the frontiers of the Soviet Union, there was some talk of the shape and nature of post-war Poland and the Baltic States, where the Western

Allies already showed their concern for democracy, and Stalin made a distinction between the Baltic States (part of the Russian Empire before 1917 and recently annexed in 1940 as part of the Nazi-Soviet Pact) and Poland (partitioned between the Russian, German and Austro-Hungarian empires up to 1914 and recently divided in 1940 between Nazi Germany and the Soviet Union by the same Pact). To some extent, the Western Allies accepted this distinction. Consideration of the treatment to be accorded defeated Nazi Germany included reduction, even dismemberment. With the launching of Operation Overlord, there would need to be coordination of the Eastern and Western Fronts. Considerable attention, too, was given to the Balkans and Turkey. Would the Soviet navy be able to make full use of Black Sea warm-water ports through access to the Mediterranean? And, after the war, would the expanded Soviet merchant fleet have access to warm-water ports either in Europe or in the Far East?

In the plenary sessions as well as in his conversations with Stalin, Roosevelt in particular showed that he was already concerned with the Far East, in particular how to bring the war with Japan to an end. Stalin, who had not forgotten the Soviet Far East, lent a willing ear to Roosevelt's request even if focused primarily on driving back the German invaders. Churchill was less interested in the Pacific than in the Mediterranean, expanding on this subject in meetings with Stalin in particular and the Big Three in general.

In his vision of the post-war world, Roosevelt sought a global United Nations, while Churchill and Stalin both thought in a more regional manner. The British prime minister was most concerned to protect the British Empire but did not forget the French, while the Soviet marshal and the American president were in agreement on the need to bring an end to empires and colonies. In other words, the three members of what Roosevelt had called the 'new family' at their first plenary meeting were far from seeing eye to eye on a number of key questions.

The Declaration on Iran recognized its facilitation of the transport of supplies to the Soviet Union, while promising economic assistance, guaranteeing 'independence, sovereignty and territorial integrity' and reaffirming the Atlantic Charter. Under the cover of pious sentiments, however, the British and Americans were thinking about Middle Eastern oil, even though Roosevelt assured Churchill that the United States was 'not making sheep's eyes at your oil fields in Iraq and Iran'.[16]

By the end of 1943, the United States bore the major responsibility for fuelling the Allied war machine from its own resources. Indeed, by some way, the United States was by the time of the Tehran Conference the leading great power, although its planners recognized that geographical position and economic potential would make the USSR another military power of the first magnitude after the defeat of Japan. Paul Kennedy, in his celebrated book, *The Rise and Fall of the Great Powers*, suggests that the years from 1943 to 1980 were marked by 'Stability and Change in a Bipolar World'.[17] However, throughout 1944, there was not only much specific reference to the Big Three but also early mention of a further designation involving all three, for in this year, W. T. R. Fox published a book entitled *The Super-Powers* with the subtitle *The United States, Britain and the Soviet Union – Their Responsibility for Peace*. Many years later, in 1980, Fox asked himself why he had included Britain along with what he called the two peripheral powers. The label 'peripheral' is a large part of the answer. In 1944, Europe was still widely seen as the centre of the world, and the offshore UK worthy of its seat at the top conference table not only for its location but also for its global empire on which the sun had still to set.[18] Churchill's personal charisma, born of long experience of war and peace, was obviously of influence here, too.

He certainly put a firm stamp on the tripartite discussions. For example, at the dinner on 29 November, when Stalin suggested that 50,000 or even 100,000 German officers should be shot and Roosevelt said 49,000 or more, Churchill objected strongly to the cold-blooded killing of soldiers fighting for their country. While all three leaders were aware at this time that 8,000 or more Polish officers had been shot along with thousands more police and members of the intelligentsia by the Red Army at Katyn after the signing of the Nazi-Soviet Pact, and while they knew something of the Nazi extermination camps in Eastern Europe, even Stalin, the most informed of them about German cold-blooded killing, probably did not know that *millions* of Red Army men were perishing in captivity, either through execution or starvation or in gas chambers.[19]

Certainly, the extermination of Soviet POWs has received less than its fair share in the historiography of the Second World War, even less in the Western popular treatment of the subject of POWs concentrating on a range of escapes in which the prison guards are treated more as dupes abiding by the Geneva Convention than as cold-blooded killers looking upon their charges as subhuman. The reasons for this disparity must be sought in the *longue durée*, in a perspective stretching back to the First World War and centuries beyond.

Yalta: 'The Same Goal by Different Means'

Before Yalta

From 6 June onwards, Operation Overlord began the largest seaborne invasion in history while the Red Army was completing some of the greatest victories ever on land. Japan was in retreat both in the Pacific and in Southeast Asia. Continuing to leave the description of the war itself in other capable hands, let us proceed to the further deliberations of the statesmen charged with formulating policies for bringing the great conflict to an end and overseeing the post-war settlement. In July 1944, an international conference on post-war world finance was held at Bretton Woods, New Hampshire, clearly foreshadowing the dominance of the dollar as it set up the IMF (International Monetary Fund) and World Bank, both largely controlled by the United States with the Soviet Union remaining aloof, a senior Soviet official commenting that the American plans at first sight looked like 'a tasty mushroom' but turned out to be 'a poisonous toadstool'.[1] In August, an Anglo-American agreement on the sale of Middle Eastern oil 'at fair prices and on a nondiscriminatory basis', in the authoritative evaluation of Warren Kimball 'used the niceties of diplomatic language to create the appearance of disinterested liberal economic reform, but it was reform on American terms'.[2] From August to October, another conference in the United States at Dumbarton Oaks, Washington, DC, considered the question of world organization, ensuring the dominance of the Big Three plus China and France as permanent members in the Security Council of the United Nations.

On 13 September, the first plenary meeting took place of the Second Quebec Conference. Now that operations were nearing completion in Italy, Churchill considered the case for an attack on Vienna to forestall any Soviet advance into the Balkans. He was by now also anxious that Britain would make a full contribution to the war in Asia after victory had been achieved in Europe. Roosevelt himself welcomed this, although some of his chiefs of staff were not so enthusiastic. In later meetings, there was some discussion of the Morgenthau Plan for the deindustrialization of post-war Germany, and of the subdivision of Germany among the victorious powers. A target date of eighteen months after victory in Europe was set for victory in Asia, and there was some mention of the contribution that might be made towards this end by the Soviet Union. A Hyde Park Agreement concerning the atomic bomb suggested that 'it might perhaps, after mature consideration, be used against the Japanese, who should be warned that the bombardment will be repeated until they surrender'.[3]

From 9 to 17 October 1944, the British prime minister and the Soviet marshal had a series of meetings in Moscow, discussing several problems including Poland, Turkey and Germany. Yet the meetings are most remembered for the first of them, when Churchill considered the moment propitious for discussion of the Balkans, and the two leaders agreed on percentages of spheres of influence as follows: Romania: Russia 90 per cent, the West 10 per cent; Greece: the West (Great Britain in accord with the United States) 90 per cent, Russia 10 per cent; Yugoslavia: West 50 per cent, Russia 50 per cent; Hungary: West 50 per cent, Russia 50 per cent; Bulgaria: Russia 75 per cent, the West 25 per cent. According to Churchill's own account, he wrote his suggestions on a half-sheet of paper and then passed them to Stalin who put a large tick on it with a blue pencil and then handed it back. After a considerable pause, as Churchill later recalled the incident, he asked: 'Might it not be thought rather cynical if it seemed we had disposed of these issues, so fateful to millions of people, in such an offhand manner? Let us burn the paper.' Stalin replied: 'No, you keep it.'[4]

As the historian Geoffrey Roberts has pointed out, 'There is no contemporary record of this dialogue, and it is reasonable to assume a certain poetic licence on Churchill's part.' However, as Roberts tells us, in the British ambassador's report, there is the following account: 'PM then produced what he called a "naughty document" showing a list of Balkan countries and the proportion of interest in them of the Great Powers. He said that the Americans would be shocked if they saw how crudely he had put it. Marshal Stalin was a realist.' The Soviet record of the meeting states that Stalin had suggested some changes in the percentages.

For Roberts, who duly records the wide variation in interpretation that has been given to the percentages agreement, the document was in fact irrelevant to the outcome in the Balkans and elsewhere. He also suggests that when Stalin told Churchill at their meeting on 14 October that the Soviet Union did not intend to organize a Bolshevik Revolution in Europe, 'he was not being untruthful or disingenuous'.[5]

Arguably, the post-war spheres of influence in Europe were decided by events as they unfolded, soon to be discussed again by the Big Three. On 22 October 1944, Churchill sent Roosevelt the message: 'I was delighted to hear from U.J. ["Uncle Joe" Stalin] that you had suggested a triple meeting towards the end of November at a Black Sea port. I think this a very fine idea, and hope you will let me know about it in due course. I will come anywhere you two desire.'[6] Was one of the Big Three already being relegated to a position lower than the other two? We must resist further speculation and turn to the meeting on the Black Sea, not in November 1944, but February 1945, at Yalta.

Before Yalta, there was at Churchill's request a preliminary meeting in Malta, both in Valetta and its Grand Harbour. Most of the discussion was between the American and British chiefs of staff, but Churchill and Roosevelt were present on board the USS *Quincy* on the evening of 2 February 1945 for a report. On the question of supplies for liberated areas in Europe, Churchill asked about its implication for British imports, which had already been less than half the pre-war amount for five years. He was told that the problem was still to be resolved. Some difference of opinion was already apparent on how the Rhine was to be crossed and how operations should proceed in the North and South of Europe.

When the focus shifted to Asia, Churchill asked if, given the vast amount of American aid to the Chinese, the results achieved by them were not rather disappointing. Roosevelt replied that China could not become a serious factor until after three generations of education and training. Churchill then observed that the British and American operations in Asia seemed to be diverging, with the latter concentrating on China as the former turned to the south. If the Americans asked the British to put more troops into China, he would be ready to consider the request, but neither the American nor the British staff chiefs were encouraging.

The prime minister asked if the attack on Japan was to be delayed until after the victory over Germany. General Marshal answered that the necessary amount of men and materiel would not be available until then. Had Germany been defeated at the end of 1944, the invasion of Japan would have been possible in the autumn of 1945.

Both leaders expressed their satisfaction at what had been achieved, and there was further conversation between them over dinner.[7]

Yalta: The priority of Europe

On Saturday 3 February 1945 in the early afternoon, Roosevelt's plane arrived in the Crimea from Malta. But he did not disembark until the arrival of Churchill's plane about twenty minutes later. Molotov explained that Stalin had not yet come down to the Crimea. Together, the two Western leaders approached a guard of honour as a band played the Star Spangled Banner, God Save the King and 'the Third [sic] Internationale'.

Leaving the airport for the eighty miles or so drive to the location of the conference, the Livadia Palace, the two parties drove through 'rolling, snow-covered country somewhat like that of our Middle West', according to the president's log, which continued: 'We saw few, if any, trees and many reminders of the recent fighting there – gutted-out buildings, burned out tanks and destroyed German railroad rolling stock that had been abandoned and burned by them in their flight.' The whole route was guarded by Soviet troops, a considerable number of whom appeared to be young girls. On arrival, all of the president's party were very tired, 'so it was a case of bathing, dining and to bed for us this evening'. The prime minister's party were housed at the Vorontsov Villa some twelve and a half miles to the south, while two US minesweepers were moored in Yalta harbour and several more US ships remained in the harbour of Sevastopol, about 80 miles to the southwest.

The Livadia Palace had been completely transformed in three weeks from 'an infested building since the German occupation and pillage, to a place that was completely habitable and comfortable', surrounded by parks and gardens stretching down to the sea. The ballroom-banquet hall was to be the main conference room. The weather was very pleasant throughout, the Russians calling it 'Roosevelt weather'.[8]

Stalin, who had arrived with his entourage in the morning of 4 February, came to see Roosevelt in the afternoon. When the president observed that he had made a number of bets on whether the Russians would get to Berlin before the Americans reached Manila, the marshal said that the Americans would achieve their objective first since the fighting along the line of the River Oder was very hard. Roosevelt went on to say that 'he had been very much struck by the extent of German destruction in the Crimea and therefore he was more bloodthirsty in regard to the Germans than he had been a year ago, and he hoped that Marshal Stalin would again propose a toast to the execution of 50,000 officers in the German Army'. Stalin replied that 'everyone was more bloodthirsty than they had been a year ago', going on to observe that the German destruction in Ukraine, which had been carried out methodically and with calculation, was far worse than that in the Crimea, which had been hurriedly improvised. The marshal added that 'the Germans were savages and seemed to hate with a sadistic hatred the creative work of human beings'. The president agreed.

More detailed discussion followed of the military situation as Germany neared defeat. Roosevelt said that the fact that the Americans had four times the number of the British in France gave them the right to have an alternative strategy. He ventured the indiscrete remark that 'the British were a peculiar people and wished to have their cake and eat it too'. He 'had had a great deal of trouble with the British in regard to zones of occupation'. As far as the French were concerned, they should probably have a zone of occupation if 'only out of kindness'. When Stalin confessed that he had found de Gaulle 'unrealistic', Roosevelt recalled that at Casablanca the French leader had compared himself to Joan of Arc as spiritual leader and Clemenceau as political leader.

An hour after Stalin met Roosevelt, the first plenary meeting of the Big Three took place in the Livadia Palace at 5.00 pm. Asked by Stalin to open the proceedings, Roosevelt thanked the Soviet leader for his hospitality before urging frank and free speech in an informal atmosphere among people with a growing understanding of each other. While the whole world was to be covered, the focus should first fall on the most important front, the Eastern European. A detailed report was given, followed by discussion of the Allied advance on Germany, and the manner in which operations on both Eastern and Western fronts could be coordinated, with implications for the manner in which the European war would be brought to an end.

Later in the evening the Big Three met again at a good-humoured dinner, agreeing that they should write the peace together. When Churchill added that they should observe the rights of smaller nations, Deputy Foreign Minister Andrei Ya. Vyshinskii conveyed to Charles E. Bohlen of the State Department that the Soviet side would never accept 'the right of the small powers to judge the acts of the Great Powers'. When Bohlen mentioned American public opinion, Vyshinskii declared that 'the American people should learn to obey their leaders'. Asked by Bohlen to repeat this statement if he would visit the United States, Vyshinskii replied that 'he would be glad to do so'. When Churchill claimed that, although he was constantly looked on as reactionary, he was the only leader of the three liable to be dismissed soon by universal suffrage, a danger in which he gloried, Stalin observed that the prime minister appeared apprehensive. Denying this, Churchill responded that not only did he not fear the elections, he was also 'proud of the right of the British people to change their government at any time they saw fit', adding: 'he felt that the three nations represented here were moving towards the same goal by different methods'. On the rights of smaller nations, Churchill recalled a quotation: 'The eagle should permit the small birds to sing and care not wherefore they sang.'[9]

When Roosevelt and Stalin left, there was some further discussion about voting in the United Nations as world organization, Churchill concurring with the Soviet view that the influence of the Big Three should be preponderant since everything depended on their unity, without which 'the world would be subjected to inestimable catastrophe'. Replying to an enquiry from Churchill about the US proposal to solve the voting problem, Bohlen said that it

> reminded him of the story of the Southern planter who had given a bottle of whiskey to a Negro as a present. The next day he asked the Negro how he had liked the whiskey, to which the Negro replied that it was perfect.

The planter asked what he meant, and the Negro said if it had been any better it would not have been given to him, and if it had been any worse he could not have drunk it.[10]

The second plenary meeting of the Big Three took place in the late afternoon of 5 February. Roosevelt said that 'they would not cover the map of the world and discuss Dakar or Indochina, but confine themselves to the political aspects of the future treatment of Germany'. They would begin with the question of zones of occupation, including one for France. Stalin asked if his two colleagues were still in favour of the unconditional surrender and dismemberment of Germany. When Roosevelt replied that the permanent condition of Germany might emerge from the zones, Stalin recalled that at Tehran the president had suggested a division into five parts and the prime minister – into two, with Prussia separated from the rest. This was just an exchange of views, however, amplified in Moscow by Churchill's idea of putting the Ruhr and Westphalia under international control. Churchill said that he agreed with the principle of dismemberment, but that its implementation would need 'elaborate searchings by experienced statesmen on the historical, political, economic and sociological aspects of the problem and prolonged study by a subcommittee'. He personally thought that the isolation and elimination of Prussia would remove 'the arch evil' as German war potential would be greatly reduced. There might be a southern state including Austria, while he recalled general agreement that some territories would be lost to Poland. The fate of the Ruhr and the surrounding area had yet to be determined, too. For the moment, however, attention needed to be given to zones of occupation including the question of one for France.

Stalin then answered his own question about the possibility of accepting unconditional surrender from Hitler or Himmler in the negative, and then went on to ask if dismemberment might be part of the terms of unconditional surrender. Churchill answered that this was the joint responsibility of the Allies, but repeated that it required careful study. Roosevelt thought that agreement now was to be on the principle, not the implementation. He recalled that when he had been in Germany forty years previously, the Reich centralized in Berlin had not really existed; he personally favoured a return to a number of states. He suggested that the foreign ministers be asked to submit a report. With the reservation of Stalin that German representatives should be told about the dismemberment, the comment of Churchill that this might stiffen their resistance and the response of Roosevelt and Stalin that the decision would not be made public, this procedure was agreed.

The Big Three took up the question of France. Churchill favoured its inclusion as a help to others, especially to the UK if the United States were to leave Europe in two years. Stalin opposed the inclusion of France as an unnecessary complication while Roosevelt thought that it should be given a zone but not included in the control machinery. The Big Three agreed to assign this problem to the foreign ministers.

Stalin turned to discussion of German reparations, and Maisky described a Soviet plan indicating the necessity for the reduction of German heavy industry by 80 per cent as part of a programme to continue for ten years. Reparations should be made according to the size of the contributions made to the victory and the losses suffered during the war. A special committee should be set up in Moscow. Churchill recalled that at the end of the First World War 'the Allies had also indulged themselves with fantastic figures of reparations but that these had turned out to be a myth'. He recognized that the Soviet Union had lost most during the Second World War. However, he continued, Great Britain had lost most of its foreign assets in spite of Lend-Lease and needed exports to pay for a half of its food supply. None of the victors would have as big an economic burden as Great Britain, which would therefore favour large reparations if they were feasible. He said that 'he was haunted by the specter of a starving Germany', adding that 'if you wished a horse to pull a wagon that you would at least have to give it fodder'. Stalin commented that this was so, but 'care needed to be taken that the horse did not turn round and kick you'. (According to the Soviet account, when Churchill changed his metaphor to an automobile needing fuel, Stalin replied that the Germans were not machines, but people.[11])

Roosevelt then recalled that the United States had made mistakes after the First World War, lending a vast amount of money to Germany but not holding on to confiscated property. The United States needed no reparations now, but did not want to have to make contributions to keeping the Germans from starvation. However, just as Americans would assist Great Britain in the expansion of its export trade, so they would support Soviet claims for reparations since 'the German standard of living should not be higher than that of the Soviet Union'. Maisky also returned to the aftermath of the First World War, arguing that reparations had failed then owing to transfer problems, while the financial policies of Great Britain and the United States had helped lead to the German refusal to pay more than a quarter of the total owed and to the extension to them of vast credits and loans. The Soviet Union did not want Germans to starve but the German standard of living should indeed not exceed that of the Soviet Union. Without military expenditure, Germany could develop light industry and agriculture sufficiently for her people to have 'a modest but decent standard of living'. After some further discussion, the question of reparations was added to those to be considered by the foreign ministers. (According to the Soviet version, Churchill observed that he liked the principle: 'to each according to his needs, and from Germany according to her abilities'. Stalin preferred another principle: 'to each according to his deserts'.[12])

The third plenary meeting ensued in the afternoon of 6 February. The foreign ministers reported their agreement on the inclusion of 'dismemberment' in the surrender terms, but they would need more time on reparations and the French zone. The prime minister underlined the importance to Great Britain of France especially after the departure of the United States from Europe. Great Britain could not guard the western approaches to the Channel alone. (According to the Soviet version, Roosevelt said that the question of the period of the presence of American troops depended on US public opinion.[13])

President Roosevelt introduced the subject of the World Security Organization, as the United Nations Organisation was first called, observing that he could not believe in eternal peace but thought that war could be avoided for fifty years at least. Since neither he nor the other two of the Big Three had been present at Dumbarton Oaks, he would ask Secretary of State Stettinius to set out the US position as already communicated to Churchill and Stalin on 5 December 1944. In summary, the position was as follows. Each member of the Security Council would have one vote, and decisions could be taken with seven votes including the permanent members, the Big Three plus China and France. The unanimity of the permanent members was necessary for the preservation of world peace, but a fair hearing for all members of the organization, small as well as large, was of particular importance to the people of the United States. A list was given of the substantive matters on which the Security Council might vote, concerning membership of the General Assembly, the settlement of disputes, the regulation of armaments and of regional agencies and agreements. A Council member was not to be allowed to vote on disputes in which it was involved.

Molotov stated that he wished to study a minor change in the draft since the Soviet government considered the question of voting in the Security Council to be of great importance. Churchill said that, as far as the British Commonwealth of Nations and the Empire were concerned and, he believed, the Self-Governing Dominions as well, the US proposals were wholly satisfactory. However, since the appearance might be given that the Three Great Powers were trying to rule the world rather than saving it from the horrors of war, they should make 'a proud submission' and allow small countries to state their grievances freely. To give an example of how British interests were to be protected, if China brought up the question of the return of Hong Kong, Great Britain could exercise its right of veto by breaking the necessary unanimity of the permanent members. Stalin interjected to ask if Egypt could be in the assembly, and Eden answered 'yes, but not on the Council unless elected'. Stalin went on to suppose that Egypt would then request the return of the Suez Canal. Churchill replied by asking Stalin to let him continue the example of Hong Kong, but went on to concede that complaints about Suez as well as Hong Kong might be brought up, giving a further example of Argentina introducing a complaint against the United States. (The Soviet version adds that in such a case, the United States could use the veto and apply the Monroe Doctrine.[14])

Roosevelt recalled that the Tehran Declaration by the Three Powers included a statement of the necessity of all nations 'to make a peace which will command good will from the overwhelming masses of the peoples of the world'. Churchill reiterated that the Great Powers, protected by the veto in case of disagreement, should allow others a hearing. Stalin said that neither China on Hong Kong nor Egypt on Suez would be content with mere expression of opinion.

Regarding Churchill's apprehension that others might suspect the three Great Powers of wanting to dominate the world, the Soviet version records that Stalin asked a series of rhetorical questions and notes the responses given in italics:

> But who was contemplating such domination? Was it the United States? No, it was not thinking of that. [*The President laughed and made an eloquent gesture.*] Was it Britain? No, once again. [*Churchill laughed and made an*

eloquent gesture.] That left the third – the USSR. So was it the USSR that was striving for world domination? [*General laughter.*] It was clear that talk of striving for world domination was pointless. His friend Churchill could not name a single Power that wanted to dominate the world.[15]

After Churchill's comment that he was talking of impressions rather than reality, Stalin asserted that, apparently, only two of the Big Three had so far accepted the document avoiding any accusation that they were trying to rule the world. But there was a more important question than voting procedure or world domination. Stalin asserted:

> They all knew that as long as the three of them lived none of them would involve their countries in aggressive actions, but after all, ten years from now none of them might be present. A new generation would come into being not knowing the horrors of the present war. He felt that there was, therefore, an obligation to create for the future generation such an organization as would secure peace for at least fifty years.

Conflict between the three great powers themselves constituted the greatest danger, but German aggression could hardly be renewed if they preserved their unity. He apologized for giving so much attention to voting rights but feared that conflict might break this unity. His colleagues could not forget the expulsion of the Soviet Union from the League of Nations in 1939, instigated by Great Britain and France along with the mobilization of world opinion against the Soviet Union and even talk of a crusade. Churchill replied that Great Britain and France were very angry at the time but that the new proposals would avert any such action. Roosevelt felt that the unity of the three Great Powers would be preserved by full and friendly discussions in the Council serving 'to demonstrate the confidence which the Great Powers had in each other and in the justice of their own policies'.

Attention turned to the Polish question. Roosevelt said that he wanted to see the creation of a government that would have the support of all the main parties and maintain good relations with the Soviet Union in particular. He favoured the adoption of the Curzon Line first suggested after the Russian Revolution of 1917 as Poland's new eastern frontier. (According to the Soviet version, Roosevelt added that 'the Poles, like the Chinese, were always worried about "losing face" '. Stalin interjected: 'which Poles were meant, the real ones or the émigrés? The real ones lived in Poland.'[16]) Stalin expressed the hope that the Polish government would have friendly relations with the other Allies, too. Churchill said that like the United States, Great Britain would support the Curzon Line as Poland's eastern frontier, with representation in the government of all interested parties. Seeking a home for the Poles where they could live as they wished, Great Britain could not forget the debt of honour incurred by its entry into the war to protect Poland from the aggression of Germany.

Stalin observed that the question involved not only the Soviet Union's honour but also its security; indeed the question was one of life and death. Twice in thirty years, Germany had attacked Russia through Poland. A strong Poland was necessary to prevent further repetition. In this respect, the Soviet government differed from its tsarist predecessor that had sought the suppression and assimilation of Poland. On the question of the eastern frontier, he recalled that the line had been fixed not by Lenin but by Curzon and Clemenceau. Stalin and Molotov could not return to Moscow to face the people saying that they had defended Russian interests less certainly than these Western statesmen. Stalin would prefer the present war to continue rather than accepting any modification of the line. He added that, in a slip of the tongue, Churchill had talked of the creation of a Polish government, but the participation of the Poles themselves was necessary. The government recently set up in Warsaw had a base as at least as democratic as that of de Gaulle in Paris. Stalin complained that agents of the exiled government in London had killed more than 200 Soviet soldiers while claiming to act on behalf of the underground resistance. Churchill agreed that anybody who attacked the Red Army should be punished but added that the British government could not recognize the Lublin or Warsaw government while remaining apprehensive that clashes with the underground army would lead to 'great bloodshed, arrests and deportations.'[17]

At the fourth plenary meeting on 7 February, Roosevelt opened the proceedings with the statement that he was less interested in the frontiers of Poland than its government. Moreover, this government's continuity and legality were not important since at times there had been none. However, the first substantial topic was the dismemberment of Germany, with Molotov reading out the results of the meeting of the three foreign ministers, himself,

Stettinius and Eden. France was to be allotted a zone of occupation, and the Soviet sacrifices to receive specific mention. The question of reparations was still to be decided, although the Reparations Committee was definitely to be located in Moscow. Churchill argued again that France could not have, and would not accept, a zone of occupation without membership of the Control Commission, although this would not give France the automatic right to join Big Three conferences. It was agreed to attempt to settle the question at Yalta but also to go on for the moment to the Polish question. Stalin said that he had received a suggestion from Roosevelt that two representatives should come from the Lublin government and two or three more from other representatives of public opinion, including the London government. Together they should organize a provisional government pledged to holding free elections. However, Stalin said, this suggestion could not be carried out at Yalta.

Moving on to the problem of the world organization, Molotov said that the Soviet delegation felt that Western proposals 'fully guaranteed the unity of the Great Powers in the matter of preservation of peace'. For this purpose, the Soviet Union would be satisfied with admission to the assembly of three or at least two of its constituent republics, in particular Ukraine. Belarus and Lithuania, which had been the first to be invaded and the most to make sacrifices. He compared these republics to the British Dominions that 'had gradually and patiently achieved their place as entities in international affairs'. Roosevelt said that he had found Molotov's remarks of great interest, adding that the British Empire, the Soviet Union and the United States differed greatly in structure and tradition. However, he felt that to give larger nations more than one vote would be to infringe the principle of one vote per member. Churchill talked of the part played by the Dominions for a quarter of a century in both peace and war. Great Britain could not agree to them being excluded from, nor diminished in, any international organization. Therefore, he had great sympathy with the Soviet request, adding: 'His heart went out to mighty Russia which though bleeding was beating down the tyrants in her path.' After some further discussion of the difficulties involved as the war was still to be concluded, it was agreed that the foreign ministers would consider the possibility of holding a conference to consider the Soviet proposal and the problem of whom to include in the assembly.

It was also agreed that the foreign ministers might look at Iran and other matters of minor importance. Roosevelt considered that Iran, formerly known as Persia, gave a good example of the problems to be encountered in the expansion of world trade. Iran had been prosperous before the arrival of the Turks, but he had never seen a poorer country than it was now. Parallels could be found in certain countries in Europe. He felt it wrong that some countries had abundant sources of electric power while others had none. He mentioned that the Soviet Union had thought in terms of the whole, while in the United States the TVA (Tennessee Valley Authority) had covered a complete area.

However, after Roosevelt's observation, the conference returned to consideration of the Polish question. Molotov put forward proposals that the Curzon Line should form the basis for the eastern frontier, the Oder-Neisse line for the western frontier, while some democratic leaders from *émigré* circles should be added to the provisional government. Roosevelt thought that progress had been made, although he did not like the word *émigré*. In any case, enough Poles could be found in Poland to form a government. Churchill also disliked the word *émigré* that had come to mean in English at the time of the French Revolution a person expelled from his own country by his compatriots. He preferred the phrase 'Poles temporarily abroad'. While always supporting that the Polish frontiers should move westwards, he said that 'it would be a pity to stuff the Polish goose so full of German food that it got indigestion'. Moreover, many Britons would be shocked by mass removal, but if it were confined to East Prussia, the six million Germans could probably be managed apart from moral considerations. Stalin pointed out that most Germans in the areas concerned had already flown from the Red Army. Churchill added that the six to seven million or more German casualties would allow space in Germany for those deported. With the addition of the words 'and from inside Poland' to replace 'from Polish *émigré* circles', it was agreed to leave further discussion for the next meeting.[18]

Before that took place, Roosevelt met Stalin on the afternoon of 8 February. The main subject of discussion was the Far East. The president said that the Pacific War was entering a new phase with the fall of Manila in the Philippines. The United States was intending to establish bases within striking distance of Japan in order 'by intensive bombing to be able to destroy Japan and its army [4 million strong] and thus save American lives'. The marshal had no objection to two American bases in the Soviet Maritime Provinces in the Far East, as previously provisionally agreed with the Soviet general staff. He also agreed to the Americans using airfields in Hungary and making surveys of areas previously bombed in Eastern and Southeastern Europe. Thanking Roosevelt for a suggestion that the Soviet Union might purchase surplus US ships on credit at the end of the war, Stalin went on to emphasize that Lend-Lease was 'a remarkable invention, without which victory would have been delayed'. Roosevelt asserted that 'the British had never sold anything without commercial interest but that he had different ideas'. The scheme of Lend-Lease had come to him while he was resting on his small yacht and thinking of a way to avoiding the problems connected with loans.

Returning to the subject of the Far East, Roosevelt had no difficulty in accepting a previous suggestion that the southern half of Sakhalin and the Kuril Islands should go to Russia at the war's end. Concerning a warm water port, a subject already discussed at Tehran, he suggested that Dairen might be leased from the Chinese or made an internationally controlled free port. He preferred the second alternative because it bore on the problem of Hong Kong, whose sovereignty he wanted given back to China. But he was aware that Churchill would strongly object to any such suggestion. Roosevelt would have no objections to Soviet use of the Manchurian railways if with some reservations regarding sovereignty. Stalin asserted that if the port and railway conditions were not met, it would be difficult for the Soviet people to understand why they were entering a war in which, unlike that against Germany, their very existence was not under threat. He would be talking to the Chinese soon about moving twenty-five divisions to the Far East as soon as possible. He would have no objection to an internationalized free port.

Moving on to the question of trusteeships, Roosevelt aired the answer for Korea of a three-way control by Soviet, American and Chinese representatives. In the Philippines, about fifty years of trusteeship had been necessary, but in Korea he considered that the people could be prepared for self-government in twenty to thirty years. Stalin thought the shorter the better, and preferably without foreign troops. To the president's tentative suggestion that the British might be excluded from Korea, Stalin responded that the prime minister might 'kill us' in such a case and that the British should be invited. Regarding trusteeship for Indochina, Roosevelt said that the British would want to give it back to the French for fear of implications otherwise for Burma. Stalin commented that the British had lost Burma by relying on Indochina, and he was not sure that they could protect this important area. Roosevelt observed that 'the Indochinese were people of small stature, like the Javanese and Burmese, and were not warlike'. France 'had done nothing to improve the natives since she had the colony' and he was unable so far to find the ships requested by de Gaulle for transport of French troops to Indochina. On China, the president and the marshal agreed that China should be kept alive under the leadership of Chiang Kai-shek. Roosevelt said that the Americans had achieved more progress than the Kuomintang in bringing in 'the so-called communists'. Stalin recalled that some years previously there had been a united front in China and that he did not understand why it had not been preserved.[19] (In the Soviet version, Stalin stated that 'it would be good to combine these forces in the interests of a united front against Japan'.[20])

The fifth plenary meeting took place in the late afternoon of 8 February. Regarding the proposed world organization, Eden reported that the UK was against the status of membership of the United Nations merely for participation in the conference, but he understood that the United States thought otherwise. Stalin found it strange that there were to be ten states represented at the conference to discuss future world security without diplomatic relations with the Soviet Union. To explain this situation, Roosevelt referred to the influence of the Catholic Church and then explained that several Latin American republics had taken American advice to break relations with Germany rather than declaring war. Realizing that this advice had been a mistake, he was now urging these republics to make such a declaration, and believed that this would help to sap German morale. He added that Iceland, the newest United Nations republic, was also to be considered. Churchill said that his government had advised Egypt not to declare war, feeling 'that it would be more useful and convenient to have Egypt a non-belligerent in order to protect Cairo from systematic bombings'. Its army having rendered good support services, Egypt should now have the opportunity to enter the war if it so chose. Iceland had made a great contribution both before and after the US entry into the war, violating her neutrality by allowing in British and American troops and keeping open a vital communications route. When Stalin said that ex-enemy states recently declaring war on Germany should not be admitted, Roosevelt and Churchill concurred. The prime minister would be against the inclusion of Eire, since it still had relations with both Germany and Japan. However, since Turkey had made an alliance with Great Britain at a difficult time even though 'not up-to-date for modern war', it might be admitted. Stalin said that he would accept a Turkish declaration if made before the end of February and Churchill thanked him. It was agreed to delay the admittance of Denmark, Stalin insisting that it 'had let the Germans in'.

Stalin's hope that the recommendation of the foreign ministers on the inclusion of Ukraine and Belarus (although not Lithuania) be accepted met with general agreement. Churchill commented that it would be wrong to take in small countries that had done little by declaration of war alone while excluding the two Soviet Republics whose 'martyrdom and sufferings' were very much on his mind. Roosevelt referred to the technical difficulty of giving one of the Great Powers three votes, but he believed that this could be overcome.

On Poland, there was confirmation that recognition would be withdrawn from the London government at the point when the government of national unity received it. Molotov argued that the Lublin or Warsaw provisional government enjoyed great popularity and prestige since it had been closely involved in the liberation, but that it could be augmented by democratic elements from home and abroad. He noted the general agreement on the eastern boundary before going on to say that the Polish provisional government supported the Soviet proposals for the western frontier. Churchill observed that 'the crucial point of this great conference' had now been reached. The world would see a split between the UK and United States on the one hand and the Soviet Union on the other if they recognized two different Polish governments. According to the information at his disposal, there was no majority support for the Lublin or Warsaw government. Furthermore, there would be a great protest in Great Britain by the Polish army (about 150,000-strong) if support for the London government was suddenly withdrawn. This could be done only if a new start was to be made on both sides on equal terms. If free elections by secret ballot and with universal suffrage were held and all democratic parties could put forward their candidates, then Great Britain would welcome the ensuing government and disregard the government in London. Roosevelt said that they were all agreed on free elections, but the question remained as to how the country was to be governed meantime.

Stalin asserted that Great Britain and the United States could send people into Poland to acquire information. He insisted that the provisional government was popular since it was led by individuals who had stayed to fight for the underground during the war. Perhaps the Polish people were somewhat primitive in their attitude concerning those who had stayed and those who had left. Moreover, their mentality had changed as a consequence of their liberation by the Red Army. Previously they had been justified in hating the Russians who had joined in three partitions of their country during tsarist times. Since Churchill was worried about differences in information and attitude, the best way forward would be to invite Poles of different persuasions to come and give their views pending free elections at the end of the war. Stalin saw a close resemblance between the position of the Polish provisional government and that of de Gaulle. Neither had been elected and nobody could say who was more popular, yet de Gaulle had been recognized even though he had done nothing to achieve popularity while the Polish provisional government had carried out a number of widely welcomed land reforms. Surely it would be better to think of reconstructing the government that existed rather than setting up a new one. Roosevelt asked Stalin how long it would be before elections could be held. Stalin replied that it might be in a month if there were no catastrophes at the front.

Stalin asked why there was a delay in the formation of a unified Yugoslav government. He also wanted to know what was happening in Greece, although he meant no criticism. Churchill answered that the Greek situation was complicated and would have to wait for the next meeting. (In the Soviet version, Churchill said that to tell the whole story now would spoil the forthcoming dinner.[21]) In Yugoslavia, the King would be ignored if he refused to accept a regency and an agreement involving Tito had been reached. Stalin observed that Tito might not welcome advice since he was the proud and popular leader of a new regime. To Churchill's reply that Stalin might risk Tito's resentment, Stalin countered that he was not afraid. On Greece, Churchill expressed the hope that peace might result from an amnesty for all except war criminals, but he feared that a government might not be set up since the parties hated each other. Stalin said that the Greeks had not yet learned to discuss their differences as each cut others' throats. Churchill said that British observers were experiencing a difficult time in Greece and thanked Stalin for holding back from excessive interest in it. Stalin emphasized that, far from criticism or interference, he only wanted to know what was happening in Greece.[22]

Conclusion

In other words, Stalin was adhering to the percentages deal made with Churchill in Moscow, giving a 90 per cent interest in Greece to the British in accord with the Americans. In a letter to the prime minister in April 1945, the marshal reiterated his understanding of Greece's significance for Great Britain while insisting on the Soviet Union's right to strive for a friendly government in Poland, to which, he declared, 'we are pledged, apart from all else, by the blood of the Soviet people, which has been profusely shed on the fields of Poland in the name of the liberation of Poland'.[23]

Halfway through the Yalta Conference, then, the major clashes of the Big Three were on Poland. For Churchill, it was a matter of honour to adhere to the commitments made at the outbreak of war in 1939, while Roosevelt was concerned about voters of Polish extraction as well as those originating in the Baltic states. Stalin argued that for the Soviet Union alone, this was a matter of life and death. However, the Big Three were in reasonable agreement on the question of the Balkans. Regarding the post-war treatment of Germany, there were indeed differences of viewpoint, with some uncertainty about how it should be divided and how much reparation should be paid, with Churchill more insistent that France should be involved. Roosevelt and Stalin were in favour of harsher punishment. On the question of the rights of smaller nations, the Soviet side took a less liberal line than its Western counterparts.

As far as the wider world was concerned, there was a hint of approaching dissension on the post-war settlement in the Far East as the terms of the Soviet Union's contribution to the victory over Japan were considered. There was also intimation of the longer-term problem of the end of empire in references to Hong Kong, Indochina and Egypt, with Churchill's perspective differing from that of Roosevelt and Stalin.

Deliberations on the United Nations Organisation included the common wish not only to settle post-war problems in general but also to make allowances for the particular concerns of the Big Three, for example, allowing Belarus and Ukraine representation to allay Stalin's apprehension that the Soviet Union would be in a minority, and bringing in China and France at the suggestion of Roosevelt and Churchill. Churchill noted that the UK could veto any proposal injurious to the integrity of the British Empire, while Roosevelt showed his big brotherly concern for Latin America.

The Big Three continued to exude confidence in themselves, their relationship and the importance of the decisions that they were making. Their personal bonhomie was indicated by their laughter at the suggestion that any of their countries would want to dominate the world. Let us recall Stalin's observation that 'as long as the three of them lived none of them would involve their countries in aggressive actions, but, after all, ten years from now none of them might be present'. In fact, Roosevelt was to die in April 1945, while Churchill would be defeated in a general election in July.

Yalta: World 'Security and Well-being' and the Death of Roosevelt

Yalta: Europe and beyond

On the evening of 8 February 1945, a jovial Stalin hosted a dinner at which forty-five toasts were proposed. The nature of most of them went unrecorded, but one of them was to Churchill by Stalin, who called the British prime minister 'the bravest governmental figure in the world'. Largely due to his courage and staunchness, Great Britain had carried on the struggle alone and regardless of allies actual or potential. Stalin knew of 'few examples in history where the courage of one man had been so important to the future history of the world'. His toast was to Mr Churchill, 'his fighting friend and a brave man'. Returning the compliment, Churchill toasted Stalin as 'the mighty leader of a mighty country, which had taken the full shock of the German war machine, had broken its back and had driven the tyrants from her soil'. He was confident that the marshal would lead his people from success to success in peace as much as in war. Stalin then asked the party to drink to the health of Roosevelt. Whereas Churchill and he were fighting for their lives, 'there was a third man whose country had not been seriously threatened with invasion, but who had had perhaps a broader conception of national interest, and even though his country was not directly imperilled, he had been the chief forger of the instruments which had led to the mobilization of the world against Hitler'. In the latter connection, Stalin praised Lend-Lease as 'one of the President's most remarkable and vital achievements'. Responding, Roosevelt compared the spirit of the evening to that of a family dinner, and he liked to think in a similar way about the relations between the three countries. While each of the leaders was working for the interests of his own people, they all hoped to bring 'the possibility of security and well-being' to all the peoples of the world. Stalin offered a toast to the Big Three alliance, whose duty was to address the difficult task of maintaining in peacetime relations as strong as they had been in war. Churchill gave voice to his feeling that 'we were all standing on the crest of a hill with the glories of future possibilities stretching before us'.

Leaders in the modern world had the task of taking their peoples 'from the forests into the broad sunlit plains of peace and happiness'. This achievement was nearer than ever before, and 'it would be a tragedy for which history would never forgive us if we let this prize slip from our grasp through inertia or carelessness'.[1]

Churchill and Roosevelt attended a meeting of the Combined Chiefs of Staff at noon on 9 February. The prime minister said that to persuade Russia to join in an ultimatum to Japan with the United States, the British Empire and China would be very valuable. While the decision must rest with the United States, he thought that some mitigation of unconditional surrender might be worthwhile if it meant the avoidance of a year or more of bloody and costly conflict. The president thought that the suggestion might well be put to Stalin, but he did not think that the ultimatum would influence the Japanese, locked off from the rest of the world and still under the impression that they could bring the war to an end with a compromise. After listening to the report of the Combined Chiefs of Staff, the two Western leaders had lunch together, talking over voting procedure in the assembly of the world organization that was soon to be known as the United Nations Organisation and agreeing on representation for the Soviet Republics equal to the United States and the UK. On the same afternoon, the American and Soviet Chiefs of Staff discussed the establishment of US bases in the Soviet Far East as a means of bringing the war against Japan to a speedier end.[2]

The sixth plenary meeting opened at 4.00 pm on 9 February with further discussion at Churchill's request of what he called 'the urgent, immediate and painful problem of Poland'. The Soviet side accepted with minor amendments a draft composed by Stettinius concerning the democratic election of a national provisional government. Time was allowed for the United States and UK to consider these amendments, Churchill arguing that 'it is better to take a few days of latitude than to endanger bringing the ship into port'.

After a brief discussion of reparations, the focus switched to trusteeships. This subject provoked Churchill to a long and vigorous assertion 'that under no circumstances would he ever consent to forty or fifty nations thrusting interfering fingers into the life's existence of the British Empire'. As long as he was prime minister, he insisted, 'he would never yield one scrap of their heritage'. To the assurance of Stettinius that trusteeship was to concern Japanese islands in the Pacific and other areas under the control of the enemy, Churchill responded with the request that the British Empire be explicitly excluded. He asked what Stalin's response would be to the suggestion that the Crimea might become an internationalized summer resort. Stalin said that 'he would be glad to give the Crimea as a place to be used for meetings of the three powers'.

On Yugoslavia, Churchill asserted that Tito was a dictator and Stalin denied it, before the Polish question was taken up again. Roosevelt observed that 'it was very important for him in the United States that there be some gesture made for the six million Poles there indicating that the United States was in some way involved with the question of freedom of elections'. For his part, Churchill wanted explicit reference to the necessity for a broadly based government in the new situation created by the Red Army's liberation of Poland. He also appealed to Stalin regarding the difficulty of acquiring adequate information on Poland, where apparently the Lublin government was intending to bring Home Army and underground fighters to trial for treason. He believed that Tito would accept foreign observers for future elections, while he would be happy for American and Soviet observers to be present at elections in Greece and Italy. In Egypt, the situation was different since the government always won elections. Stalin talked of his understanding that Egyptian politicians bought each other and that Egypt could not be compared with Poland where there was much more literacy. Churchill said that he had not meant to make this comparison but was obliged to assure the House of Commons concerning free elections. Stalin asserted that the Poles were 'good people' formerly including many scientists such as Copernicus. Nevertheless, some Fascists remained in Poland and therefore there should be explicit reference to 'non-Fascist and anti-Fascist' in addition to 'democratic parties' in the provisions for the Polish elections. Roosevelt commented 'I want this election in Poland to be the first one beyond question. It should be like

Caesar's wife. I did not know her but they said she was pure.' Stalin riposted: 'They said that about her but in fact she had her sins.'

The meeting concluded with some brief exchanges between the Big Three. When Churchill said that he had given Wilkie (who had been Roosevelt's Republican opponent in 1940 and subsequently performed several missions for him) a copy of his statement to the House of Commons to the effect that the British Empire already observed the principles of the Atlantic Charter, Roosevelt asked 'if that was what had killed Mr. Wilkie'. Stalin remarked that he thought that it would be dangerous to allow forces other than British into Greece and that he had complete confidence in British policy there. Churchill said that a Soviet observer would be welcome to Greece and thanked Stalin for his confidence. On war criminals, Churchill considered that those whose crimes were without specific location should be tried as soon as their identity was confirmed and then shot. To questions from Stalin, he replied that prisoners of war should also be included if they had broken the laws of war, adding that 'we should merely have an exchange of views here and no publicity should be given to the matter'. Churchill assured Stalin that the offensive had begun on the Western Front, albeit not yet as promised.[3]

On 10 February, Churchill and Eden met Stalin and Molotov to discuss what the prime minister called 'a most unfortunate business', the latest Soviet proposals on Poland. To be frank, all he could find out about Poland came from the London government. Stalin insisted that Great Britain could have appropriate representation in Poland itself, as had already been accorded de Gaulle's France, and accepted Eden's proviso that there be no restriction on British representatives. Churchill moved on to the question of prisoners of war, the two sides agreeing that all should be repatriated as soon as possible. Turning to the problem of reparations, Stalin suggested that Churchill was sorry for the Germans. Eden responded that it was not a question of pity but of experience of reparations after the First World War. Churchill added that German factories under Soviet control could promote trade. He then asked about German generals in Soviet hands. Would the Soviet government use them simply for propaganda, or would it use them in Germany? 'God forbid!', answered Stalin. Churchill complained that the Soviet government paid American businessmen compensation owed them more readily than it did British, and Stalin asked about progress on the revision of the Montreux Convention of 1936 on Turkey (allowing Turkey to refortify the Straits).[4]

At the seventh plenary meeting on the afternoon of 10 February, Eden read out the draft of the agreement on Poland. Churchill commented that it made no mention of frontiers. While the eastern had been agreed, agreement on the western could not be reached but it was necessary to make some mention of the settlement or 'the whole world would wonder what had been decided on the question'. Roosevelt said that there should be consultation with the Polish government and the US Senate before any statement was issued regarding the western frontier. Stalin thought that there should be a statement on the agreed eastern frontier, and did not object to the suggestion of Churchill supported by Roosevelt that the French provisional government should be invited to associate itself with the statement. On Yugoslavia, there was general confirmation of the agreement between Tito and his chief rival with an anti-Fascist assembly being set up in addition.

On reparations, Churchill believed that the reparations committee should arrange figures, and Roosevelt cautioned that if any figures were mentioned, 'the American people would believe that it involved [their] money'. Stalin said that the sum of $20 billion mentioned in the Soviet proposals was no more than an indication of the value of reparations in kind, and that these had already been mentioned in treaties with Finland, Hungary and Romania. If the British wanted the Russians to receive no reparations, they should say so. Churchill immediately denied this. Stalin considered that the conference could agree that there should be reparations and that the Reparations Commission convening in Moscow should determine the amount in the light of the American-Soviet proposal that 50 per cent of reparations to the value of $20 billion should go to the Soviet Union. Roosevelt and Churchill reiterated their reservations, the prime minister adding that the figure of $20 billion was too great since it was beyond Germany's capacity to pay. After further haggling, it was agreed that Germany would have to pay reparations but that the Commission in Moscow would discuss the amount. (In the Soviet account, Stalin asked ironically: 'You will not go back on this tomorrow?'[5])

Turning to the question of the Straits, Stalin asserted that the Montreux Convention of 1936 was now out of date, since the Emperor of Japan had played a greater part in its composition than the Soviet Union and the treaty was associated with the League of Nations that no longer existed. The Turks had been given the right to close the Straits not only because of war but also because of what they considered to be threat of war. The convention had been drawn up when Anglo-Soviet relations were not so good. He did not believe that Great Britain would want Turkey to have a hand on Russia's throat with the help of the Japanese. Roosevelt observed that for more than a hundred years there had been no armed forces on the frontier of the United States with Canada stretching for more than 3,000 miles. He hoped that other frontiers would eventually follow suit. Churchill recalled that Stalin and he had already had a constructive talk on the Straits during his visit to Moscow the previous October, and that he sympathized with Stalin's wise view. But he thought that the Turks should be given some assurance on the maintenance of their independence and integrity. Stalin commented that 'it was impossible to keep anything secret from the Turks and that such assurance should be expressed'. Roosevelt agreed. Churchill commented that the UK's position in the Mediterranean was more important than that of the United States and that a meeting of the foreign ministers in London would be an appropriate place for discussion of the question of the Straits. Referring to the ill-fated expedition of the First World War, he recalled how some years earlier the Russian government of the time had made available armed forces, unfortunately without success, when 'he had tried very hard to get through the Dardanelles'. Stalin said that the Germans and Turks had been on the brink of surrender and that Churchill had withdrawn his troops too quickly. Churchill responded that he had nothing to do with the decision to withdraw from the Dardanelles because he was by the time it was taken already out of the government as a consequence of the campaign. Stalin then asked who was recording decisions being taken at Yalta.

Roosevelt asked for minor amendments to the statement on Poland to conform with the requirements of the American Constitution. 'The three heads of government' should be substituted for 'The three powers' and 'feel' for 'agree'. Instead of a reference to 'substantial accessions of territory in the North and West', Molotov proposed 'with the return to Poland of her ancient frontiers in East Prussia and the Oder'. When Roosevelt asked how long ago these lands had been Polish and Molotov answered 'very long ago', Roosevelt replied that this might persuade Great Britain to ask for the return of the United States. Stalin asserted that the ocean would prevent this and that it was important for the Poles to say something specific about frontiers. While Churchill shared Roosevelt's reservations about mention of the frontier in the west, he was not in principle against a line on the Oder if that was what the Poles themselves wanted. It was agreed to leave delineation of the western frontier to the Peace Conference. Roosevelt observed that he would have to leave Yalta by 3.00 pm the following afternoon, and there was some discussion of how a communiqué might be completed in time.[6]

At the beginning of a Tripartite Dinner Meeting at 9.00 pm on 10 February, Churchill began with a toast to His Majesty the King, the president of the United States and the president of the Supreme Soviet of the Soviet Union, Kalinin. He asked the only Head of State present to reply to the toast. Roosevelt recalled that soon after he had become president in 1933, his wife had gone to open a country school and had noticed a blank space on the map where the Soviet Union should have been. She was told that it was forbidden to mention this place. Roosevelt had then written to Kalinin suggesting that they should begin negotiations concerning diplomatic relations. Talking to Churchill, Stalin expressed a fear about telling his people that, because of British opposition, they were not going to receive reparations. Churchill denied that this was so, hoping indeed that Russia would receive large amounts of reparations. However, he remembered that the amount set at the end of the last war had been too much for Germany to pay. Both the prime minister and the president agreed to Stalin's suggestion that Germany was now to pay reparations because of the damage it had inflicted on the Allies in the present war. Churchill then proposed a toast to Stalin, expressing his feeling that 'the common danger of war had removed impediments to understanding and the fires of war had wiped out old animosities'. He foresaw a Russia already glorious in war 'as a happy and smiling nation in times of peace'.

Roosevelt recalled that he had sat at a Chamber of Commerce meeting in a small town in the South between a Catholic and a Jew who both turned out to be members of the Ku Klux Klan. This illustrated the fact that if you really knew people it was difficult to be prejudiced against them. Stalin observed that 'this was very true'. Then, talking over British politics, Stalin gave his view that there would never be a Labour government. Roosevelt gave his view that any leader must look after his people's needs. He himself had become president at a time when his country was 'close to revolution' because the American people were short of food, clothing and shelter. He had kept his promise to give them what they lacked and there had thereafter been very little social disturbance. Roosevelt went on to propose a toast to Churchill, who already had been in the service of his country for many years when he himself had begun his political life at the age of 28. He went on to suggest that Churchill's service might have been greater when he was out of government because he had made people think. Churchill replied that he would soon face elections that would be difficult because 'he did not know what the Left would do'. Stalin observed that Left and Right were terms used in parliaments. Who was more to the left, Churchill who had never hampered trade unions in Great Britain or Daladier, a radical socialist, who had dissolved them in France? (Needless to say, recalling Churchill's policy during the General Strike and at other times, British trade unionists would not have agreed with Stalin's assertion.) Roosevelt recalled that in 1940 he had been obliged to deal with three French prime ministers in a week, and there had been eighteen parties in France at the time. But at a meeting the previous summer, de Gaulle had told him of his intention to make comprehensive changes.

Churchill suggested that it was much easier for Stalin who agreed that 'experience had shown one party was of great convenience to a leader of a state'. Churchill went on to say how much easier his own task would be if the British people would give him full support. He had been unhappy about losing votes during the Greek crisis. But, whatever the results of the election, he was sure that both he himself and Eden would continue their own support for the interests of Russia and the United States irrespective of who was in power. The British were opposed to Communism, but this was because of their beliefs on 'the old question of the individual versus the state' rather than 'any attachment to private property'. However, in war, 'the individual was necessarily subject to the state'.

Reiterating his opinion that there would never be a Labour government in Great Britain, Stalin asked Roosevelt if there was such a party in the United States. Roosevelt replied in the negative although pointing out that organized labour was very powerful nevertheless.

When Stalin gave his view that more time was necessary to deal with the conference agenda, Roosevelt replied that he had three kings including Ibn Saud waiting for him in the Near East (no doubt to consider oil among other questions). Stalin went on to talk about the difficulties of the Jewish problem. When they had attempted to set up a national home for them in Birobidzhan (Jewish autonomous region in the Soviet Far East), the Jews had gone off to the cities after just a few years. Although the Jews were traders by nature, however, small groups of them in some agricultural regions had been quite successful. Roosevelt declared himself a Zionist, and asked Stalin if he was one too. Stalin replied that 'he was one in principle but he recognized the difficulty'. Later, on another troublesome subject, Stalin observed that the Soviet Union would never have agreed to the non-aggression treaty with Germany in 1939 if it had not been preceded by the Munich Agreement of 1938 and the German-Polish Non-aggression Treaty of 1934. When Stalin doubted again that the conference could complete its work the next day, Roosevelt said that he would stay over for another day if necessary. But there was tentative agreement that there should be a final plenary session and farewell luncheon.[7]

The eighth plenary meeting, indeed the last, took place at noon on Sunday 11 February. The communiqué was discussed and accepted after some discussion on certain phrases and even words. For example, Churchill argued that the word 'want' means 'privation, not desire', and that 'reparation' sounded better than 'reparations'. Both Churchill and Roosevelt were concerned about the inclusion in the world organization of Belarus and Ukraine. The prime minister wanted to consult the British dominions, the president wanted 'to avoid a war with the Irish in the United States'. When Churchill said that he expected criticism from the Poles in London, Roosevelt said that there were ten times as many Poles in the United States. Demurring from Roosevelt's suggestion that he should sign before the others because he had been such a wonderful host, Stalin suggested that the signatures should be in alphabetical order in Russian: Roosevelt, Stalin, Churchill. Churchill responded that in English, he would come first, and Stalin accepted this order. The farewell luncheon at 1.00 pm avoided business matters for the most part, although Stalin made a none too indirect reference to Iran in his assertion that any nation that would not let its oil be exploited was 'working against peace'.[8]

After Yalta

A communiqué was released to the press on 12 February 1945, beginning with the defeat, occupation and four-power control of Germany and going on to reparation by Germany. A conference of the United Nations as world organization along lines proposed at Dumbarton Oaks would be held in San Francisco on 25 April, with the Big Three plus China and France as the main sponsors. On liberated Europe, the signatories declared their intention of eliminating Nazism and Fascism and introducing democracy as proclaimed in the Atlantic Charter. On Poland in particular, the three powers were resolved to settle differences regarding the establishment of a country 'strong, free, independent and democratic'. There was agreement also on a new government for Yugoslavia as part of a review of Balkan questions. Provision was made for periodic meetings of the three foreign secretaries in their respective capitals, the first to be in London. And a common determination was reaffirmed for unity in peace as well as in war.

A protocol of proceedings, released to the press on 24 March 1947, reiterated much of what was in the communiqué with some amplification. However, the item on world organization included a section on the proposed membership of Ukraine and White Russia (Belarus) and another on Territorial Trusteeship, making clear that subsequent agreement would be necessary on which former League of Nations, ex-enemy and other territories should be placed under this heading. Items were added on major war criminals, Balkan frontiers, Iran and the Montreux Convention and the Straits. A further Protocol also released on 24 March 1947 concerned German reparations.

The Agreement Regarding Entry of the Soviet Union into the War against Japan was released to the press on 11 February 1946. This confirmed that the Soviet Union would enter the war against Japan two or three months after the surrender of Germany with certain conditions. First, the status quo would be preserved in Outer Mongolia. Second, 'The former rights of Russia violated by the treacherous attack of Japan in 1904 shall be restored', viz. the southern part of Sakhalin; an internationalized commercial port of Dairen and a leased naval base at Port Arthur. The Chinese-Eastern Railroad and the South Manchurian Railroad would be placed under the control of a Soviet-Chinese Company with China retaining full sovereignty in Manchuria. Third, the Kuril islands would be 'handed over to the Soviet Union'. President Roosevelt undertook to obtain the agreement of Generalissimo Chiang Kai-shek with the advice of Stalin, who accepted that the Soviet Union would ally with China in order to help remove the Japanese yoke.

There was also a bilateral Agreement between the United States and the Soviet Union concerning Liberated Prisoners of War and Civilians released to the press on 8 March 1946.[9]

We must be careful to note the dates on which the documents just summarized were released to the press. Only the communiqué was made public immediately after the Yalta Conference, with the United Nations and liberated Europe as its principal subjects. Announcements on the Far East and other matters were held back until well after the victory over Japan. A misleading Eurocentricity was thus encouraged as the war with Germany was coming to an end.

However, the importance of Yalta for Europe was indeed considerable, especially for Poland whose liberation was being completed as the conference convened. Was Poland indeed being liberated? Like any other important question, this one can be answered to a considerable extent via the *longue durée* of history. The struggle between Russia and Poland was age-old, and in earlier times, as is often forgotten or ignored, Poland was in the ascendancy. In particular, at the beginning of the seventeenth century during a period of early modern Russian history consisting of civil war and foreign intervention and known as the Time of Troubles, the Poles invaded and installed their puppet on the Muscovite throne. By the end of the eighteenth century, however, the boot was very much on the other foot with the partition of Poland by Russia, Prussia and Austria. The great pendulum of power swung again after the Russian Revolution of 1917, which was followed by another Time of Troubles involving more civil war and foreign intervention, taken advantage of by a resurgent Poland to invade Soviet Russia. As the Red Army counterattacked, the British foreign minister stepped in to propose the Curzon Line of which we have heard so much in the previous chapter. Then, in 1939, as also noted above, the Soviet Union and Nazi Germany subjected Poland to a further partition. Many Polish patriots believed that, with the defeat of Nazi Germany in 1945, the Soviet Union did not so much liberate Poland as enslave it. For Stalin, a Polish government sympathetic to the

Soviet Union was necessary after the two German invasions in the First and Second World Wars.

Misleadingly, the idea has grown that Yalta marked a great giveaway, with the UK and United States yielding in an unnecessary manner to the Soviet Unions takeover of Eastern Europe. Amid the vast amount of historical writing on the subject, *Yalta* by Diane Shaver Clemens stands out as a work that manages to be both global in its coverage and balanced in its evaluation of the significance of the conference. Some critics would say overbalanced, for Clemens argues that 'The decisions at Yalta involved compromise by each nation, probably more by the Soviets than by the Western nations' and, furthermore, that it was the United States rather than the Soviet Union that changed its interpretation of the Yalta agreements on both Poland and reparations among other questions.[10] On the other hand, S. M. Plokhy asserts that 'Stalin was an imperial conqueror who never fully shed his revolutionary ideology.... His sphere of influence would be secured by brute force and maintained through the intimidation, incarceration and elimination of his opponents'. But he also suggests that, while beyond doubt 'Yalta was a stepping stone to the insecure world of great-power tensions and the threat of nuclear annihilation ... the main decisions leading to the Cold War were made after the Yalta Conference.... With the passage of time, Yalta became much more important than its participants intended it to be, both as political reality and as historical mythology'.[11]

Bearing this welcome caveat in mind, we may nevertheless conclude that the conference in the Crimea marked the high point of the Big Three as individuals and perhaps as great powers too, sometimes synonymous for Churchill, Roosevelt and Stalin. The relationship prepared by correspondence and a number of bilateral meetings, then consolidated at Tehran, was taken to a new degree of intimacy at the conference in the Crimea. Simultaneously, however, fatal flaws in the association were revealed as never before, between the UK and United States as represented by Churchill and Roosevelt on the one hand and the Soviet Union led by Stalin on the other on questions concerning Eastern Europe, on Poland especially, which, to reiterate the point crudely, Churchill saw primarily as a matter of honour, Roosevelt of votes and Stalin of security. But there was disagreement between the Western Allies as well: indeed, regarding the end of empire, Roosevelt seemed on occasion to be closer to Stalin than to Churchill. On Asia in particular, there were already some hints of the Big Three being replaced by the Super Two, although ambiguities persisted concerning the powers and the personalities.

During the months between the Yalta Conference in February and the Potsdam Conference in July, there were further developments of considerable significance, most notably the end of the war with Germany and the change of emphasis to bring to a conclusion the war with Japan. In personal terms, the Big Three were deeply affected by the death of Roosevelt.

In March, the armed forces of the Big Three closed in on Germany. As victory in Europe approached, however, political differences widened, most notably over Poland. On 8 and 10 March, Churchill sent to Roosevelt a complaint that the Soviet Union was moving towards the settlement of the question of the Polish government in a unilateral manner. He suggested that a communication to this effect be sent to Stalin. On 11 March, Roosevelt agreed about what was happening, but was against direct confrontation for fear of provoking Uncle Joe to an unhelpful reaction. On 13 March, the prime minister wired the president: 'Poland has lost her frontier. Is she now to lose her freedom?' He did not wish 'to reveal a divergence' between their two governments, but he had to make it clear that 'we are in presence of a great failure and an utter breakdown of what was settled at Yalta'. In his reply of 16 March, Roosevelt could find 'no evidence of any divergence of policy', but believed that the main purpose should be 'without giving ground to get the negotiations moving again'. In a further communication of 16 March, Churchill remained impatient since 'At present all entry into Poland is barred to our representatives. An impenetrable veil has been drawn across the scene', but he emphasized in yet another of 18 March that 'Our friendship is the rock on which I build for the future of the world so long as I am one of the builders. ... There will be a torn, ragged, and hungry world to help to its feet: and what will Uncle Joe or his successor say to the way we should both like to do it?' Yet the Polish problem remained, Stalin insisting in a letter to Churchill on 7 April that the *émigré* Prime Minister Mikolajczyk had 'come out openly against the decisions of the Crimea Conference' and that 'if British or other foreign observers were sent into Poland the Poles [the provisional government] would regard this as an insult to their national dignity'.[12]

Churchill's next major concern expressed to Roosevelt on 1 April 1945 was that Eisenhower was not firm enough in his dealings with the Russians and in his resolve to advance to the Elbe and into Berlin, the fall of which would be 'the supreme signal of defeat to the German people'. There was no doubt that the Russians would take most of Austria including Vienna. 'If they also take Berlin', he asked, 'will not their impression that they have been the overwhelming contributor to our common victory be unduly imprinted in their minds, and may this not lead them into a mood which will raise grave and formidable difficulties in the future?'[13]

On 3 April 1945, Stalin wired Roosevelt with the complaint that preliminary negotiations between representatives of the Western and German High Commands at Berne, Switzerland had ended 'in an agreement ... to open the front and permit the Anglo-Americans to advance to the east, and the Anglo-Americans have promised in return to ease for the Germans the peace terms'. Stalin said that he could not understand the silence on this matter of the British who had instigated these negotiations. On 5 April, Roosevelt replied that negotiations at Berne concerned terms for the German surrender in Italy and in no way meant any deviation from the agreed policy of 'unconditional surrender'. He concluded: 'Frankly, I cannot avoid a feeling of bitter resentment toward your informers, whoever they are, for such vile misrepresentations of my actions or those of my trusted subordinates.' On learning about this interchange, Churchill immediately communicated his astonishment to Roosevelt, suggesting that the Russians had been surprised by the rapidity of the advance of the Western Allies, and adding:

> We must always be anxious lest the brutality of the Russian messages does not foreshadow some deep change of policy for which they are preparing. On the whole I incline to think it is no more than their natural expression when vexed or jealous. For that very reason I deem it of the highest importance that a firm and blunt stand should be made at this juncture by our two countries in order that the air may be cleared and they realize that there is a point beyond which we will not tolerate insult. I believe this is the best chance of saving the future. If they are ever convinced that we are afraid of them and can be bullied into submission, then indeed I should despair of our future relations with them and much else.

On 6 April, Churchill sent Stalin a message recording the British government's decision not to reply to the 'most wounding and unfounded charge' regarding 'the silence of the British' and associating himself with Roosevelt's explanation of the Berne negotiations and with the president's feeling of resentment.

On 7 April, Stalin sent a reply to Roosevelt, with a copy to Churchill. The Marshal insisted that the matter was not one of integrity and trustworthiness but of different views on what was admissible. All three Allies together should meet German representatives no matter what the subject. Moreover, Stalin found it difficult to admit that the lack of resistance by the Germans on the Western Front was solely due to the fact that they had been defeated. They had 147 divisions on the Eastern Front and could easily have transferred fifteen to twenty of them to the West; instead, they were continuing 'a crazy struggle' for an insignificant railway station in Czechoslovakia, as much use 'as hot poultices to a corpse' while giving up important towns in Germany without a fight. Such behaviour was 'more than curious and unintelligible'. Furthermore, the marshal insisted that his informants were 'extremely honest and modest people', discharging their duties conscientiously. In his copy to Churchill of 7 April, Stalin reiterated that it was important to express differences of view, continuing: 'If however you are going to regard every frank statement of mine as offensive it will make this kind of communication very difficult.' On 11 April, Churchill wired Roosevelt that the Russians had come as near to an apology as they could get. On 12 April, Roosevelt thanked Stalin for his 'frank explanation of the Soviet point of view of the Berne incident, which now appears to have faded into the past without having accomplished any useful purpose'. Sending a copy to Churchill on the same day, the president added later: 'I would minimise the general Soviet problem as much as possible. ... We must be firm however, and our course thus far is correct'.[14]

On the same day 12 April 1945, President Roosevelt suddenly died. This was a huge shock to the surviving members of the first Big Three. Churchill paid fulsome tribute to him in a speech in the House of Commons on 17 April, while Stalin wrote of him on 15 April as 'a distinguished statesman and an unswerving champion of close co-operation between the three States'. The significance of this death is difficult to assess. Evidently trust between the Big Three was already breaking down. On the other hand, Roosevelt's vision of world security was more complete than that of Churchill or Stalin, even though it seems that in his mind the interests of the United States overlapped to some extent with the aims of the United Nations. But nothing can be said with complete confidence about FDR's views on later developments, including the use of the atomic bomb.

The new president, Harry S. Truman, soon asked for notes on foreign policy, while one of his hobbies was known to be the history of military strategy.[15] He was not slow to move into action, proposing to Churchill a joint note to Stalin on the Polish question, which was duly sent on 15 April. Churchill considered an early meeting between Stalin, Truman and himself to be vital. At least the new Big Three were able to agree on the simultaneous unconditional surrender of Germany to them all. This was ratified early on 9 May.

Meanwhile, on 25 April, just a few days after the death of its principal architect, the United Nations Conference opened in San Francisco, with fifty nations present, including many who had not been actively involved in the war and including some, for example Turkey, who had joined in towards the end of hostilities in Europe. President Truman broadcast an address of welcome to the delegates including the British and Soviet Foreign Ministers Eden and Molotov – the latter's reluctant presence in what he might well have seen as a headquarters of the 'capitalist camp' was said to be in tribute to the late President Roosevelt. The future British prime minister Attlee was there in his capacity of deputy to his predecessor Churchill, stopping off in Washington to meet Truman and finding him 'one of the best. Of course he'd just come new to things. He didn't know much. But his instincts were right and he was learning fast. A very courageous fellow and a good friend.'[16] Not surprisingly, the United Nations was soon bogged down in arguments about organization and procedure.

On 30 April, Truman agreed with Churchill that Trieste, which Roosevelt had seen as a key outlet to the Adriatic Sea from the Danube basin, should be put under the control of the Western Allies to forestall Tito's incorporation of it in Yugoslavia. Truman also agreed that there was no need to ask the Russians about the operations to this end already under way. But the president's tone on Trieste and other Yugoslav matters soon changed as his advisers argued against too close an involvement in Europe incurring the risk of further war.

Stalin entered the discussion on 21 June with a note to Churchill asking for satisfaction of what he called legitimate Yugoslav interests in Trieste and adjacent Istria. Churchill replied on 23 June complaining that, although he and Stalin had agreed on a 50–50 influence in Yugoslavia, it was looking more like 90–10, with even the 10 under pressure from Tito supported by the Russians. Before then, Truman had clashed with de Gaulle on the question of another frontier, the Franco-Italian, where there was tension between French and American troops.[17]

Already by Victory in Europe (VE) Day on 7 May, in Churchill's later appraisal, 'The Soviet menace, to my eyes, had already replaced the Nazi foe. But no comradeship against it existed.' The prime minister, soon to face also a general election at home, believed that another meeting of the three Great Powers, with Truman passing through London en route, would be advisable. However, the dominant thought in Washington appeared to be opposed to the United States being dragged into a rivalry with the Soviet Union that would advance British interests in Poland and elsewhere in Europe at a time when the major American effort had to be directed against Japan. Churchill commented: 'These pressures must have been very strong upon Truman. His natural instinct, as his historic actions have shown, may well have been different. I could not of course measure the forces at work in the brain-centre of our closest Ally, though I was soon conscious of them.' Meanwhile, Churchill 'could only feel the vast manifestation of Soviet and Russian imperialism rolling forward over helpless lands'.

To Churchill's suggestion of 11 May for a further tripartite meeting, Truman replied that he would rather have the proposal come from Stalin and that the Western leaders should travel to the conference separately in case they should appear to be 'ganging up' on Stalin. On 12 May, Churchill sent Truman the telegram on which he said later he would most liked to be judged. Concerning Soviet advances, he asserted that 'An iron curtain is drawn down upon their front. We do not know what is going on behind', he feared that, with the withdrawal of American forces from Europe to the Far East, the way would soon be open for the Russians to advance to the North Sea and the Atlantic. An understanding with the Russians could be achieved only through 'a personal meeting'.

On 14 May, Churchill sent the following message to Lord Halifax, the British Ambassador in Washington:

We desire the entry of the Soviets into the war against Japan at the earliest moment. Having regard to their own great interests in the Far East, they will not need to be begged, nor should their entry be purchased at the cost of concessions prejudicing a reign of freedom and justice in Central Europe or the Balkans.

Then, on 22 May, Truman sent Churchill the message that he had asked Joseph E. Davies, well known for his sympathetic pre-war view of the Soviet Union, to come to England for a discussion before the Big Three meeting of a number of matters best omitted from telegrams. Much to the prime minister's astonishment and dismay, the principal suggestion put forward by Davies was that Truman should meet Stalin alone before he met Churchill. In a long note of 27 May, Churchill reiterated the urgent necessity for a conference of the three major powers, adding that many visits had been made to Moscow and that the previous conference had been on Russian soil. He went on to declare: 'London, the greatest city in the world, and very heavily battered during the war, is the natural and appropriate place for the Victory meeting of the three Great Powers.' Moreover, he emphasized that the British government could not attend any such meeting 'except as equal partners from its opening'. He understood that President Truman would like to meet Premier Stalin, while he himself wanted to make the personal acquaintance of the president: he had 'indulged the hope that he might have some private talks with the President before the general sittings commence'. While at such sittings, 'the principals meet together how they like, when they like, and for as long as they like, and discuss any questions that they may consider desirable', this would not prevent 'certain lunches and dinners at which the strong bonds of unity which have hitherto united the three major Powers are vivified by agreeable intercourse and often form the subject of congenial toasts'. The prime minister would prefer the meeting to take place after 5 July, when the British general election would be completed, but it should take place as soon as Stalin could agree, even as early as 15 June, 'before the United States forces in Europe are to a large extent dissolved'.

Churchill went on at some length to describe the differences between the ideologies of the two Western powers on the one hand and Soviet Communism on the other before asserting: 'The great causes and principles for which Britain and the United States have suffered and triumphed are not mere matters of the balance of power. They in fact involve the salvation of the world.' Churchill then set out the threats posed throughout Central and Eastern Europe by 'the imperialistic demands of Soviet Communist Russia'. Davies replied to Churchill on hearing such assertions that he 'wondered whether he, the Prime Minister, was now willing to declare to the world that he and Britain had not made a mistake in not supporting Hitler'.

In his report on the meeting, Davies observed that the prime minister was 'tired, nervous, and obviously working under great stress'. Churchill was 'a very great man' but 'bedevilled by the consciousness that his Government no longer occupies its position of power and dominance in the world'. He was 'bitterly hostile to the Soviets' and 'bitterly disappointed by the President's decision' to meet Stalin first.[18]

Truman responded to Churchill's note on 29 May saying that he was looking at dates for the conference. On 30 May, Stalin wired that Hopkins had told him that he thought 15 July to be the most convenient date for the proposed meeting. Truman had sent Hopkins to Stalin at about the same time that he had sent Davies to Churchill. In his report on this meeting, Ambassador Harriman wrote that Stalin 'was gravely concerned over the adverse developments during the past three months in the relations between our two countries'. It was 'difficult for him to understand why we should want to interfere with Soviet policy in a country like Poland, which he considers so important to Russia's security, unless we have some ulterior motive'. However, he did appear to understand that American and British help would be necessary to obtain 'a stable political situation' there. Harriman feared that Molotov was far more suspicious than Stalin, and did not always report to his leader accurately and truthfully. Frequent direct access could overcome many difficulties. Already, although Stalin had said that he did not consider that 'a country is virtuous because it is small', he had overruled Molotov's obduracy on voting procedure in the United Nations.[19]

On 1 June, Truman told Churchill that Stalin had agreed to a meeting of 'the Three' in Berlin on or about 15 July. Churchill suggested that, in view of the urgency of the questions to be considered, the meeting should take place earlier, but deferred to Truman's response that neither he himself nor Stalin wanted to bring the date forward. He insisted, however, that each delegation should have its own quarters with its own guards.

The leader of the Labour Party Clement Attlee (soon to replace Churchill as prime minister) accepted Churchill's invitation to accompany him as 'a friend and counsellor'. The British prime minister was concerned about the arrangements of the Allied zones in Germany and Austria, and about Soviet advances and Communist takeovers in East Europe. But he had to exercise patience until the meeting in Berlin at Potsdam.[20]

Potsdam: The Arrival of Truman and 'A Critical Juncture'

Victory in Europe: Potsdam

On 8 May 1945, a leader in *The New York Times* declared that 'The evil power that unsheathed the sword has been destroyed. The greatest threat that has ever been directed against modern civilization exists no longer.' 'The myth of German invincibility' had been overcome 'by the armies and navies of the United Nations and by the millions of plain people who supported them on the home fronts'. Inevitably, however, some names stood out: 'the indomitable Churchill, who roused Britain to her finest hour; Marshal Stalin, who turned the Nazi tide at the gates of his own capital', President Roosevelt and General Eisenhower. The late president would have a special place for Americans as the first to proclaim that 'Nazism represented a mortal threat to the United States', who 'beyond all others, aroused the moral forces of humanity and in their name united all the separate and sometimes divergent forces into the Grand Alliance of the United Nations'. The victory vindicated the fateful decision to concentrate on Europe, but now the 'costly lessons' learned in the course of the defeat of Germany had to be applied to the ongoing war against Japan. In particular, 'an ill-prepared and premature landing' in response to pressure for a 'second front ... would have been doomed to failure'. Moreover, no modern war could be won without airpower, but the nation 'beaten in the air must eventually be beaten on the ground'. While the Japanese army was smaller and weaker than the German, 'the individual Japanese is imbued with a religious fanaticism such as was shown only by the most insane Nazis'. Now, superiority must be built up for an 'all-out effort' in the Pacific. Many might feel that it was time for others to take on the chief burden, but too many might be 'basing overoptimistic hopes on a quick entry of the Soviets'. Emotions must not be allowed to run that way, and all hearts, brains and energy concentrated on completion of a victory so far only half won.

On 8 May 1945, too, a leader in *The Times* of London announced VE (Victory in Europe) Day, along with 'the uttermost catastrophe of defeat'. 'In a score of the great cities of Germany', *The Times* continued, 'scarcely a building stands intact; the Russian armies have swept like an avenging hurricane over the shattered avenues and palaces of Berlin'. From the ruins of Hitler's 'new order', Germany would have to be reconstructed through re-education.

Was the idea of the inferiority of their neighbours to the East completely rejected as more chilling evidence of the extermination of Jews and of Slavs came to public light? To look at this question in the *longue durée*, both anti-Semitism and the struggle between German and Slav had roots in medieval times, as Hitler demonstrated in his choice of the name of a medieval German emperor for his invasion of the Soviet Union in 1941 – Barbarossa. As far as the twentieth century was concerned, a quotation from Hitler's *Mein Kampf* (*My Struggle*) illustrates his warped thinking: 'When fate abandoned Russia to Bolshevism, it robbed the Russian people of the educated class which once created and guaranteed their existence as a State. The Germanic element may now be regarded as entirely wiped out in Russia. The Jew has taken its place.'[1]

At the end of March 1945, the Georgian Stalin himself had declared on behalf of his adopted race that 'we Slavs must be prepared for the Germans to rise again against us. That is why we, the new Slavophile-Leninists are so insistent on calling for the union of the Slavic peoples'.[2] Respect for the Slavs and their comrades in the Red forces was not easily learned as they swept into Germany in a manner often described as the incursion of barbarian hordes. If not repeating the mass extermination meted out by the Germans and their satellites in earlier years, it has nevertheless been associated with an inordinate amount of rape and pillage. No doubt, having fought their way from Stalingrad to Berlin and come across Treblinka and other death camps, many Red Army soldiers were in no mood to exercise restraint. But the actual extent of the violations and depredations remains a matter of controversy, the charge that at least two million women were raped being rejected by post-Soviet historians as unfounded: 'Murder, robbery, rape – these crimes, inevitable attributes of war, were committed by soldiers of the Soviet and other Allied armies. But, on the whole, they treated peaceful Germans humanely.[3] Whatever the fact of the matter, there is no doubt that reports and rumours were to influence the attitude of Western representatives at the Potsdam Conference. Even before that, from late May onwards, the British Chiefs of Staff were discussing the first drafts of a plan, 'Operation Unthinkable', for war against the Soviet Union. Too much should not be made of this, for Churchill called it 'a purely hypothetical contingency'.[4] Nevertheless, although classified 'top secret', it was passed on to Moscow by Kim Philby, and increased Soviet suspicions of Churchill.[5]

On 6 July, the British Ambassador in Washington Lord Halifax sent a personal and secret communication for the prime minister in London. President Truman was hoping to accept an invitation from King George VI to stay at Buckingham Palace, and was looking forward to meeting the prime minister and working very closely with him while being 'quite prepared to be friends with U.J. ["Uncle Joe" Stalin] where the ground is good'. Halifax hoped that Churchill was 'none the worse for all your election labours and that you have a good feeling about it'. Churchill replied that he had been advised that his government would probably have achieved a majority in the general election that had been held on 5 July, although there could be a surprise. But he would not resign unless there was 'a very extreme expression of national displeasure'. In any case, the British delegation would leave the forthcoming conference on 25 July to await the declaration of results on 26 July. The delay was caused by the necessity to await the votes of the armed forces overseas.[6]

On 10 July, Sir A. Clark Kerr, the British Ambassador in Moscow, reported that a 'gush of self-praise has left little room to the allies of the Soviet Union for a share in the credit for victory'. According to the newspaper *Red Star*, the Soviet Union under Generalissimo Stalin had 'saved civilisation from fascist obscurantism and barbarism, and had emerged from the war more mighty, still more monolithic and with still greater vitality'.[7]

A comprehensive British memorandum on the political scene entitled 'Stocktaking after VE-Day' was submitted by Sir Orme Sargent on 11 July. The end of the conflict in Europe had left the UK facing two problems completely different to those faced at the end of the First World War: the military occupation of the East by the Soviet Union along with its future policy in general; the economic rehabilitation of the continent as a whole. Moreover, control of Europe was not disputed by the UK and France as in 1918, but by the Soviet Union and the United States. British interests would have to be asserted for the principle of cooperation between the three Great Powers to be continued. True, the United States sought collaboration with the UK to fortify its position in Europe and elsewhere, while the Soviet Union recognized the UK as a European power with which it would certainly have to reckon. However:

> the fact remains that in the minds of our big partners, especially in that of the United States, there is a feeling that Great Britain is now a secondary Power and can be treated as such, and that in the long run all will be well if they – the United States and the Soviet Union – as the two supreme World Powers of the future, understand one another. It is this misconception which it must be our policy to combat.

As the weakest and smallest of the three Great Powers, the UK should seek to increase its diplomatic, military and economic strength by seeking the collaboration of the Dominions and especially France, not to mention the lesser Western European powers. Only thus could the two big partners be forced in the long run to treat the UK as an equal. Nevertheless, to collaborate with the United States and the Soviet Union would be difficult owing to wide divergences between respective outlooks, traditions and methods.

Sargent's memorandum considered the Soviet Union first, stressing the danger of assuming that the foreign policy of a totalitarian power would be 'opportunist and fluctuating' like that of a liberal counterpart, obliged to justify its policy to its own people and subject to changes of government. Free of such restrictions, a totalitarian foreign policy could be 'consistent and persistent' over a long period, although never needing to disclose its basic principles. For the time being, the Soviet Union was so weakened by the war coming to an end that Stalin would not want and could not afford any repetition. In any case, he was impressed by the economic strength of the United States and the potential of Western air forces, having seen what had happened to Germany and what was happening to Japan. Nevertheless, the Soviet Union would be able to exploit for its own purposes the economic crisis likely to engulf and even paralyse many European governments in coming months. Hence the necessity for the wholehearted support of the only country with the material means of coping with this crisis, the United States.

In Sargent's estimation, the UK must be prepared for the United States 'to falter from time to time when called upon to pull their weight in Europe', preferring the role of mediator to active political and economic involvement. For the liberalism of the constitution rendered US foreign policy 'fluctuating, uncertain and emotional'. However, 'We must have a policy of our own and try to persuade the United States to make it *their own.* ... [Sargent's italics] We must face the fact that they will feel that being the richest and strongest Power they must also be the wisest and the most fair-minded, and will therefore resent any contradiction by us'. For the time being, Europe's major political problem would be the Soviet Union, but a resurgent Germany could cause difficulty if it did not develop a new economic and political system. In this connection, 'If we hesitate or allow our German policy to be at the mercy of the emotions and ignorance of the people of the United States, we shall be lost'. For Germany might well then be in a position to play off each of the three Great Powers against the other two, and the eventual winner could well be the Soviet Union.

Turning to the Far East, acknowledging that the UK's position there would be weaker than in Europe, Sargent believed it all the more important to organize under UK leadership what he called 'the lesser colonial Powers who have a stake in the Far East' France, the Netherlands and Australia. While the Soviet government might well be 'less security-haunted than it is in Europe', and possibly therefore its policy 'less coldly realistic and more opportunist', the United States would be more likely to be 'more aggressive and pertinacious'. In the last resort, all would depend on the part played by Japan and China. Almost inevitably, the Soviet Union and the United States would eventually struggle 'for the body and soul of China' unless her latent economic and human resources could be harnessed in the interests of national unity and independence. In the course of the American-Soviet struggle, Japan would almost inevitably be brought in to help one of the protagonists.

In his summary, Sargent stressed the necessity for the UK to promote the collaboration of the three world powers while not shrinking from pursuing an independent foreign policy consonant with 'British fundamental traditions', but opposed to totalitarianism of both Right and Left in a manner that would appeal to the United States, the Dominions and to smaller countries in Europe, especially those in the West. In pursuit of such a liberal policy, Sargent considered, 'we shall have to take risks, and even live beyond our political means at times', not shrinking from diplomatic intervention in the internal affairs of other countries or taking the offensive against Communist penetration to the East and in Germany and Italy, Greece and Turkey. The UK must not be discouraged even if the United States pursued a policy of appeasement towards Soviet domination. Every effort must be made to tackle Europe's economic crisis, not only because a prosperous Europe would be the UK's best export market, but also to use British material resources along with American to counterweigh Communist propaganda.[8]

The British foreign secretary Eden considered Sargent's memorandum 'excellent', agreeing that the UK should 'speak frankly to the Soviet [*sic*] and to show no subservience' while fearing that the Soviet Union did not need Anglo-American aid and might indeed develop rapidly.[9]

'Britain as Member of the Big Three' was the title of one of the briefing papers prepared for the US delegation to Potsdam. It concluded:

> At meetings of the 'Big Three', Mr. Churchill, representing the United Kingdom which controls India and the colonial empire, acts for a power which is part of a larger association of powers of a very special character. The United Kingdom, though more populous and powerful than all the Dominions put together, and though a great power in its own right under existing world conditions, cannot be disassociated from the co-belligerent Dominions. Britain's two great allies, conscious of the Dominion statesmen behind the scenes, must gauge the limitations of the influence of those gentlemen upon Mr. Churchill, and of his upon them, remembering always that Mr. Churchill often offends the susceptibilities of the Dominions by forgetting that the British Empire has changed since Kipling's day.[10]

For their part, the US Chiefs of Staff looked to a foreseeable future in which there would be only three great military powers, the UK, the United States and the Soviet Union. In order to avoid conflict, regard should be taken of 'the inherent suspicions' of the Russians. In such circumstances, 'to present Russia with any agreement on such matters as between the British and ourselves, prior to consultation with Russia, might well result in starting a train of events that would lead eventually to the situation we most wish to avoid.'

However, the danger was not only military. In another background report prepared for the US delegation to Potsdam, the warning was given of the 'resumption of more radical policies by communist movements'. In spite of strict censorship and professed applause for democratic practices, 'those Communists in power in Eastern Europe have applied terror, intimidation, mass deportation and murder under the guise of necessary purges, all of which has proved shocking to our concept of democracy and free speech'. In Western Europe, notably Italy and France, communist parties had played a moderating part with the main aim of winning the war, but now they were turning to a more radical policy. In the United States, the party was attacking the State Department and the president after two years without such criticism.[11]

Warned of the dangers of Churchill's outdated views of empire, of misunderstandings among the Allies and of the spread of communism, and with other preparatory advice, the US delegation sailed for Europe, discussing the forthcoming meeting of the Big Three en route. In particular, receiving intercepts of Japan's 'peace feelers' sent to the Soviet Union, Truman and Secretary of State Byrnes discussed the policy of 'unconditional surrender' confident in the knowledge that the United States would soon be in possession of the atomic bomb.

Making use of his own intelligence services, Stalin was aware of this new weapon. No doubt, he bore this in mind as he ordered a huge effort to prepare the Cecilienhof Palace and other buildings in Potsdam so that the Soviet hosts could demonstrate their power in general and their seizure of Berlin in particular.[12]

On 16 July 1945, a member of the British delegation to the Potsdam Conference reported from Berlin that their accommodation was much better than at Yalta. He continued:

> The overwhelming impression we got flying in on Saturday [14 July] was of the total devastation and the stillness of all the built-up areas. In the whole flight over Germany I did not see a single train moving.... One saw a few chimneys smoking but they were noticeably the exception.

However, the sun was shining brightly and the Rhine wine was beginning to come in. Spirits were flowing freely. The official concluded: 'It will be rather a blow when we really have to get down to work.'[13]

Potsdam: Settlement in Europe

Before formal proceedings began, both Churchill and Stalin called on Truman. The first meeting was something of a courtesy call by the prime minister, the second a rather more substantial visit from the marshal. In his memoirs, Truman wrote:

> There were many reasons for my going to Potsdam, but the most urgent, to my mind, was to get from Stalin a personal reaffirmation of Russia's entry into the war against Japan, a matter which our military chiefs were most anxious to clinch. This I was able to get from Stalin in the very first days of the conference.

While the American and Soviet records of the conversation differ somewhat, they agree that Stalin committed his forces to entry into the war against Japan by mid-August.[14]

On the afternoon of 17 July, the Big Three as individuals came together at Cecilienhof, Potsdam, for their first plenary meeting. Stalin with the support of Churchill proposed that Truman should take the Chair throughout the conference. Accepting this proposal, Truman said how conscious he was of the responsibilities of the leaders of the three Allied Powers as they approached decisions at a 'critical juncture in the world's history'. He believed that some kind of mechanism needed to be set up for arranging peace talks in a manner avoiding the many flaws of the Versailles Conference. He therefore proposed that a special Council of Foreign Ministers be set up. Truman was also conscious of his own difficulties in following President Roosevelt who had become a close personal friend of the other two. Churchill seconded by Stalin talked of the warm regard and even affection for the late president and hoped that similar bonds might be formed with his successor. Churchill and Stalin agreed that the introduction of a special Council might be discussed after a report from the foreign ministers.

As discussion turned to liberated Europe, Truman talked about the necessity of free and fair elections throughout the continent. Churchill expressed some reservations about the entry of Italy into the United Nations in view of her behaviour during the war, although he did accept it. The UK's goodwill towards Italy had been demonstrated by its provision of fourteen out of fifteen ships sent to the Soviet Union against its claim for a share in the Italian fleet. Stalin urged UN pressure on Spain to allow the people to make a choice of political regime. On Tangier, Churchill said that no decision could be taken without French representation. Stalin argued that views could be given nevertheless, suggesting that Syria and Lebanon could be brought into discussion, too. Concerning Poland, Churchill stressed the importance of free elections, with some attention being given to the exiled Polish government in London and to the Poles who had fought for the Allies under British protection. Asked by Stalin why he was reluctant to allow the Soviet Union a third of the German fleet, Churchill responded that the question was whether the fleet should be divided or sunk. Reiterating his preference for division, Stalin said that other countries could sink their share if they so chose.

Attention turned to the proposal for the creation of a Council of the Ministers of the UK, the United States, the Soviet Union, France and China with a first task of drawing up peace treaties with Italy, Romania, Bulgaria and Hungary along with consideration of territorial questions. Stalin was not clear why, in view of prime attention being given to European problems, China should be included in the Council. Truman responded that China's inclusion followed from its membership of the Security Council of the United Nations. Churchill suggested that China could be brought into talks about world peace, but not about the settlement of detailed European questions. The foreign secretaries of the Big Three were instructed to choose items for consideration at the next plenary meeting.[15]

Later on 17 July, at a private meeting, Stalin told Churchill that, just before he had left Moscow, a communication had been received from the emperor of Japan stating that 'unconditional surrender' was unacceptable. Churchill urged Stalin to pass the message on to Truman, adding his opinion that the American people were now asking: 'was it worth while having the pleasure of killing ten million Japanese at the cost of one million Americans and British?' Stalin observed that the Japanese were frightened as 'unconditional surrender' was realized in Germany.

Asked by Churchill 'Where was Germany?', Stalin replied 'nowhere and everywhere'. He could not understand how Germans were brought up, since they were like sheep, always needing a man to give them orders and never thinking for themselves. Churchill agreed, adding that the Germans also needed a symbol to believe in, and that there would have been no Hitler had a Hohenzollern emperor been restored to the throne after the First World War. Turning to more personal matters after a further meeting had been agreed, Stalin revealed that he had begun to smoke cigars. Churchill commented that a photo of this new habit would cause a great sensation throughout the world. Stalin also confessed that he had become so used to working at night that he could not get to sleep before four in the morning even now that night work was not necessary. Churchill thanked Stalin for the warm reception accorded to his wife during her visit to Stalingrad and elsewhere in the Soviet Union. Welcoming Russia 'as a Great Power and in particular as a Naval Power', he expressed the opinion that 'The more ships that sailed the seas the greater chance there was for better relations.' Stalin stated that Russia's fleet, great or small, 'could be of benefit to Great Britain'. In reply to a question from the prime minister, the generalissimo hoped that the prime minister would address him as before as marshal.[16]

On the same day, 17 July, Foreign Secretary Eden sent Prime Minister Churchill a note agreeing with him that Russian policy was now one of aggrandisement, using international meetings to 'grab' as much as possible. Accepting that at Tehran and Yalta Russia was bearing the heaviest burden in casualties and devastation of all the Allies, it was no longer losing a single man. Not at war with Japan, it was doing all it could to impose heavier demands on China than had been agreed. The UK did not hold many cards, but one of them was possession of the German fleet. Not one ship should be handed over until such British interests as the independence of Persia (Iran) were guaranteed. Russian interests in access to the Mediterranean were fair enough, but care should be exercised to avoid the subjection of Turkey to Russia. Moreover, Eden insisted, 'while we agree that the Russians should be free to enter the Mediterranean, they have not yet freedom to get out of it. Would they now seek a presence in Tangier, and were they moving towards an interest in Egypt, 'quite the last place where we want them, particularly since that country with its rich Pashas and improverished [*sic*] fellahin would be a ready prey to Communism?' Eden asked Churchill to forgive 'this sermon' although he felt that the prime minister agreed with all of it, to be summarized as deep concern 'at the pattern of Russian policy, which becomes clearer as they become more brazen every day'.[17]

Eden sent a copy of his note to the deputy prime minister and Labour Party leader, Clement Attlee, who agreed that Russian pressure needed to be resisted while asserting: 'We ought to confront the Russians with the requirements of a world organisation for peace, not with the needs of the defence of the British Empire.' Old strategic considerations should be abandoned.[18]

On 18 July, Churchill had lunch with Truman, who asked him first about the best time to tell Stalin about the successful testing of the atomic bomb on 16 July. Churchill accepted that best policy would be simple disclosure of the fact without any addition of the particulars. Regarding division of the German fleet, Churchill thought that the Russians should be allowed their third share and accorded a warm welcome to the high seas. However, he believed that naval concerns should be tackled along with those on Central Europe. Truman seemed to agree, and was determined to insist on 'free, full and unfettered elections' as a guarantee of 'true independence'. The US president also appeared to be in full accord with the British prime minister's remarks about Persia (Iran), Turkey and Greece.

On Lend-Lease and other financial matters, Churchill spoke of 'the melancholy position of Great Britain' and Truman of 'the immense debt owed by the United States to Great Britain for having held the fort at the beginning', justifying the United States in looking upon these matters 'as above the purely financial plane'. Churchill added: 'Until we got our wheels turning properly once more, we could be of little use to world security or any of the high purposes of San Francisco [the United Nations].' Truman said that he would do all he could in this connection, and possible disagreements on such questions as tariffs were for the time being postponed. Both leaders expressed their support for the idea of reciprocal arrangements for post-war bases, although Truman pointed out his great difficulties in regard to the enormous expenditure involved in construction of airfields on British territory, and the consequent necessity of 'a fair plan for common use'.

Concerning Japan, Truman spoke of 'the terrible responsibilities that rested upon him in regard to unlimited effusion of American blood'. Churchill gained the impression that, although Truman believed that the Japanese lost their military honour with the attack on Pearl Harbor, he might not insist rigidly on unconditional surrender. However, when Churchill told Truman about the Japanese approach to Stalin, the president made no comment.

As he set off for a meeting with Marshal Stalin, Truman said this had been his most enjoyable luncheon in years and hoped that he could continue the good relations with Churchill established by Roosevelt. To Churchill, the new American president seemed 'a man of exceptional character and ability, with an outlook exactly along the lines of Anglo-American relations as they have developed, simple and direct methods of speech, and a great deal of self-confidence and resolution'.[19]

At his meeting with Stalin, when told about the Japanese peace feelers, Truman agreed that the best response would be a stalling request for more details. The president found the marshal 'honest – but smart as hell'.[20]

The second plenary meeting on 18 July began with a renewed agreement to exclude the press from the conference. (According to the Soviet version, Churchill observed: 'I don't want to be a lamb led to the slaughter. I could talk to them [the press] if the Generalissimo guarantees to rescue me with troops in case of need'.[21]) The Big Three then turned to subjects for discussion as suggested by the three foreign secretaries: peace negotiations and territorial settlements in Europe; the control of Germany; and the Polish question. On Europe, there was general agreement that the ultimate authority should be the United Nations, although Stalin considered that the Great Powers should represent the interests of all and the word 'ultimate' was unnecessary. Churchill and Truman wanted 'Germany' to mean the state as defined by pre-war boundaries, while Stalin argued that it should be accepted as 'a geographical section or concept' on its post-war basis of four zones, and that agreement might be advanced if attention were first given to the western frontier of Poland. As Churchill agreed with Truman on taking the frontiers of Germany as they existed in 1937, Stalin accepted them as a formal starting point. The Polish question was more intractable, with a considerable amount of reiteration and amplification of points already made at Tehran and elsewhere. It was decided to refer the matter including the holding of free elections to the three foreign secretaries again.[22]

The same evening, on 18 July, Churchill had dinner with Stalin. The first topic of conversation was the British general election, Stalin suggesting that Churchill would achieve a majority of about eighty seats. To the prime minister's doubts about how the soldiers had voted, the marshal responded that the army would prefer a strong, Conservative government. Moreover,

Stalin volunteered the opinion 'that no country needed a Monarchy as much as Great Britain, because the Crown was the unifying force throughout the Empire, and that no one who was a friend of Britain would do anything to weaken the respect shown to the Monarchy'. Stalin went on to say that his government had given a non-committal reply to the Mikado's note and that the Soviet forces would begin to attack Japan on 8 August, or a fortnight later.

Churchill welcomed Russia as a naval power, adding that, as far as the narrow exits from the Baltic and Black Seas were concerned, it had been like 'a giant with his nostrils pinched'. However, the Turks were very frightened about Russian policy. Explaining his government's position, which included a claim to Kars and Ardahan taken away from Russia at the end of the First World War, Stalin went on to ask again for his share of the German fleet, while thanking Churchill for the ships delivered by the UK after the surrender of the Italian navy. The two leaders went on to consideration of the situation in Greece, Hungary, Yugoslavia, Romania and Bulgaria and on some of their frontiers, making some reference back to their 'percentages agreement' of October 1944. Stalin insisted that 'in all the countries liberated by the Red Army, the Russian policy was a strong, independent, sovereign State'. For his part, Churchill talked of the anxiety of the peoples living east of a line from North Cape to Albania, and his impression of Russia rolling westwards. Stalin responded that five million Russians had been killed or were missing as a result of the war. (Of course, this figure was later shown to be an underestimate, the actual figure turning out to be twenty-seven million or more.) The Russians had mobilized twelve million apart from industry, the Germans eighteen million. The Russians had already demobilized two million men and sent them home. More would follow them when adequate rail transport could be found.

Expressing his hope that agreement could be reached on all land and sea questions before the end of the conference, Churchill went on to observe that 'the Three Powers gathered round the table were the strongest the world had ever seen, and it was their task to maintain the peace of the world'. The two leaders agreed that, although satisfactory for them, their victory was a tragic defeat for the Germans, who were 'like sheep'. Churchill went on to tell the story of young Lieutenant Tirpitz, which remains obscure, while Stalin recollected an experience from his time in Germany in 1907, when 'two hundred Germans missed a Communist meeting because there was no-one to take their railway tickets at the station barrier'.

Stalin apologized for not yet giving official thanks to Great Britain for the supplies sent during the war, and said that Russia was ready to talk about trade with the UK. Replying to a question, he described the Collective and State farm system, and agreed with Churchill that there was no fear of unemployment in both Russia and Britain.

The prime minister stated that 'the happiness and well-being of her people' would be 'the best publicity for Soviet Russia abroad'. The marshal referred to the continuity of Soviet policy, saying that he was thinking thirty years ahead, and that: 'If anything were to happen to him, there would be good men ready to step into his shoes.'[23]

On 19 July, the third plenary meeting took place. Beginning with some reference to the complex situation in the Balkans, including frontier problems, and then to Poland, on which a draft statement was being reworked, the conference turned to the question of the German navy and merchant marine, considering at length the number and nature of the losses sustained by the Allies and of compensation for them. Truman said that he 'did not want to upset the apple-cart' and would rather leave settlement of the problem in Europe until after the end of the war with Japan. If Russia came into that war, it would share in the allocation of resources in Asia. Among other observations, Churchill spoke out for the sinking of the bulk of German U-boats that had brought the British Isles to 'the brink of disaster'.

Spain was the next item on the agenda, the Big Three concurring in a negative view of the Franco regime. However, while Stalin gave emphasis to the danger to Europe posed by the regime and the advisability of using diplomatic means to show the Spanish people and others that the Allies supported democratic principles, Churchill said that this would infringe the principle of non-intervention in the internal affairs of another country not involved in the war. Truman commented that there had been enough war in Europe and that he did not want to become involved in another Spanish Civil War. Since there was no possibility of immediate agreement, he suggested that the question be taken up again later. On Yugoslavia, Truman opposed the other two who wanted Tito and other leaders to appear before the conference, pointing out that he had come to Berlin for a discussion of world affairs, not to sit on a court. Again, any decision had to be postponed, as it had to be on Romania, too.[24]

The fourth plenary meeting ensued on 20 July. One of the first subjects discussed was the Yalta Declaration on Liberated Europe, with general agreement on the necessity for free elections and a free press in the Balkans, although the Soviet government was not happy with the supervision of the elections. Churchill suggested that 'observation' might be a better word. On the establishment of a Council of Foreign Ministers, the only question to be decided was the time and place of its first meeting. Churchill argued that it was the turn of the UK. London had been 'the capital most under fire, and longest in the war' while it had claims to be 'the largest city in the world and one of the oldest' as well as being located halfway between the United States and the Soviet Union. Attlee agreed with Churchill, asserting: 'The people of London had a right to see some of these distinguished people, and moreover the geographical argument was very strong.' Stalin and Truman agreed with this location, although adding that the foreign secretaries would have to give further attention to the manner of the inclusion of France and China in their Council.

Next, detailed attention was given to Italy. Like Spain, this was a subject arousing the emotions of Churchill in particular. It was not just that Italy had been the first enemy power to surrender. Unaided, and with very heavy losses, throughout the Mediterranean the UK had resisted the aggression of Italy that had made 'a most dastardly and utterly unprovoked attack upon Greece' and previously seized Albania 'by a most lawless act'. He therefore favoured caution in making peace with Italy, and the further consideration of the question of reparations. Stalin insisted that not only had some Italian forces had been among those invading the Soviet Union but Romania, Hungary, Finland and Bulgaria had also made significant contributions to the invasion. However, he was against revenge, which would impede the creation of 'a gulf between Germany and her satellites' and the adherence of these satellites to the Allied camp. Truman agreed 'most cordially' with Stalin's remarks about revenge: 'Sinners must be punished, but revenge was the wrong start.' Churchill said that he was in agreement with such sentiments. He was not thinking of reparations from Italy for the Allies but for Greece.

Churchill complained about Soviet delays in allowing access to Vienna and zones in Austria. Truman also expressed dissatisfaction on this matter, but proposed acceptance of Stalin's assurance that the occupation could now proceed.[25]

The much more vexed question of Poland was a major theme of the fifth plenary meeting on 21 July. After insisting that the liabilities as well as the assets of the Polish governments be taken into consideration, Truman said that he would not want the US and UK governments alone to announce that they were carrying out their obligations. When Stalin asked if the British government proposed to make the new government in Lublin responsible for the debts of the old one in London, Churchill said that this was a matter for discussion with the Poles. Stalin went on to assert that the Soviet Union had extended credits to both governments, but that the Polish forces had redeemed them through their actions, and that the matter should be closed. When the focus turned to questions of human rights, freedom of the press and elections, Stalin argued in favour of protecting 'the dignity of Poland' and not giving emphasis to freedom when it already existed. Truman said that there were six million Poles in the United States and that therefore he was keen to see free elections, as well as freedom of the press. Stalin put forward the following version of the paragraph in question, which was generally agreed:

The Three Powers note that the Polish Provisional Government, in accordance with the decisions of the Crimea Conference, has agreed to the holding of free and unfettered elections as soon as possible on the basis of universal suffrage and secret ballot in which all democratic and anti-Nazi parties shall have the right to take part and to put forward candidates; and that the representatives of the Allied Press will enjoy full freedom to report to the world upon developments in Poland before and during the elections.

The western frontier of Poland aroused more dissension. Stalin argued that general agreement had been reached at Yalta on the eastern frontier following the Curzon Line and the western extending into what had previously been German territory, albeit without specific definition. Truman argued that zones of occupation should be introduced in Germany as they had been agreed at Yalta, and that reparations and other matters would be difficult to settle otherwise. But he would have no objection if the Soviet government brought a Polish administration into its own zone of occupation. Stalin said he would like to explain how the Russians fought the war. The Red Army had concentrated on winning the war, a task that necessitated a quiet, preferably friendly area behind the lines. Obviously, Poles could set up an administration sympathetic to the Allies better than the Germans. In any case, the Germans had fled. Debate ensued about how many Poles and Germans would have to be moved in accordance with the new frontiers, and how the peoples of both nations should be fed. Churchill said that a movement of so many millions of people would bring about 'a great shock to the people of Great Britain'. Moreover, he was concerned about feeding the German population, particularly in the industrial Ruhr in the British sector, fearing that: 'If enough food could not be found to feed this population, we should be faced with conditions in our zone of occupation such as had existed in the German concentration camps, only on a scale a thousand times greater.' When Stalin suggested that the Germans could buy food from Poland, Churchill countered that the British government could not accept part of pre-war Germany as Polish territory, and he was concerned not only about agriculture but also industry, in particular the takeover of coalmines in Silesia. Stalin asserted that if the Poles were not allowed to do the work, all production would have to be stopped, especially since forcibly deported labourers were now returning home. Moreover, better that Germans should experience difficulties than the Poles. Mr Attlee said that the definition of the western frontier could be postponed, while emphasis should be given to the present chaos and how the occupying Powers could deal with it. The resources of Germany as it was in 1937 should be used on behalf of the peoples living in that area. The arbitrary annexation of part of Germany to Poland would result in a heavy burden for the other zones. Stalin exclaimed that 'perhaps Mr. Attlee should bear in mind that Poland was also an ally, and should not be put in a very stupid position'. But Truman said that he could not regard parts of eastern Germany as annexed from the rest of the country from the point of view of supplies and reparations. Further discussion was postponed until the next meeting.[26]

Duly, at the sixth plenary meeting on 22 July, arguments on Poland were reiterated and amplified. Churchill hoped that the Big Three could bridge the gap between them before the subject was discussed by 'all the Parliaments of the world'. Moreover, delay could be dangerous since: 'The Poles, who had assigned to themselves, or had been assigned, this area, would be digging themselves in and making themselves masters.' Truman read out the Yalta agreement on the problem, including the advisability of consulting the Polish Provisional government. Stalin pointed out that this government had already declared itself in favour of the Oder-Western Neisse line, but the Russians and circumstances were more responsible for the incursion into pre-war Germany than the Poles themselves. It was agreed to ask the Polish government to send representatives to the conference.[27]

The problem of Territorial Trusteeship led to more debate. Churchill was inclined to doubt if the question should be discussed by the Big Three since it was already in the hands of the world organization. Truman observed that the trusteeship question could be discussed just as appropriately as, for example, Poland. Stalin then said that Mr Eden had told the British Parliament that 'Italy had lost her colonies once and for all.' But who had made this decision, where were the colonies now and who had found them in the first place? Churchill replied that the British Army had conquered them through 'heavy losses and indubitable victories'. After Stalin interjected that the Red Army had taken Berlin, Churchill conceded that British heavy losses 'were nothing like as great as had unhappily been those of the valiant Soviet Armies', but went on to point out that the UK was now the world's greatest debtor and could not hope to regain parity with the US Navy. Nevertheless, the UK had made no territorial claims: 'For us there was no Königsberg, no Baltic States, nothing.' With 'a sense of perfect rectitude and complete disinterestedness', he went on to suggest that Italy might have some of her colonies returned to her on certain conditions. He had himself seen admirable reclamation work carried out by the Italians in Tripolitania and Cyrenaica. Truman said that the United States certainly did not want these colonies or trusteeship over them, adding that 'they already had enough poor Italians'. Churchill pointed out that the Jews were 'not very smitten' by the thought that one of these countries might suit them, going on to emphasize that any changes in the status quo in the Mediterranean would need long consideration on the part of Great Britain since it had 'great interests' there. Stalin said that if discussion of this subject were considered premature, it could be temporarily postponed, but not forever. Churchill said that, if indeed the Soviet government was wanting 'large tracts of the North African shore', the question would have to be looked at in the context of many other factors. The conference agreed to hand the question over to the foreign secretaries.

Another difficult problem was that of Turkey and the Straits. Reiterating that he was in favour of Russian warships or merchant ships moving in and out the Black Sea, Churchill went on to point out that Turkey was alarmed by the presence of Russian troops in Bulgaria, the continuous criticism of it in the Soviet media and Molotov's demands for Kars and Ardahan on the eastern frontier as well as military bases on the Black Sea as conditions for an alliance with Turkey. In response, Molotov confirmed that Turkey had indeed suggested an alliance, that Russia had asked for the return of Kars and Ardahan taken away in 1921 and that Soviet military bases would be used in addition to Turkish to prevent 'the use of the Straits by other countries for the purposes inimical to the Black Sea Powers'. In response to Churchill's comment that the military base issue was 'entirely fresh', Molotov mentioned that the Russo-Turkish Treaties of 1805 and 1833 had provided that Turkey and Russia alone were to control passage through the Straits.[28] As before, tsarist agreements were adduced in support of Soviet policy, as the *longue durée* once again made its presence felt in discussions focused mainly on the circumstances of 1945.

To sum up Potsdam so far, from the Straits through Syria and Lebanon to Egypt and on to the Balkans, Italy and Spain, the Western Allies were still apprehensive about Soviet encroachment into the Mediterranean which they saw as their own preserve, with Churchill especially concerned about the route to India via the Suez Canal. The prime minister was also sensitive to any threat posed to the integrity of the British Empire, which he saw as the basis for the UK's future prosperity and influence, during discussions of trusteeship under the aegis of the world organization increasingly known as the United Nations Organisation. On the whole, the arrival of the United Nations Organisation received a welcome from the Big Three, although warmer from the UK and the United States in the spirit of the Atlantic Charter than from the Soviet Union which had a different tradition. The main source of disagreement remained the inextricably connected problem of Poland and Germany, with the UK and the United States especially unhappy about the Soviet proposal for the western boundary between them on the Oder-Neisse line which expanded Poland into the pre-war configuration of Germany.

Although they did not object to the Soviet transformation of Königsberg into Kaliningrad, they could not accept Eastern Europe as Russia's traditional sphere of influence.

We need to remember that, although fully conscious of the preponderance of the United States' power, Truman wrote later: 'There were many reasons for my going to Potsdam, but the most important, to my mind, was to get from Stalin a personal reaffirmation of Russia's entry into the war against Japan, which our military chiefs were most anxious to clinch.' The new American president soon achieved his primary aim, while, on the whole, Truman began and Churchill continued good relations with Stalin, even if something of the warmth of the tripartite relationship seems to have been lost through the absence of Roosevelt, probably also because of the Big Three's knowledge of the arrival of the atom bomb, successfully tested on 16 July.

Potsdam: From Churchill to Attlee and a 'New Weapon'

Potsdam: From Europe to Asia

Having already changed once with the death of Roosevelt, the composition of the Big Three was to change again before Potsdam was over with the replacement of Churchill by Attlee. However, we should not forget that, even before the British general election results were announced, Attlee was already participating in the conference in his capacity as Churchill's deputy, a role which he had carried on with self-effacing efficiency throughout the war. For example, on 23 July, he sent Churchill a minute on the Montreux Convention and the Straits, elaborating points that he had already made on 18 July and arguing that although the Russians appeared to be carrying out 'a crude exercise of power politics', it was necessary 'to look at the matter from the Russian angle'. Noting the lack of Russian access to the world's wider waterways, contrasting with the Anglo-French dominance of the Mediterranean and Suez, Attlee feared that the British disinterestedness in further acquisitions might prompt 'the subconscious retort by the Russians' – 'Why should you, you have all you want.' Seeing the present position as 'the result of the power politics of the past', they were making demands to acquire full freedom of the seas and to enforce it, and this was 'not unnatural in the second greatest power in the world'. Past precedents and old treaties were useless in a new situation in which 'air power transcends all frontiers and menaces all home lands'. Moreover, the United States would be unlikely to give the UK much support 'although they would be stiff enough over their own control of the Panama Canal zone'. The best policy would be to have constructive proposals appropriate to the new world situation for submission to the United Nations Organisation.[1]

The seventh plenary meeting on 23 July briefly noted progress made by the foreign secretaries and made some provision for future meetings before taking up again the question of Turkey. Churchill said that he could not accept that the Straits might be fortified by a Russian base. In response to Churchill's earlier assertion that Russia had frightened Turkey with its military presence in Bulgaria, Stalin claimed that there were fewer troops there than the British had in Greece, although Churchill interjected his disagreement. Continuing, Stalin conceded that the restoration of pre-First World War tsarist frontiers might indeed have frightened the Turks, but pointed out that Kars was part of Armenia and Ardahan part of Georgia. An alliance was first suggested by the Turks themselves: if they did not want to rectify their frontiers, the question of an alliance should be dropped. Regarding the Straits, the Russian position was desperate. The Montreux Convention of 1936 was directed against the Soviet republic, allowing Turkey to block the Straits when it alone deemed that a threat of war existed. Moreover, according to the Convention, Soviet Russia had the same rights as the Emperor of Japan. A small power, Turkey, supported by a great power, Britain, held another great power, Russia, by the throat. What kind of British and American reaction would there be if a similar situation arose regarding the Suez or Panama Canal? Asked by Churchill if the freedom of the Straits should be guaranteed by law or by force, Stalin responded by saying that it should be the first backed up by the second, as it was in Suez by the British navy and in Panama by the US Navy. When Churchill said that it would be unacceptable for Russia to have a base in the Straits, Stalin said that it should be given one elsewhere for the Soviet navy to refuel, be repaired and work with its Allies to keep order in the area.

Truman was in favour of the revision of the Montreux Convention, and a guarantee of the freedom of the Straits by the Great Powers. He added that after much study, 'he had come to the conclusion that all the wars in the last 200 years had originated in the area bounded by the Baltic Sea and the Mediterranean on the North and South and by the Eastern border of France and the Western border of Russia'. In the two world wars, first Austria and then Germany had upset the peace of the world. The present conference and the later Peace Conference should see to it there should be no further such happening. The free exchange of goods in the part of Europe that he had previously mentioned, just as in the United States, would go a long way to securing this desirable end. He favoured free access for all to all the seas of the world as well as unrestricted navigation on all inland waterways bordered by two or more states, beginning with the Danube and the Rhine, but applying also to the Kiel Canal and the Straits. Churchill agreed with Truman in general, and in particular that the freedom of the Straits and other international waterways should be guaranteed by the Great Powers. He hoped that Stalin might consider this as an alternative to a Russian base near Constantinople. Stalin said that the president's proposals would have to be examined carefully.

Attention turned to the Soviet Union's suggestion that its western frontier should incorporate the Königsberg area, Stalin underlining that, as already discussed at Tehran, Russia should have an ice-free port at the expense of Germany. Moreover, he added, 'Russia was anxious to secure some piece of German territory, so as to give some small satisfaction to the tens of millions of her people who had suffered in the war.' Truman raised no objection, although the US delegation thought that there might have to be some examination of the Soviet proposal 'on ethnological grounds'. Churchill said that he had already mentioned the proposal in a speech to the House of Commons on 15 December 1944, and that the British government was in sympathy with it. But there remained the legal question of the transfer and he would like to look at the exact line of the frontier on the map. The Big Three agreed that the final settlement of the question would be made at the Peace Conference.

Another conference was proposed by Stalin, on the Levant States including Syria and Lebanon, and attended by representatives of the Big Three and France. Churchill pointed out that the task of keeping peace and order in these two states had fallen to the British. However, in view of France's long ties with them, he had already informed General de Gaulle that as soon as he had made a satisfactory treaty with them, the British troops would leave. The transition should be smooth, or the French troops and civilians already there might well be massacred. This might produce 'very great excitement throughout the Arab world', making it more difficult to control Palestine and Iraq, and affecting Egypt, too. Thus, passage through the Suez Canal might be interrupted as British and American troops and supplies were on their way to join in the war against Japan. General de Gaulle had most unwisely already sent 500 troops to Syria, but a settlement was still possible with both Syria and Lebanon, guaranteeing their independence and securing France's historic cultural and commercial interests. Since the matter concerned the UK, France and the Levant countries themselves, Churchill was against the Soviet proposal, although the fact that US diplomatic support had been given when the UK bore the whole burden encouraged him to say: 'If the United States were prepared to take our place that, of course, would be a different situation.' Truman said that the US government did not want to take on this responsibility. But he was against the French keeping their privileged position in the region, 'especially after the troubles which they had provoked in that part of the world'. In any case, his government were against privileges anywhere, but in favour of equal rights for all. Churchill replied that the British would 'smile benignly' on a French agreement with the countries concerned, since they already had schools, archaeological institutes and many people there as well as special interests stretching back as far as the Crusades. Having been assured by Churchill that the French would have to secure their privileges from the governments of Syria and Lebanon, and heard the view of Truman that such concessions were unlikely, Stalin agreed with Truman, thanked Churchill for his explanation and withdrew his suggestion for another conference.

The Big Three turned their attention to Iran, then known as Persia, and the problem of the withdrawal of Soviet and British troops. Stalin agreed to the British proposal for an orderly withdrawal from Tehran, but he was not prepared to go further before the Council of Foreign Ministers met in London in September 1945. Truman proposed to withdraw all American troops from Iran within sixty days or so since they were needed for the war against Japan.

After some discussion of the problem of feeding the population of Vienna, Churchill stated that he and Attlee had to return to London on 25 July for the results of the British general election, but it would be possible to hold a plenary meeting in the morning of 25 July, and another in the late afternoon of 27 July. This was agreed.[2]

The eighth plenary meeting took place on 24 July. After the report of the foreign secretaries, Byrnes summarized the views of the Polish government. If the proposed Oder-Neisse line were adopted, between 1 and 1.5 million

Germans would have to leave but, along with adjustments to the east, Poland would be losing 20 per cent of its former territories as opposed to Germany losing its 18 per cent. There would be considerable economic advantages to the new arrangement, while the line would be the shortest possible and the easiest to defend. It was agreed to postpone discussion to a later meeting.

After further explanation by Byrnes, Molotov and Eden, the Big Three took up the question of the admission to the United Nations of neutral and ex-enemy states, in particular Romania, Bulgaria, Hungary, Finland and Italy. Stalin complained of an 'artificial distinction' between Italy and the other four which were being treated 'as lepers'. Italy had been the first to surrender, but had done more harm to the Allies than all the others. If diplomatic relations were to be resumed with Italy, it would be just to resume them with the others, too. Truman argued that free access was possible to Italy, but not to Romania, Bulgaria and Hungary. When these three complied with the US government's requirements, they would receive the same recognition as Italy. Stalin said that restrictions had been placed on Russian representatives in Italy, and that the other three governments were more democratic and closer to the people than the Italian. He added that the words 'responsible and democratic' should generally be deleted since they discredited all the governments under discussion. To Truman's assertion that he could support these governments only if he was satisfied that they were indeed responsible and democratic, Stalin responded that these governments were much less Fascist than that of Argentina, which had been admitted to the United Nations. To disparage them was to throw discredit on the Soviet government. Churchill pointed out that it was nearly two years since the surrender of Italy, no more than a few months from the surrender of the others. There was no censorship in Italy, where he himself had frequently been under attack in the newspapers, and a considerable growth of political liberty there. But about Romania, still more about Bulgaria, he knew almost nothing because of restrictions imposed on them: 'An iron curtain had been rung down.' Churchill refuted Stalin's interjection that his remarks were 'fairy tales', and gave more details of the ways in which the activities of the British missions had been hampered, contrasting their predicament with the free access of Soviet officials to Italy. Stalin insisted that this was not the case, but added that neither had the Soviet government sought rights in Italy. Truman said that the US missions had experienced great difficulties in Romania and Bulgaria, but he did not wish to disparage the Soviet government or its representatives. Stalin accepted the suggestion of Byrnes that the phrase 'responsible and democratic Governments' should be replaced by 'recognised and democratic Governments' but proposed the addition to the agreement of the statement: 'The three Governments agree to consider, each separately, in the immediate future, the question of the establishing of diplomatic relations with Finland, Romania, Bulgaria and Hungary.' It was agreed that the foreign secretaries should consider the draft further.

As discussion returned to Turkey, when Stalin objected that a paper submitted by the US delegation concerned the Danube and the Rhine rather than Turkey and the Straits, Truman replied that he wanted both questions to be looked at together. When Churchill pointed out what he called a 'remarkable, indeed a tremendous fact', that is to say Truman's suggestion that there should be an international authority including the Big Three to guarantee the freedom of the Straits, Stalin insisted that Soviet bases in the Straits were still necessary, similar to those on the Suez Canal. Churchill riposted that that the Canal was open in peace and war, and an agreement had worked well for sixty or seventy years. Molotov claimed that there had been many complaints, and that Egypt's views of the matter would be interesting. Churchill reiterated his support for the international treaty, although accepting 'that it was not suitable, in time of war, or just because Turkey saw a threat of war, for a Great Power like Russia to have to go cap in hand to a small country like Turkey'. Again, it was agreed that the matter be postponed while the three governments had further talks with Turkey, Churchill remaining certain that the Turks would be unlikely to accept 'a large fort being erected near Constantinople' while Stalin thought it very unlikely but not certain.

After further discussion of Ukrainians in a British Prisoner of War camp and problems of food supply and administration in Austria, Truman suggested that work begin on a communiqué to be issued at the end of the conference a week or more on; Churchill observed that 'it was wise to put the fish in the basket as they were caught' and the suggestion was generally accepted.[3]

At a recess in the meeting on the evening of 24 July, Truman told Stalin: 'We have a new weapon of unusual destructive force.' Stalin appeared to show little interest, but expressed the hope that the weapon would be used to good effect against the Japanese. (In fact, via Soviet intelligence, Stalin already knew about the bomb, and was concerned about its implications for the extension of American power in Europe and Asia. He sought to accelerate production of a Soviet bomb.[4])

Unlike all previous plenary meetings, the ninth was held in the morning, of 25 July, to allow Churchill and Attlee to fly back to London for the election results. After the Big Three had agreed to postpone discussion of the German fleet and merchant navy, they turned to the question of transfers of population. Churchill said that they must look at mass movements such as the transfer of 2.5 million or more Germans from Czechoslovakia back home. Would they all find themselves in the Russian zone? Stalin said that most of them would go there and many had already arrived, summarily evicted by the Czechs. However, he agreed that the transfer of Germans not only from Czechoslovakia but also from Hungary and Poland should be considered by the foreign secretaries. Those in Poland were mentioned again by Churchill as discussion was resumed of its western frontier. While further conversations were continued with the Polish representatives, Truman thought that discussion might be postponed, but he wanted to make plain his view that Poland seemed to be acquiring the status of a fifth occupational zone. He added that while any Peace Treaty accepted by him would have to be ratified by the US Senate, he was in Potsdam to represent the views of the American people, who had a particular interest in the Polish question. Without popular support, he was unlikely to secure popular ratification. His wartime powers were without restriction, but he would not abuse them for other purposes.

While Churchill talked of reparations and food, Stalin argued that supplies of coal and metals from the Ruhr were even more important. When Churchill riposted that the miners could not work without food, Stalin claimed that Poland was short of food and that 'there was still a good deal of fat left in Germany'. Recognizing that the Soviet government had been asked to supply the Poles until the harvest, Churchill went on to assert that Great Britain faced 'the most fire-less winter of the war' owing to shortage of miners. To Stalin's suggestion that German prisoners of war should be used in the mines, Churchill countered that the UK had been exporting coal to liberated France, Holland and Belgium, while Poland was exporting coal to Sweden and elsewhere from areas not yet recognized as Polish. Stalin asserted that the Polish coal was coming from previous Polish, not former German, territory and that, although he did not want to dwell on the Soviet Union's difficulties, it was extremely short of labour having lost more than five million men in the war. To Churchill's offer that coal could be sent from the Ruhr in exchange for food, Stalin said that it needed careful consideration. Churchill agreed. There was some attention given to questions for the consideration of the foreign secretaries before the Big Three met again.[5] At the next such meeting, of course, Churchill would be replaced by Attlee.

During the lull, in the late evening of 26 July, Truman issued an ultimatum of unconditional surrender to the Japanese government in the form of what became known as the 'Potsdam Declaration'. The proclamation began with reference to the US president, the Chinese president and the British prime minister in that order, Chiang Kai-shek having pointed out that to put him ahead of the British prime minister would help him back home, and that, in any case, the US president and himself were both 'supreme heads of nations', while the prime minister was 'a secondary official'. In the limbo between Churchill and Attlee, British assent to this change appears to have been tacit. Certainly, Truman signed on behalf of Churchill after he had actually left Potsdam. Churchill had given his assent to the proclamation, albeit with the provision that it be issued to the Japanese government rather than to the Japanese people. But the prime minister had not specifically agreed to his third place in the order of leaders issuing the proclamation (a subject on which he had previously shown considerable sensitivity at Yalta as far as signatures were concerned). Molotov protested to the Americans at the exclusion of the Soviet Union, but he was told that since the Soviet Union was not yet in the war against Japan, the president did not want to cause it any embarrassment. Copies of the proclamation were issued to the press at seven in the evening, exactly the same time as Churchill went to Buckingham Palace to tender his resignation to the King.[6]

Soon after the change of the British government, Sir Alexander Cadogan was referring to 'the Big 3 [or 2½!]'. To some extent, Cadogan's remark might have been occasioned by his evaluation of the new prime minister and foreign secretary. Bevin, he wrote on 31 July, 'effaces Attlee, and at Big Three meetings he does all the talking while Attlee nods his head convulsively and smokes his pipe'. Churchill himself made his views known to Cadogan on 5 August: 'A very formidable event has occurred in Britain, and I fear it will diminish our national stature at a time when we need our strength.'[7] Ironically, however, Churchill's loss of power in 1945 saved his historical reputation, since it absolved him from responsibility for the loss of British influence in the later months of that year, especially in the Far East, which his charisma could not have averted.

On the evening of 28 July, on his return from his triumph over Churchill in the British general election two days before, Attlee met Truman and Stalin in turn. The American president showed the new British prime minister the boundary changes proposed by Stalin for Germany, Poland and the Soviet Union. The new foreign secretary Ernest Bevin forcefully opposed these changes. The Soviet leader asked the new prime minister to explain Labour's great victory. Attlee agreed that it had been unexpected, but there had been a favourable 'wave of opinion'. He did not agree with Stalin that the British people were turning their attention to the problems of peace, having decided that the war was over and that the Americans could finish off the distant war against Japan. On the contrary, the people understood that peace and liberty went together and that the Americans should be supported, even though they were also thinking of reconstruction. To Stalin's suggestion that while their leaders were committed to the conclusion of the war against Japan, the people had a feeling that the most important war was over, Attlee replied that Britain believed it a duty to carry on the war in the Far East, with a million men in Burma, and great casualties. Bevin added that £1 billion was owed to India. Molotov offered his view that some great event must have happened to produce such a surprising election result. Attlee observed: 'Labour enthusiasts were sometimes led away by great meetings in which the electors would cheer and applaud a Labour candidate, but they forgot the silent voters. The reverse had happened in this case.' As far as Churchill was concerned, the people had made a distinction between him as war leader and Conservative Party leader: 'The people wanted a parliament based on a definite programme. Many people looked upon the Conservatives as a reactionary party which could not carry out a policy answering to peace requirements.' Moreover, the middle and 'technical' classes had voted Labour. Bevin added that the trade unions had given great support, too. After mentioning that Japan had approached the

Soviet Union for mediation a second time after turning down an ultimatum from the United States, the UK and China, Stalin observed that Truman was in a hurry to bring the conference to an end, and agreed with Attlee that it might end in two or three days.[8]

Unusually, the tenth plenary meeting began at 10.30 pm. After the report from the foreign secretaries, Truman said that he was ready to consider any subject, and Attlee said the same, adding his regret that the progress of the conference had been delayed by the UK's domestic affairs. Stalin relayed Japan's second request for Soviet mediation, which had contained nothing new, and had therefore been summarily turned down. On the admission to the United Nations of neutral and ex-enemy states, Stalin said that of the countries under discussion, only Finland had an elected government, and that, therefore, he could see no distinction between Italy and the other states in Eastern Europe. To Bevin's interjection that Italy had been recognized because much more was known about it than the others, Stalin responded that the UK could find out more about the governments in question while adding that the Soviet Union had known very little about the Italian government when recognizing it. Attlee emphasized that the UK could not establish relations with countries with which it was technically still at war, while Bevin agreed with Byrnes that the whole question of recognition should be withdrawn. This was generally accepted.

On reparations from Austria and Italy, Stalin suggested that Austria should be exempt since it had been forced into the war by Germany but Italy, which had contributed to the devastation of the Soviet Union as far as the Volga, should pay up. Truman expressed his government's unwillingness to send money to any country if some of it was to be used to pay reparations, and that the first demand on exports from Italy should be for the repayment of loans already advanced. Referring again to the devastation inflicted on the Soviet Union, Stalin said that Finland, Hungary and Romania had each promised $300 million worth of reparations and went on to ask the total amount due, including military equipment, to be expected from Italy. Attlee pointed out that the UK too had suffered under Italian attacks and had also sent assistance to Italy. To a question from Bevin, Stalin answered that military factories could turn to peacetime production. It was agreed that no reparations should be imposed upon Austria, while those from Italy would be considered again at a later meeting. In conclusion, there was agreement with Attlee's suggestion that the conference had reached a point at which progress was more likely at plenary meetings and that these should therefore be held more frequently with meetings of the foreign secretaries suspended in order that the conference might be drawn to an end as quickly as possible.[9]

At noon on 29 July, Molotov informed Truman and Byrnes that Stalin was ill and would not be able to come to meet them later that afternoon. Nevertheless, a discussion ensued on the western boundary of Poland. Byrnes said that the American side could accept all the suggestions except for the area between the Eastern and Western Neisse, which would in effect make Poland a fifth occupying power. There was an inconclusive exchange of views, too, on reparations, including the delivery of German ships to the Soviet navy. Regarding the Soviet Union's entry into the war against Japan, Molotov suggested that the best way to proceed would be for the other Allies to make a formal request to this end. He was given an evasive answer.[10]

The Soviet foreign secretary entertained his British counterpart to lunch on 31 July. Although little of the recorded conversation was on the conference as such, it certainly threw light on the relationship between the Big Three both as individuals and countries. The first topic was again the British general election, Bevin admitting surprise but attributing the result to the negative influence of Lord Beaverbrook's newspapers, with their concentration on anti-socialist propaganda. In any case, all agreed that Churchill was a great war leader, Bevin adding that his place would be among his country's elder statesmen. On the question of nationalization, Bevin said that the new government was considering coal, transport and the Bank of England for such a takeover. When Molotov gave his estimate of Eden as a capable foreign secretary, Bevin said that continuity in foreign policy would be maintained while inspiration would be drawn from Arthur Henderson, Secretary of State from 1929 to 1931. Then, 'Some amusing exchanges were made on the subject whether the [war] criminals should be shot before or after making a statement before the Tribunal', with Molotov insisting that their statements should be heard. He went on to ask Bevin 'how soon the Labour Government proposed to establish their Gestapo. He was surprised to hear in reply that the British government was going to consult Russia but was relieved when he heard that the reason was that most of the Gestapo documents were in Russian hands'. (This interchange presumably resulted from the Conservative allegation during the general election that a Labour government would introduce a Gestapo into Britain.)

The two foreign secretaries agreed that the conference would come to an end when each had accepted the other's proposals. Bevin went on to say how he would have to report the agreements to, and receive their ratification from, the House of Commons, assuring Molotov that 'Russia would find no better guarantee in the world for the fulfilment of all that was undertaken'. When Bevin made reference to 'England [*sic*] as a great, powerful and free country with an enlightened public opinion', Molotov agreed but insisted that 'the USSR was an equally powerful country, rich in natural resources', and that it would be wrong to think that 'there was no influential public opinion in Russia'. Both foreign secretaries hoped that a lasting peace could be established. Molotov wanted the United Nations Organisation to be stronger, while Bevin thought that its strength lay 'in the goodwill of the three great democracies'. When Bevin advised against following the ideas of old teachers blindly, adding that 'Karl Marx was a brilliant economist but the world had progressed since his day', there was agreement that the same applied to 'the great British economists'. Molotov agreed that the theories of Marx 'had to be further developed before they could be applied to present-day problems'. Asked by Bevin if he was prepared to accept English as the language for diplomacy, Molotov responded that the English and Americans were lucky to be able to understand each other and that the importance of their language was recognized in his country.[11]

Later on the same day, 31 July, the eleventh plenary meeting took place. The first item on the agenda was the question of German reparations, complicated by the circumstance that the Soviet Union would be taking resources from the other zones of occupation as well as its own. After much discussion, appropriate figures were agreed for a drafting committee to complete. US Secretary of State Byrnes then proposed that the Provisional Polish government should administer on a provisional basis the eastern part of pre-war Germany that it claimed for its western frontier. On being asked by Bevin if each Power could transfer to other countries territories within its occupation zone, Stalin replied that Poland was a special case and had been recognized as such at the Yalta Conference. He added that Soviet troops had been withdrawn from the area except those necessary to keep lines of communication open to the Soviet zone, and that he would strive to establish air lines from London to Moscow. However, he stipulated that Russian pilots would have to be used between Warsaw and Moscow, and assumed that British or French pilots would have to be used from Paris to London. It was agreed to accept the US proposal pending the final peace settlement.

On the admission of neutral and ex-enemy states to the United Nations, Byrnes put forward a revised draft providing for each of the three governments to establish diplomatic relations with Bulgaria, Finland, Hungary and Romania as much as possible before 'the ratification of peace treaties'. Moreover, the draft continued, the three governments expressed the desire that representatives of the Allied press in those countries should have 'full freedom to report to the world on developments'.

The focus shifted to Germany, with renewed discussion of reparations, including appropriate figures, the problem of the Ruhr and the nature of a central German administration. On the Transfer of Populations, there was some disagreement between the Western view that Germans were being forced to flee and Stalin's that they chose to leave countries where they could not remain. But Stalin said that he would not object to a statement proposed by Attlee that the Polish and Czechoslovak governments should be made aware that 'the activities of their peoples were laying an intolerable burden on the occupying Powers'.[12]

Some inconclusive discussion ensued on the question of the German navy and merchant marine, which was held over. Concerning the Yalta Declaration on Liberated Europe, there was a gulf between Western views on Romania, Bulgaria and Hungary and those of the Soviet Union on Greece and Yugoslavia. It was agreed to drop the matter. On war criminals, with Attlee and Truman reluctant to name names in case there should be discrepancies between various lists, Stalin emphasized that 'if the Conference did not name some of the most hated major War Criminals, the declaration on the matter in the Protocol would not have its full worth'. This matter was deferred. Truman repeated his conviction that Central Europe had been 'the hotbed of war for the last 200 years' and that proper control of the inland waterways would help to prevent future wars. The problem was added to the list to be considered by the foreign secretaries at their meeting in September 1945. The conference agreed to meet twice the next day in order to conclude its deliberations.[13]

On the afternoon of 1 August, the twelfth plenary meeting took place. After the report from the foreign secretaries, the Big Three returned to the question of German reparations. Stalin cut through previous disagreements with the suggestion that the Soviet Union would have exclusive rights to assets in its own zone and the United States and UK such rights in theirs. This would mean, for example, that assets in Finland, Bulgaria and Romania would be at the disposal of the Soviet Union, while the United States and Great Britain would exert control in like manner over France, Belgium, Holland and the Western Hemisphere. Bevin sought further clarification from Stalin, who agreed that his proposal meant that German assets in Czechoslovakia and Yugoslavia would be under the Western powers while those in Austria would be shared between all Three. On a suggestion from Attlee, France was invited to become a member of the Allied Commission on Reparations. Stalin asserted that Poland had suffered more than France and therefore had a greater claim to reparations, but did not press the point when Truman hoped that they would not have to return to ground already covered.

The conference turned to some German problems, beginning with supplies for the Berlin area, on which agreement was impossible since Stalin argued that he could not make any commitment until he found out the quantities of supplies to be delivered and exchanged. However, it was agreed that the Control Council take over external assets owned by Germany but not yet under United Nations control and that reparations payments should be of a size to allow the German people subsistence without assistance from abroad. On war crimes, Stalin wanted a list of names to be published in order to satisfy public opinion and to make clear that some German industrialists were to be included in the trials. But he accepted Truman's point that such a list might handicap the preparatory work of the judges and was assured that a first list would be published as the trials started in thirty days. Concerning Allied Control Commissions in Bulgaria, Hungary and Romania, there was an agreement including free movement for American and British representatives in those countries provided that the ACC was informed of the time and route of such movement. The delegation of the Polish provisional government thanked all three governments for their statement on Poland's western frontier. Truman wanted radio correspondents to be added to those from the press in the agreement on reporting in Poland and elsewhere, but Attlee agreed with Stalin that they should be excluded. All Three agreed that the Soviet Union would provide Poland with merchant ships from its share of the overall amount, and that discussion of Allied property in 'satellite states' should be deferred for the evening meeting. After Truman expressed strong reservations about secret agreements, it was generally accepted that the decision on inland waterways would be included in the conference protocol but not the communiqué.[14]

Before the final meeting, Attlee wrote to Churchill assuring him that the new Big Three had been 'building on the foundation laid by you, and there has been no change of policy'. The vital questions had been reparations and the Polish western frontier. On the first, the Russians were 'very insistent on their pound of flesh', but the Western Allies insisted that food and other supplies were needed from the Eastern zone and that reparations should not be more important than the maintenance of 'a reasonable economy in Germany'. On Poland, the Americans had yielded to Soviet insistence on the Western Neisse line, but the West had gained specific pledges on elections, press arrangements and repatriation of Polish combatants. Attlee commented:

> Uncle Joe was not in a good mood at the start caused I think by an indisposition which kept him in bed for two days. Thereafter he was in good form. The President was very co-operative. My having been present from the start was a great advantage, but Bevin picked up all the points extremely quickly and showed his quality as an experienced negotiator in playing his hand. I think that the results achieved are not unsatisfactory having regard to the way the course of the war had dealt the cards. I hope you have been able to get some rest. If you would care to come and see me to hear more details I should be delighted.

Attlee thanked Churchill for a letter on 'T.A.' (Tube Alloys, codename for the atomic bomb), which he had passed on to Truman. The president made no comment, adding that 'Uncle Joe had not cross-examined him on the matter.'[15]

After Potsdam

The thirteenth and final plenary meeting of the conference met in the late evening of 1 August. It concentrated on the contents of the communiqué and protocols. On Germany, it was made clear that all three powers would share German external assets and that renunciation of their claims in the zones of others concerned reparations only. It was agreed to leave final determination of the frontiers of Königsberg and surrounding area to the Peace Conference. It was also agreed to make minor revisions to the statement on ex-enemy states and their admission to the United Nations, and to omit some subjects from the communiqué.

Potsdam ended with a discussion of the order in which the Big Three would sign the communiqué, Molotov pointing out that it had previously been agreed by Roosevelt and Churchill that Stalin should come first on the next occasion after Yalta. So Stalin came first, then Truman followed by Attlee. The other two accepted Attlee's suggestion that greetings and thanks be sent to the absent surviving member of the old Big Three. So a message was sent to Churchill recognizing 'the untiring efforts and the unconquerable spirit with which at earlier conferences and throughout the war he served our common cause of victory and enduring peace' and concluding with the observation: 'The whole world knows the greatness of his work, and it will never be forgotten.' A somewhat less fulsome message was sent to Eden.[16]

Bringing the business of the conference to an end, Truman expressed the hope that the next meeting would be in Washington. 'God willing' said Stalin.[17] In fact, of course, Potsdam was the last conference of the Big Three, and peace was never formally concluded.

A communiqué was issued to the press.[18] A somewhat longer protocol which may be taken also as something of a summary of the proceedings was published in 1947. Section I began with the establishment of a Council of Foreign Ministers representing the Big Three, China and France, and beginning its work with the composition of peace treaties with Italy, Romania, Bulgaria, Hungary and Finland to be submitted to the United Nations. Proposals for settlement of outstanding territorial questions would also be drawn up. Moreover, 'the Council shall be utilised for the preparation of a peace settlement for Germany when a Government adequate for the purpose is established'. Section II listed the political and economic principles to govern the treatment of Germany in the initial control period. These included thorough elimination of Nazi principles and activities, and decentralization. Section III was concerned with reparations from Germany, Section IV with the disposal of the German navy and merchant marine. Section V dealt with the city of Königsberg and the adjacent area, Section VI with war criminals and Section VII with Austria, from which no reparations were to be exacted. Section VIII referred to the formation of 'a Polish Provisional Government of National Unity' and the 'free and unfettered elections' that it had agreed to hold. The Oder-Western Neisse line was accepted as the provisional western frontier of Poland.

Section IX looked at the conclusion of peace treaties and admission to the United Nations Organisation, with special reference to those countries referred to in Section I. The three governments made clear that they would not favour any application for membership submitted by the then Spanish government, founded as it had been with the support of the Axis powers. Section X, on territorial trusteeship, mentioned specifically the question of Italian colonial territory which would be considered by the Council of Foreign Ministers. Section XI was concerned with revised procedure for the Allied Control Commission in Romania, Bulgaria and Hungary, Section XII with the 'orderly and humane manner' in which the transfer of German populations should be effected. Section XIII said that within ten days, on the spot, bilateral commissions would consider the question of the removal of oil equipment from Romania, while Section XIV said that Allied troops would be withdrawn immediately from Tehran, with further stages of such withdrawal to be considered by the Council of Foreign Ministers. Section XV recorded agreement that the strategically important Zone of Tangier should remain international for the time being, Section XVI recorded agreement that each of the three governments would discuss with the Turkish government the manner in which the Montreux Convention 'should be revised as failing to meet present-day conditions'. Sections XVII and XVIII looked forward to discussion of European international inland waterways and transport. Section XIX recorded the agreement that each government would send a directive to its representative on the Allied Control Council for Germany, Section XX left agreement on the use of Allied property for satellite reparations or 'war trophies' to be worked out through diplomatic channels. Section XXI simply recorded that there had been meetings of the Chiefs of Staff of the three governments 'on military matters of common interest'. The protocol was signed by Stalin, Truman and Attlee on 2 August 1945.[19]

As a bald summary of the Proceedings at Potsdam, the protocol also hides certain significant aspects of the proceedings, most notably through the comparative lack of reference to the Middle East and total absence of any mention of the Far East.

On 28 July, Harry Truman wrote to his mother and sister: 'Well here another week has gone, and I'm still in the Godforsaken country awaiting the return of a new British Prime Minister. I had hoped we'd be finished by now, but there are some loose ends to clean up, and we must do it again....'[20] 'Loose ends' is a description that could be applied to Potsdam more widely, with its focus on problems of left over from Yalta, including Polish and German boundaries and reparations. Turkey and the Middle East were also discussed again to some extent. Yet the approach was without clear direction. For example, the new prime minister agreed with Stalin that the American president was in a hurry to bring the conference to an end. Attlee then agreed with Truman that any subject could be considered, which suggests that the attention of Truman in particular was switching to the problem of bringing to an end the war against Japan through the Potsdam Declaration while contemplating the awful question of how to use the atom bomb and wondering how this would affect the significance of Soviet collaboration, while not forgetting the impact that events in Asia might have on developments in Europe. The nature of victory over Japan, although not normally considered in such detail at the Big Three conferences as victory over Germany, is important enough to deserve more detailed attention at the beginning of the next chapter. For the moment, let us just note that, in the informed view of Cat Wilson, for the ex-prime minister Winston Churchill 'Asia was a distraction and a sideshow' and his policy was 'for America to attend to Japan'.[21]

Before we leave Europe, however, let us conclude with a comment on Truman's observation that, after much study, 'he had come to the conclusion that all the wars in the last 200 years had originated in the area bounded by the Baltic Sea and the Mediterranean on the North and South and by the Eastern border of France and the Western border of Russia'. Indeed, most of the discussion not only at Potsdam but also at Tehran and Yalta concerned this troublesome region, over which Germans and Slavs had fought for centuries and the post-war settlement of which involved the migration of about ten million Germans, Slavs and others, in the informed estimate of Arnold Toynbee constituting the greatest migration of population since the fourth to the seventh centuries CE but restoring the ethnic map to something like that of 1200 CE.[22]

On his way home, on 2 August, Truman fulfilled a previously discussed engagement in a meeting with George VI, not in the shape of a state visit to London, however, but a brief encounter in Plymouth Harbour. The president 'was impressed with the King as a good man', and there was a friendly luncheon. In response to a polite communication from the monarch, the republican leader replied 'I am sure that our two nations will cooperate in peace as they are now cooperating so effectively in war.'[23]

But this was not to be. On 9 August, Mr J. Balfour, the British *chargé d'affaires* in Washington, reported to Bevin that 'Almost all thoughtful Americans are … imbued with the belief that, by reason of her vast size, limitless resources in men and raw materials, and industrial potential, Soviet Russia is the only world power comparable in stature to the United States'. The idea of the Big Three was being replaced by 'the Big Two concept'. On 20 August, the British government received formal notification of the termination of Lend-Lease. British officials had to work strenuously to obtain a loan from the United States, offering bases for the American air force and markets for American business both in the UK and in the Empire in part exchange. Possibly, the Americans drove a harder bargain because of their apprehension concerning economic policies likely to be pursued by a Labour government. In the informed appraisal of M. E. Pelly, one of the editors of the British documents on the subject, neither Bevin nor Churchill appears to have realized 'how little leverage was left to an impoverished Britain in the partnership with the United States which they sought'. Thus, wrote Pelly, 'acceptance of the loan, together with American possession of atomic know-how, increasingly cast Britain as an American client, and thus unable to function with the complete independence of a power of the first rank on the world stage'.[24]

Great Powers and Superpowers

Victory over Japan

In 1945, the Big Three concentrated heavily on the European theatre of war at both Yalta and Potsdam. Little was said among them about the termination of the war in the Far East. This was partly for security reasons, but partly also because of emerging differences between the Western Allies and a developing consciousness that US-Soviet rivalry would become a factor in the final struggle against Japan. Nevertheless, at the Big Three conferences, the United States made clear its wish for the Soviet Union to share the burden of bringing the Emperor Hirohito's forces to submission, and the Soviet Union exacted large concessions in return. For its part, while making a significant contribution to victory in the Far East, the UK was most anxious to restore its empire, especially in Malaya, Singapore and Hong Kong, in the face of American reservations.

Towards the end of the war, then, the UK had ceased to be a major player in the Far East and its status as a major power was in jeopardy. Meanwhile, the United States exerted its influence to an unprecedented degree in the Pacific and on the Asiatic mainland, while the Soviet Union was accelerating its preparations for the restoration of losses conceded by its tsarist predecessor to Japan in the war of 1904–5 and the resumption of its own hostilities with Japan begun in 1938 and 1939. Both of the UK's partners in the Big Three were on their way to a new status, superpower.

In the Potsdam Declaration of 26 July 1945, the United States, China and the UK, while disavowing any intention to enslave the Japanese as a race or destroy them as a nation, called for 'the unconditional surrender of all the Japanese forces'.[1] At the time, however, before the use by the United States of atomic bombs and the invasion of Manchukuo by the Soviet Union, a window of opportunity appeared to open for the Japanese government to avoid unconditional surrender and to achieve peace by negotiation along the lines of other points made by the Potsdam Declaration. There seemed to be a real chance of saving some of the Japanese Greater East Asian Co-Prosperity Sphere.

While fully expecting an attack by the Soviet Union, the Japanese High Command nevertheless believed that, by playing the Soviet Union off against the United States, there could be a way of limiting US dominance over their empire. Since the defeats by Soviet forces on the frontiers of Manchukuo in 1938 and 1939, the Japanese had abandoned their Northern strategy and aimed at the promotion of new orders in Asia and Europe through the Tripartite Pact of September 1940 with Germany and Italy and the Soviet–Japanese Neutrality Pact of April 1941. The Nazi invasion of the Soviet Union in June 1941 and the Japanese attack on Pearl Harbor followed by Germany's declaration of war on the United States in December changed the situation radically. While the Soviet and Japanese forces were preoccupied by events remote from the border between them for some years from 1941 onwards, arguments that the Soviet and Japanese peoples could maintain peace and friendship as part of their shared Eurasian affiliations and destinies were somewhat contrived on both sides and already wearing thin by the end of 1944. Indeed, Stalin's Russian Revolution anniversary speech of 9 November included the denunciation of Japan as an aggressor, a clear warning that the Neutrality Pact had become a scrap of paper.

Nevertheless, negotiations were already under way for a measure of compromise as the war in the Far East was not all that far behind war in Europe in reaching the final stages. By June 1945, indeed, the Japanese were offering to restore all the losses incurred by the tsarist government in 1904–5, and more, surpassing (however unwittingly) the concessions offered to Stalin by Roosevelt and Churchill at Yalta in February. Historian Yukiko Koshiro comments:

> While pursuing these diplomatic guessing games with Moscow, the Japanese
> policymakers regarded Stalin not as a revolutionary [Lenin II] but rather as

a legitimate successor to Alexander III and Nicholas II, the last two tsars of the Romanovs – an imperialist with territorial ambition. They guessed that Stalin would naturally attempt to reestablish a Soviet foothold in Manchuria and also Korea and eventually expand out into the Pacific Ocean, a course that would sooner or later collide with that of the United States.

Similar observations have been put forward by Western and post-Soviet analysts, as we shall see later.

Of course, whether or not Stalin's policies were following those of the tsars, there were powerful Japanese voices raised against the threat of communist expansion in the Far East and in favour of post-war integration in the capitalist world via accommodation with the United States. However difficult this might be for a country like Japan without a colonial hinterland, there was also at least the dawning of the realization that the United States would also want a reconstruction aimed against the spread of communism in China and elsewhere in the Far East.

While the best way of securing maximum advantage for Japan would be to play one side off against the other, this stratagem would involve it in at least some resistance to the expected Soviet invasion of Manchukuo as well as to ongoing American attacks from the Pacific.

When Molotov announced on 5 April 1945 that the Soviet–Japanese Neutrality Pact would not be renewed after it had run for five years by April 1946, a Soviet attack was expected later in 1945. On 6 August, the first atomic bomb was dropped over Hiroshima. On 8 August, the Red Army's invasion of Manchukuo took the Japanese army by surprise. On 9 August, as the invasion intensified, the Soviet Union declared war on Japan, and a second atomic bomb destroyed Nagasaki. On 10 August, Japan accepted the terms offered in the Potsdam Declaration, but with the condition that the status of the Emperor would remain unchanged. The United States rejected this condition. The end of the war was then recognized by the Emperor himself in two recorded broadcasts: one on 14 August to the people as a whole making reference to 'a new and most cruel bomb'; the other on 17 August to the armed forces in particular with the explanation 'Now that the Soviet Union entered the war, to continue under the present conditions at home and abroad would only result in further useless damage and eventually endanger the very foundation of the empire's existence.' In Tsuyoshi Hasegawa's estimation,

'Despite their destructive power, the atomic bombs were not sufficient to change the direction of Japanese diplomacy. The Soviet invasion was.' While some Japanese officials urged the United States to resist the Soviet takeover of southern Sakhalin and the Kuril Islands, others were still hoping for restraint of the United States by the Soviet Union, possibly along with the support of the Chinese Communist Party. In reality, for the time being at least, Japan ceased to be an active force in international relations.[2]

A counterfactual question remains: Would the Soviet invasion have been enough to bring about the Japanese surrender without the American use of atomic bombs? Certainly, Secretary of War Henry L. Stimson's plan to leave Washington on 10 August for a short vacation is considered by Richard B. Frank to be 'an eloquent indicator of how far official Washington believed that Japan remained from surrender even after two atomic bombs'.[3] Perhaps an appropriate way to view the Allied victory in the Far East is as part of the struggle between the United States and the Soviet Union for predominance while order could not easily be extracted from the final confusion of the Japanese government in Tokyo.

Meanwhile, what of the UK, almost totally excluded from many accounts of the final victory over Japan? According to the official history of British foreign policy in the Second World War, there was a firm decision not to accept unofficial Japanese peace proposals 'in view of American suspicions that the Japanese would appeal to Great Britain on the basis of past friendship and business connexions'. During the period before VJ Day, the three allies kept each other informed about Japanese peace-feelers and rumours of them, maintaining their agreement on the unconditional surrender of Japan. For their part, the British government accepted 'the fact that American views would probably be decisive in a sphere which United States opinion regarded as primarily an American concern'.[4]

When, on 8 May 1945, VE Day, President Truman announced that unconditional surrender did not mean the extermination or enslavement of the Japanese people, there was some Anglo-American discussion about the post-war position of the Emperor. On 26 July, the leaders of the United States, China and the UK made a joint declaration amplifying this point.

Regarding the post-war civil situation in Japan, by September 1944, the British authorities 'had as yet no official knowledge of American intentions, but had heard unofficially that the Americans had at first envisaged a thirty per cent British participation but had decided later in favour of an all-American civil affairs plan'. There was some discussion with the Dominions of Canada, Australia and New Zealand about the role to be played by the British Commonwealth and Empire in the military occupation and civil administration of Japan after the war, while some British views were communicated to the Americans who continued to keep their own ideas largely to themselves.[5]

On 10 August, with the Japanese surrender, the British government accepted the American proposal for a response insisting that the Japanese government must subject itself to the Allied Supreme Commander. But Attlee and Bevin doubted whether it was wise to ask the Emperor to sign the surrender terms, suggesting that instead he should 'authorise and ensure the signature' of the civil and military government. Molotov stated that he was 'sceptical' about the Japanese offer which fell short of unconditional surrender in its insistence that the prerogatives of the Emperor should not be prejudiced: the Soviet offensive would therefore continue.

On 11 August, Molotov said that he accepted the American proposal, which should be issued in the name of the powers at war with Japan, while representatives of the Allied High Command should be chosen forthwith. Averell Harriman complained that this last suggestion amounted to a veto on American action, and Sir A. Clark Kerr suggested that '*by force of circumstance* [italics added] the Supreme Command would fall to the Americans; he was sure that the British government would accept their choice'. Molotov objected strongly, wondering if the Soviet government would learn of the appointment of the Supreme Commander from the press. Why not Marshal Vassilevsky, the Soviet Chief of General Staff, as well as General MacArthur? Harriman curtly reminded Molotov of 'America's four-year effort in the Far East in contrast with Russia's two-day excursion into Manchuria'. Molotov referred to the part played by the Soviet Union 'in the liberation of Europe'. Altogether, as Clark Kerr commented later, this was 'ding-dong, tempers ever rising'.[6]

On 11 August, too, the US government sent Japan the terms of surrender on behalf of the Four Powers (the Big Three plus China) incorporating the British suggestion concerning the Emperor. On 12 August, Truman confirmed to Attlee his choice of MacArthur as Supreme Commander. A British representative would be present in Tokyo at the surrender, which would be accepted in SE Asia by Mountbatten or a subordinate. However, the US government did not consult their British, Chinese or Soviet allies about the act of surrender. Still less was there any reference to a partition of Japan between the Four Powers as had been discussed previously. After the Japanese government had accepted the terms of the surrender on 14 August, Truman ordered the cessation of offensive operations on 15 August. The formal Instrument of Surrender was signed on the USS *Missouri* in Tokyo Bay by the representatives of the Four Powers and Japan on 2 September. The Soviet armed forces completed their takeover of the Kuril Islands two days later.

Chiang Kai-shek asserted that he should receive the surrender in Hong Kong since it was part of China. But Truman accepted Attlee's request that Hong Kong should surrender to the British, although adding that its status might be discussed in due course and recalling later that Roosevelt had wanted it to be returned to China. Already by the end of the war, then, there were rifts threatening not only between the Soviet Union and its allies, but also between the UK on the one hand and the United States and China on the other, clearly indicating a decline in the UK's influence.[7]

The fall of the Big Three

After Potsdam, the Big Three never met again, and any remaining bonhomie was dispelled in the meetings of the Council of Foreign Ministers that followed. Towards the end of Potsdam, anyway, the concept of a Big Three was already disappearing with the emergence of the two superpowers. Let us look at what actually happened to the concept of the Big Three after the end of the Second World War, first in some of the words of surviving members of that select group.

On 27 October 1945, in a speech to mark Navy Day, Truman referred to 'a sea power never before equalled in the history of the world', 'one of the most powerful air forces in the world' and a strong army reserve based on the adoption of universal training. In collaboration with the United States' allies, these forces would be used for four main purposes: to enforce the terms of the peace; to fulfil the obligations made to UNO; 'to preserve the territorial integrity and the political independence of the nations of the Western hemisphere'; and, as stated in the Constitution, to 'provide for the common defense' of the United States. While the atomic bombs must act as a signal 'not for the old process of falling apart but for a new era ... of ever closer unity and ever closer friendship among peaceful nations', Truman declared that 'We have learned the bitter lesson that the weakness of this great Republic invites men of ill-will to shake the very foundations of civilization all over the world.' For Truman, then, the Big Three had been replaced by a superpower, militarily, economically and ideologically.

On 9 February 1946, in a speech to the voters of the Stalin Electoral Area of Moscow, Stalin underlined the Marxist-Leninist concept of 'the unevenness of development of the capitalist countries' and their division 'into two hostile camps [British and American] and war between them'. As long as capitalism continued to exist, further war would be inevitable. Consequently, the Soviet Union would have to force the pace and demand sacrifices in the implementation of three or more further Five Year Plans. Stalin, then, believed that the Soviet Union would have to become a superpower to counterweigh the strength of the two other former members of the Big Three and the persistence of capitalism. This would involve the development of atomic power and the assertion of Marxism-Leninism as well as economic recovery.

On 5 March 1946, in his famous speech at Fulton, Missouri, Churchill stressed the importance of 'a special relationship between the British Commonwealth and Empire and the United States'. The secrets of the atomic bomb should be retained by this association, especially by the United States. While an 'iron curtain' had fallen on Europe to the east of a line drawn from Stettin on the Baltic to Trieste on the Adriatic, 'in a great number of countries, far from the Russian frontiers and throughout the world, Communist fifth columns are established in complete unity and absolute obedience to the directions they receive from the Communist center'. Outside the area of the special relationship, 'the Communist parties or fifth columns constitute a growing challenge and peril to Christian civilization'. War was not inevitable, however since, as he had understood 'our Russian friends and allies during the war', they admired nothing so much as strength.

Strict adherence by the Western democracies to the principles of the United Nations Charter would avert molestation. Otherwise, 'indeed catastrophe may overwhelm us all'.[8]

The British Prime Minister Attlee and Foreign Secretary Bevin were somewhat alarmed at the influence that Churchill's speech might have on American public opinion. While hoping along with Bevin that UNO might be able to avert confrontation with the Soviet Union, Attlee strove mightily to avert the exclusion of the UK from further development of the atomic bomb. He made an unsuccessful visit to Washington for this purpose in November 1945. Then, after further frustrations, he sent a long letter to Truman on 6 June 1946, setting out the history of wartime collaboration before asking for more. Attlee concluded by urging strongly that 'our continuing co-operation over raw materials shall be balanced by an exchange of information which will give us, with all proper precautions in regard to security, that full information to which we believe we are entitled, both by the documents and by the history of our common efforts in the past'. Truman, restricted by the passing by Congress of a bill restricting disclosure of the kind of information that Attlee was requesting, made no reply. The UK would have to make its own bomb, and Attlee gave this policy his full support.[9] While Churchill strove to maintain British power through the 'special relationship', Attlee realized that, to a considerable extent, Britain would have to go it alone in a client relationship that was less than special.

Further light may be thrown at the post-war collapse of the Big Three by examining some of the analysis of the new global situation made by diplomats at the behest of their governments. Here, we shall look in chronological order of appearance at three 'long telegrams' sent respectively by an American, a Briton and a Russian in 1946. In 1946, too, let us recall, Fernand Braudel was beginning to enunciate his concept of the *longue durée*, which will make a framework for an analysis of the 'long telegrams'.

The first and most celebrated of them is George F. Kennan's, sent on 22 February 1946 in response to a State Department request for 'an interpretive analysis' of what to expect as implementation of policies recently announced by Stalin and his associates in, for example, the leader's 'election' speech. In the Soviet view as evaluated by Kennan, threats of intervention from outside the socialist camp could be resisted 'if USSR remains militarily powerful, ideologically monolithic and faithful to its present brilliant leadership'. Some enlightened elements existed in the capitalist world, although the most dangerous were those whom Lenin had called false 'friends of the people', moderate socialists serving the ends of capital although using some socialist means. (Possibly, although Kennan made no explicit reference to them, Attlee and his Labour government would come into this category.) However, advantage could be taken of differences between the capitalist powers, and any imperialist war between them must be transformed into revolutionary upheavals.

Regarding the background of these perceptions, Kennan began by observing that the natural outlook of the Russian people was outgoing, keen to experience the outside world but also to compete with it in a peaceful manner while enjoying 'fruits of their own labor'. But the party line, whose dominance was ensured by the backing not only of the Communist Party itself but also of the secret police and the government, was based on false premises. The Kremlin's 'neurotic view of world affairs' arose from a 'traditional and instinctive Russian sense of insecurity'. Originating from the apprehensions of 'a peaceful agricultural people trying to live on vast exposed plain in neighborhood of fierce nomadic peoples', the sense of insecurity intensified through contact with the economically and socially more advanced West. But the people were less affected than the rulers, who 'invariably sensed that their rule was relatively archaic in form, fragile and artificial in its psychological foundations, unable to stand comparison or contact with the political systems of Western countries'. Later, after the Revolution of 1917, 'Marxist dogma, rendered even more truculent and intolerant by Lenin's interpretation, became a perfect vehicle for the sense of insecurity with which Bolsheviks, even more than previous Russian rulers, were afflicted.' Moreover, asserted Kennan, 'There is good reason to suspect that this Government is actually a conspiracy within a conspiracy; and I for one am reluctant to believe that Stalin himself receives anything like an objective picture of outside world.' In other words, distortion and disinformation were rife in an 'atmosphere of oriental secretiveness and conspiracy'. Consequently, 'there is ample scope for the type of subtle intrigue at which Russians are past masters', and foreign governments found themselves unable to present their case fairly and squarely.

In official relations, there would be emphasis on the 'prestige of Soviet Union and its representatives and with punctilious attention to protocol, as distinct from good manners'. However, in addition, the attempt would be made to further Soviet aims by such 'subterranean means' as 'a concealed Comintern', the exploitation of the rank and file of foreign Communist parties and of a wide variety of supportive organizations.

Responses would have to be flexible since 'Soviet power, unlike that of Hitlerite Germany, is neither schematic nor adventuristic', but careful as well as more likely to give into force rather than argument. Weaker than that of the Western world, Soviet power had not yet withstood the test of time and had still to survive 'the supreme test of successive transfer of power from one individual or group to another'. The first such occasion, the death of Lenin, had led to fifteen years of travail. Stalin's death would be the second such test, but not the final one.[10]

Less than a month after Kennan's 'Long Telegram', Frank K. Roberts, *chargé d'affaires* in the British Embassy, Moscow, sent three cables to London on 14, 17 and 18 March 1946. Like Kennan, Roberts considered the mainsprings of Soviet policy in post-war circumstances. In his view, the attempt was being made to drive a wedge between the UK and the United States. Meanwhile, however, there were signs of strain within the Soviet Union in the face of 'a certain postwar lassitude' in the face of formidable tasks of reconstruction. Stalin himself had talked of the necessity for several Five Year Plans before Western capitalism could be overtaken. Meanwhile, there had been 'a tremendous revival of orthodox Marxist ideology' and all-round discipline. Possibly, the Soviet leaders no longer sought cooperation among the Big Three. Indeed, 'it may even be asked whether the world is not now faced with the danger of a modern equivalent of the religious wars of the 16th century, in which Soviet communism will struggle with Western social democracy and the American version of capitalism for domination of the world'.

In the appraisal of Roberts, there was one fundamental influence on Soviet policy originating many centuries previously: 'This is the constant striving for security of a State with no natural frontiers and surrounded by enemies. In this all-important respect the rulers and people of Russia are united by a common fear, deeply rooted in Russian history.' In 1917, the whole world appeared to be united against the new Soviet state, and the subsequent foreign intervention had provoked fears that still remained, as did Western fear of communism. However, although Russia had never achieved the security of fixed frontiers, it had expanded over the centuries both peacefully and by conquest. From the British point of view, 'The Tsarist system was regarded with the same ideological aversion as the present Communist tyranny, and Alexander I and Nicholas I were feared as Stalin is today.' There had been periods of collaboration, notably in the two world wars. But now, because of the decline of France and collapse of Germany, Britain and Russia faced each other with no buffer between them.

In such a situation, the important questions had to be asked: 'Who are the real rulers of Russia propagating the above views, and how do their processes of thought really run in regard to the outside world?' In answer to the first question, Roberts observed that, although the last word rested with Stalin, 'it would seem either that he is exceptionally crafty in dealing with foreign statesmen or that he is himself dependent upon the collective decisions of his colleagues in the Politburo. The explanation may even lie deeper, in the information or lack of information which reaches him about the outside world.'

Stalin and his colleagues had all been clandestine revolutionaries before becoming leaders of a state with enormous difficulties at home and hostile attitudes from abroad, believing their own Marxist dogma about the struggle of communism with capitalism, liberal and social democracy.

As for the people, especially the dominant Russians, although to some extent suffering from jealous xenophobia, they were friendly and unlike the Germans who had believed themselves to be the master race. However, they could be indolent, indisciplined and inefficient. Therefore, Roberts commented, 'it is essential that the Soviet people should be ruled with the greatest firmness and, at the same time, deceived about the outside world.' The vast majority of them accepted the Soviet regime.

World revolution was no longer on the agenda. Although there was 'a certain Messianic strain in the Russian outlook', there was no Communist threat closely comparable to the Nazi menace. The policy of the Kremlin differed only in degree from that of Ivan the Terrible, Peter the Great and Catherine the Great, clothed though it was in Marxist-Leninist ideology. Thus it pursued security in an expansionist manner, weakening its opponents as much as possible while attempting to drive a wedge between them. The Soviet regime was still dynamic and expanding, although 'not as yet beyond areas where Russian interests existed before the Revolution.'[11]

On 27 September 1946, Soviet Ambassador Nikolai Novikov sent a telegram from Washington on post-war US foreign policy. Molotov made underlinings which will be indicated here. The Soviet foreign minister noted in the margin the difference between pre-war and post-war US policy, which Novikov characterized as reflecting 'the imperialist tendencies of American monopolistic capital and thus characterized by a striving *for world supremacy*'. Truman and other leaders had indicated in many statements that 'the United States has the right to lead the world'. The armed forces, industry and science had been geared to this policy of expansion which was being carried out through such means as the establishment of a wide-ranging system of bases and the pursuit of an arms race involving newer and newer kinds of weapons.

The stronger post-war Soviet position, especially in Central and Eastern Europe, was inevitably seen as a barrier to their expansionism by the imperialists of the United States. The foreign policy of Roosevelt, who had striven to strengthen the cooperation of the three leading powers in the war against Hitler, had been abandoned. Power had passed to Truman, 'a politically unstable person but with certain conservative tendencies', while the appointment of Byrnes as Secretary of State had produced a strengthening of the influence on US foreign policy of the most reactionary circles of the Democratic Party. In Congress, 'an unofficial *bloc of reactionary Southern Democrats and the old guard of the Republicans*' had produced what was labelled even officially a 'bi-partisan' foreign policy. Meanwhile, there had been a decline in the influence on foreign policy of those who follow Roosevelt's course for cooperation among peace-loving countries.

Finally, Molotov underlined several phrases in Novikov's assessment of US relations with the UK and with the Soviet Union. The UK was regarded by the United States as both the greatest competitor and a possible ally, and thus there had been division of some parts of the world into spheres of influence. The UK had been obliged to make concessions to obtain a loan while receiving support or developing coordination in policies in Europe, the Near (or Middle) East, India and Indonesia. However, the idea of military alliance put forward by Churchill in his Fulton speech in the presence of Truman had not been realized. The UK's financial dependence on the United States meant that there were regions throughout the world of Anglo-American contradictions, particularly in the Near (or Middle) East.

Meanwhile, the 'hard line' policy of the United States had abandoned the idea of cooperation among the Big Three or Four and was aimed at the imposition of the will of others, upon the Soviet Union, for example through the abolition of the principle of the veto in the Security Council of the United Nations. There had been US support for reactionary forces in countries adjoining the Soviet Union, aimed at obstructing 'democratisation' and allowing the penetration of American capital. In Germany, there had been no attempts to eradicate fascist remnants through the abolition of industrial monopolies and large-scale landlordism, while there had been talk of ending Allied occupation before Germany had been fully democratized and demilitarized. There had also been talk of a 'third war' throughout the press, both 'yellow' and 'respectable', and not only on the far-right. This anti-Soviet campaign of American 'public opinion' also had the goal *'to create an atmosphere of war psychosis* among the masses, who are weary of war, thus making it easier for the U.S. government to carry out measures for the maintenance of high military potential'. These and other measures were 'only intended *to prepare the conditions for winning world supremacy* in a... *war against the Soviet Union'.*[12]

The historian Geoffrey Roberts (not to be confused with the diplomat Frank Roberts) suggests that there is nothing original in the Novikov Telegram, which is distinguished from other Soviet writings of the period by 'its relentless pessimism about the future of Soviet-American relations'.[13] Nevertheless, not only Molotov read it with interest at the time, and there are instructive commentaries on it published in 1993 and written by three historians, one post-Soviet Russian and two American. Viktor L. Mal'kov contrasts the wide publicity given to Kennan's communication with the tightly restricted nature of Novikov's, not even generally known until 1990. Yet he also points out that both diplomats did not originate new views so much as articulate views already set out in a number of speeches in the Soviet Union and the United States. Each side saw the other as bent on world domination and thus constituting the main danger to world peace.

Novikov's note was not only underlined by Molotov but was also commissioned by him after heated arguments at the Peace Conference in Paris in the summer of 1946. A year later, it was under heavy criticism for being soft on American imperialism. In October 1947, another Soviet note from Washington asserted that, beyond intimidation of the Soviet Union, US foreign policy was aimed directly at preparing for war with it. Clearly indicated by non-collaborative, even aggressive stances on the questions of Germany, Japan and the A-bomb, war had been 'predetermined' by the military party fortified with generous appropriations. This was the kind of message sent thereafter from Soviet diplomats in the US capital.[14]

Dubbing the Novikov Telegram a 'tease', Melvyn P. Leffler nevertheless suggests that while it might be taken seriously for the light that it throws on internal debate involving Stalin and Molotov, it tells us little about the aims of Soviet foreign policy. Moreover, such phrases as 'American monopolistic capital' and 'world supremacy' are pathetically superficial because they are presented without elaboration. There is very little, for example, on the economic and social difficulties being experienced in the United States at the time of writing. Nevertheless, in Leffler's estimation, Novikov's account of US policy is more accurate on the Anglo-American relationship, for example, but not without serious deficiencies, on the low level of US military preparedness to give another instance. Correct or not, Novikov's note reveals clearly a sense of Soviet vulnerability and apprehension, while failing to appreciate similar feelings influencing American leaders. In Leffler's assessment, 'Truman and his advisers knew that the country was very powerful but they also faced grave perils.' These were in Europe and Asia, although not yet apparently in the United States' own backyard, Latin America.[15]

For Steven Merritt Miner, one of the main messages of the Novikov Telegram for historians is that, in spite of his despotic power, Stalin 'was in many respects a prisoner of the information those below him chose to provide'. And he could choose to ignore it, as in the case of the information that he received on the eve of the launch of Barbarossa.

In respect of what he was told, or what his entourage dared to tell him, and how he chose to treat it and them, Stalin resembled not only Soviet successors such as Yuri Andropov but also tsarist predecessors such as Nicholas I. Moreover, the situation became even worse in 1943, when diplomats who understood the international situation, Litvinov in Washington and Maisky in London, were removed from their embassies which now became 'hothouse transplants from Stalin's jungle'. What a contrast, observes Miner, between Novikov's telegram and that of Kennan, which is important, not because of its style nor indeed its content, since others had already said much that was similar. Kennan's analysis 'is important because, from the cacophony of voices trumpeting interpretations of Soviet postwar foreign policy throughout the halls of power in postwar Washington, Kennan's clear tones struck a sympathetic chord with both the government and the public'.

While commenting that we still know nothing about the way in which the Novikov Telegram was received and by whom, Miner considers that it contains 'some shrewd observations', in particular on the tensions in the Anglo-American relationship and the threat that would appear to be constituted by the construction of US bases round the world. However, there is also 'a good deal of nonsense' about the springs of American foreign policy, and no mention of the manner in which Soviet policy, especially in Eastern Europe, was intensifying Washington's suspicions.[16]

Let us make a few further remarks about the Kennan, Roberts and Novikov telegrams in the historical perspective of the *longue durée*. Note first that they say little about the individual members of the Big Three: Kennan and Roberts certainly mention Stalin, but in context; Novikov says nothing about Roosevelt, dismisses Truman and makes more of Byrnes. Next, observe that both the American and British communications look to the pre-revolutionary tsarist period for a considerable part of their explanation of the structure and conjuncture of Soviet insecurity. To an extent, they would have agreed with the observation of V. N. Tatishchev made in the 1730s that, while aristocracy or democracy might be suitable for governments in other circumstances, 'Great and spacious states with many envious neighbours cannot be ruled by any of those mentioned above, particularly where the people is insufficiently enlightened by education and keeps the law through terror, and not from good conduct, or knowledge of good and evil'.[17] Kennan in particular recalls Tatishchev with his reference to 'a peaceful agricultural people trying to live on vast exposed plain neighbourhood of fierce nomadic peoples', while also asserting that the Soviet regime had not yet stood the test of time. (This remark would take on a new significance in 1991, when the Soviet regime collapsed.) Roberts mentions Ivan the Terrible, Peter the Great, Catherine the Great, Alexander I and Nicholas I while noting that the Soviet regime was not yet expanding 'beyond areas where Russian interests existed before the Revolution', which would have included Poland and the Baltic states in Europe and Manchuria in China.

However, neither Kennan and Roberts on the one hand nor Novikov on the other address the question of the extent to which American foreign policy in its turn might have been influenced in the early post–Second World War years by earlier developments. Novikov makes no reference to any predecessor of Truman, not even Franklin D. Roosevelt nor Woodrow Wilson, the first formulator of a new world order, let alone his nineteenth-century predecessors. This difference of approach followed from the nature of the tasks tackled by Kennan and Roberts on the one hand and Novikov on the other. However, it also reflects a wider Western view that Soviet behaviour could be understood in a deep historical perspective, while Soviet analysts themselves, who as Marxist-Leninists should have been interested in the longer view of the United States' development, mostly neglected it. (This might have been partly because of the comparatively late development of American Studies in the Soviet Union.)

But was there really more continuity in the Soviet case? If Kennan and Roberts had found a large amount there, should we not seek for some in the American case?

Influenced by the basic structure of US history, in particular the transatlantic remoteness of North and South America from Europe, the 'classic' statement of US foreign policy, the Monroe Doctrine of 1823, declared: 'In the wars of the European powers in matters relating to themselves we have never taken any part, nor does it comport with our policy so to do.' Indeed, one of the main reasons for the enunciation of the doctrine was reluctance to become involved in what was to become one of the countries of primary concern in 1945, Greece. Another of the prompters of the Monroe Doctrine was Russian and British infiltration down the northwest coast of North America. If the Russians had still been coming to California in 1945, or Alaska remained in Soviet hands because of American refusal to accept the purchase of 'Seward's Ice Box' in 1867, all hell would probably have broken loose. However, in fact, what had changed from Truman's early years to those of his presidency was not so much Russian foreign policy as the United States'. Tacitly issuing as it were his own corollary to the Monroe Doctrine, Truman now saw the difficulties in Greece and other European countries as matters relating to the United States as well as to themselves.

Let us consider another aspect of the Monroe Doctrine. The warning to European powers to keep their hands off the Americas, North and South, was put in the following manner: 'we should consider any attempt on their part to extend their system to any portion of this hemisphere as dangerous to our peace and safety'. This statement would be relevant enough in 1945, when the 'system' of communism was immediately thought to be a major threat to the well-being of the United States. But what of the Monroe Doctrine's reassurance that 'With the existing colonies or dependencies of any European power we have not interfered and shall not interfere'. If European matters were seen by Truman and his advisers as pertaining to themselves in 1945, so were European colonies in the Western hemisphere and the wider world where American bases were now being established along with the intensification of pressure for the dismantlement of European empires in general.[18]

Of course, the Monroe Doctrine does not include all the sources of American conduct. Walter LaFeber puts the wider context eloquently but succinctly:

> Mission and money or, as some historians prefer to phrase it, idealism and self-interest have for nearly five hundred years been the reasons Americans have given for their successes. From their beginnings, they have justified developing a continent and then much of the globe simply by saying they were spreading the principles of civilization as well as making profit. They have had no problem seeing their prosperity – indeed their rise from a sparsely settled continent to the world's superpower – as part of a Higher Purpose or, as it was known during much of their history, a Manifest Destiny.[19]

American 'Manifest Destiny', of course, matches the 'certain Messianic strain in the Russian outlook' detected by Roberts.

Some kind of clash was more than likely, therefore. From about 1898, the Russian threat was first perceived as seriously affecting American interests, in particular the policy of the Open Door, on the Asian mainland. The reverses suffered by the tsarist regime in the Russo-Japanese War did not stifle completely apprehension about Russian expansionist ambitions in China, revived in fresh form after the arrival of Soviet power, and intensified at the end of the Second World War.

As we have seen, American and British diplomats were not the only observers to find historical roots for later policy in the years before 1917. Stalin himself, it will be recalled, made specific mention to the losses incurred as a result of the Russo-Japanese War in the demands he put forward at Yalta. However, a most important new element in the American-Russian clash after 1917 was the ideological, between the world views of Woodrow Wilson and Vladimir Lenin.

Wilson's global ideology arose from the Fourteen Points that he put forward in January 1918, responding to a call for 'definitions of principle and purpose' made by the 'sincere and earnest' Russian representatives at negotiations between them and their counterparts from Germany and Austria-Hungary at the frontier town of Brest-Litovsk. Believing that 'the people of the United States would wish me to respond, with utter simplicity and frankness', the American president went on to call for open covenants of peace, freedom of navigation upon the seas, removal of all economic barriers, reduction of national armaments and adjustment of colonial claims. He then proposed 'evacuation of all Russian territory' and other boundary alignments between the warring powers before declaring that 'A general association of nations must be formed under specific covenants for the purpose of affording mutual guarantees of political independence and territorial integrity to great and small states alike.'[20]

The Brest-Litovsk negotiations came to an end with harsh terms for Soviet Russia involving losses in huge areas of the former empire – Poland, the Baltic provinces, Finland, Ukraine and the Caucasus. Lenin insisted that, because of the weakness of Soviet Russia, these terms had to be accepted. However, he also believed that the losses would soon be regained and more, as the world revolution developed. (In fact, of course, Poland, the Baltic States and Finland were still independent as the Second World War approached.) In March 1919, the Comintern (the Third Communist International) was formed to manage the world revolution. Then, in 1920, the League of Nations was set up following the Paris Peace Conference. Wilson hoped that this embodiment of his Covenant would lead to the maintenance of global stability, a world 'made safe for democracy'. But the US Senate rejected the idea, and the next president Harding called a further conference in Washington, DC.

The Washington Conference of 1921–2 had a dual purpose: the establishment of peace in the Far East, especially in China; and the creation of a balance between the navies of the world that was not welcome to the British government and the navy in particular. As an eyewitness reported the response to an announcement made by the American Secretary of State:

> When Hughes began to enumerate British ships to be sunk – ships whose very names are milestones in the history of British sea-power – [Admiral] Lord Beatty came forward in his chair with the manner of a bulldog sleeping on a sunny doorstep who had been poked in the stomach by the impudent foot of an itinerant soap-canvasser. [21]

The navy, of course, complete with its heroes, such as Horatio Nelson, had been an essential part of the British Empire. Even if Churchill had once dismissed its traditions as 'rum, sodomy and the lash', he saw the British navy, superior to its rivals throughout the world's oceans, as one of the guarantors of the dominance of the British Empire along with domestic stability and free trade.[22] Similarly, while there might be a case for characterizing the British Empire's traditions as 'racism, slavery and the gun', many of its subjects would want to celebrate what they saw as a glorious achievement. However it is labelled, the rise of this empire was one of the outstanding facts of world history in the eighteenth and nineteenth centuries. In the twentieth century, Churchill was determined to avert its decline and fall in the twentieth century. But his efforts were in vain. The UK could not become a superpower as it began to lose its empire, and indeed became to a considerable extent a client of the United States. In the informed estimate of Paul Kennedy, 'the illusions of Great Power status lingered on' after the Second World War, but by 1980, in comparison with the situation in 1945, the UK 'was now just an ordinary, moderately large power, not a Great Power'.[23]

To revert in conclusion to the three 'long telegrams', they all indicate how, barely a year after the end of the Second World War, the concept of the Big Three had already faded away. Kennan and Roberts see the Soviet Union as the communist enemy, while Novikov detects a rivalry in the capitalist world between the United States and the UK. In our final chapter, we shall see how the former Big Three went their separate ways in the two major post-war developments, the Cold War and the end of empire including decolonization, while examining further the problem of historical continuity, of central significance to a final assessment of the formation of the Big Three and its replacement by the Super Two, with an emphasis on the part played by individuals during and after the Second World War.

Concerning the part played by individuals, consider for now the following observation from Warren F. Kimball about the relationship between the Big Three at the time of the Second Quebec Conference in September 1944:

> The USSR was now a Great Power, while the Anglo-American relationship as it was, did not allow creation of an entente aimed at containing [cordon sanitaireing] the Soviets. The wartime alliance and Roosevelt's policy of cooperation took precedence. Moreover, regardless of whether Churchill and Roosevelt were [pick, as with a Chinese menu, any one or combination of the following] wise, naive, realists, idealists, sick, opportunists, or realpolitikers, it is hard to escape the conclusion that in 1944 any such Anglo-American entente would have achieved little or nothing.[24]

Kimball reminds us, then, that personal relationships between statesmen depend to a large extent on their circumstances. But an exception is often made for Stalin, as we shall soon see.

An exception is often made, too, for the Soviet Union as an expansionist power, while its former allies were said to be essentially defensive in their posture. But consider the following observation of the American journalist Howard K. Smith made in 1949:

> The nation that has expanded most since the outbreak of World War II has not been Russia, but America. The most distant of Russia's new areas of dominance are 600 miles from her borders. The farthest of America's are 7,000 miles. Since 1942, America has displaced Britain as rulers of the seas, including even that most British of all waters, the eastern Mediterranean. America is said to have a lien on some 400 world-wide naval and air bases. This means that any empire linked to the motherland by water exists on American sufferance, as it did in the past on British sufferance. Russian influence over other governments is blatantly visible. American influence is like an iceberg: only the smaller part can readily be seen by the naked eye.[25]

Smith makes clear the great difference that the Second World War had made to the alignment of the Great Powers. This is particularly noticeable in the oil industry in the Middle East, a region 'considered central to imperial strategy and to the governance of India'. At Tehran, Roosevelt assured Churchill that the United States was not 'making sheep's eyes at your oil fields in Iraq and Iran'. Then, after Yalta, he went to the Middle East to meet three kings in oil-rich lands, including Saudi Arabia. By the time of Potsdam, experts were beginning to realize that the days of American self-sufficiency in oil were numbered. Soon, the United States was infiltrating into the region that the UK had considered its own preserve.[26]

As far as the United States' new principal rival was concerned, a US Navy memorandum had made clear the predicament of the Soviet Union in 1946:

> The Red Fleet is incapable of any important offensive or amphibious operations … a strategic airforce is practically non-existent either in material or concept. … economically, the Soviet Union is exhausted. The people are undernourished, industry and transport are in an advanced state of deterioration, enormous areas have been devastated. … Maintenance of large occupation forces in Europe is dictated to a certain extent by the necessity of farming out millions of men for whom living accommodations and food cannot be spared in the USSR during the current winter.[27]

Evidently, the Soviet Union was finding difficult expansion even in traditional contiguous areas of interest, let alone the wider world. Some years would elapse before the Soviet Union could be considered a superpower either economically or militarily. Probably, the economy never recovered from the war, and military expenditure helped to subject it to unbearable strain.[28] Hence, the heavy emphasis given to a third defining characteristic of superpower – its ideology of Marxism-Leninism, which Stalin and his advisers clung to as a reassurance that the future was theirs.

Meanwhile, the UK remained a Great Power, but could not become a superpower, struggling to maintain its empire, handing over responsibility for maintaining order in the Eastern Mediterranean, its key area, to the United States in 1947.

Always remembering that the sequel to the Second World War, like that conflict itself, must be viewed in *world* terms, let us proceed to make a final assessment of the years preceding and immediately following 1945 with special reference to the part played in them by our Great Men.

Great Men in the Second World War
and After: Conclusion

Towards the Cold War: Stalin and Truman

This book began with the consideration of two sets of questions. First, does all power tend to corrupt? Are great men usually bad men? Second, what power do so-called great men wield anyway? In their historical context, are they not dependent on the societies that produce them? How, then, should they be judged by historians? My answers to these questions will follow the appraisal of the individual by Fernand Braudel:

> I am always inclined to see him imprisoned within a destiny in which he himself has little hand, fixed in a landscape in which the infinite perspectives of the long term [*longue durée*] stretch into the distance both behind him and before. ... In historical analysis as I see it, rightly or wrongly, the long term always wins in the end.[1]

Members of the Big Three would almost certainly not agree with this observation, nor would their supporters and opponents viewing them as heroes or villains. But let us bear it in mind as we consider each of them in turn.

On the question of morality, there is widespread agreement that Stalin was a bad man. As for power, a dictator is generally believed to have wielded an unlimited amount of it, and many would agree with Lord Acton that absolute power corrupts absolutely. Consequently, in much literature on the Cold War period, especially what we might call 'mainstream Western', a simple account is given. Stalin, an evil dictator, pursued a foreign policy as expansionist as other powers would allow it to be, both ruthless and treacherous. To quote John Lewis Gaddis in his celebrated work *We Now Know* on the question of responsibility for the Cold War: 'The answer, I think, is authoritarianism in general, and Stalin in particular.'[2]

But even if we accept Stalin as a villainous leader in a dictatorial regime, why tar all Soviet foreign policy with the same brush, to the extent that nothing good can be found in it at all, and almost any interest in affairs beyond the boundaries of the Soviet Union is condemned as completely unwarranted?

This blanket condemnation poses a problem for post-Soviet historians. One of them, Anatolii Koshkin, offers the following solution regarding in particular 'Stalinist expansionism in Asia':

> the participation of the USSR in the war in the Far East was important from the point of view of both the geopolitical and the strategic interests of our country. In the assertion of these interests, we must perceive not the 'hegemonism' of Stalin but his contribution as the leader of the state.[3]

As a development of his argument, Koshkin examines Stalin's policy on Japan in the context of the *longue durée* the twentieth century as a whole.

A similar approach is taken by Vladimir Pechatnov in an essay on Stalin's empire in general, the essentials of which are as follows. While ideological and geopolitical considerations were inextricably mixed in Stalin's policies, he adhered to the old-fashioned view inherited from his tsarist predecessors that the greater the amount of territory a state possessed, the higher was its degree of security. Hence, his attitude to Europe in particular, where he was concerned to establish defence in depth against enemy incursions. Showing itself already in the years of the Nazi-Soviet Pact, 1939–41, this policy was asserted vigorously during the Big Three meetings and realized after the Victory in Europe of 1945. Traditional pretensions in Eastern Europe were imposed by force under the disguise of 'people's democracies' in the years following VE Day. Aiming at maximum influence in Germany, Stalin was already apprehensive about US influence in Europe in 1945. By then, there were already pretensions in other traditional directions, for example in the Far East and Middle East.

In the Far East, Pechatnov continues, Stalin's ambitions for a presence in Hokkaido were nullified by the atomic bomb. Immediately in August 1945, the

United States not only refused any Soviet occupation of the Japanese mainland but also put forward its own ambitions for an air base in the Kuril Islands and the occupation of the port of Dal'ny on the Chinese mainland. Stalin forestalled the Americans on these counts, and held on tightly to what had been taken. Regarding China, he was more flexible, continuing secret negotiations with both Chiang Kai-shek and Mao Zedong, by now looking upon the Yalta agreement as an 'anachronism'. Soon after the Chinese Revolution of 1949, however, he recognized Mao's total victory with the withdrawal of Soviet forces from Dal'ny as well as Port Arthur and the Chinese Eastern Railway, giving up all the rights of occupation first achieved by his tsarist predecessors at the end of the nineteenth century in the hope of maintaining close relations with Mao. (Let us interject here to say that, officially, Stalin remains, along with Marx, Engels and Lenin, one of the founding fathers of Chinese communism, to some extent a reflection perhaps of the fact that both Russian and Chinese Revolutions occurred in societies with small proletariats and huge peasantries.)

According to Pechatnov, in his appraisal of the position of the Soviet Union as a whole, Stalin considered its weakest flank to be to the south, in Transcaucasia bordering on Iran and Turkey. Iran was important not only for security but also for oil. Stalin made the most of the fact that Azeris could be found on both sides of the frontier, but withdrew his forces under Western pressure, and after commitments, later unfulfilled, by the Iranian government. The significance of Turkey was also twofold: for immediate security and as the key to the Mediterranean. Hence, Stalin's pressure at two major junctures: at Yalta and Potsdam for a review of the Montreux Convention concerning the Straits; and in the 'war scare' of August 1946, when the US High Command for the first time devised a plan for war with the Soviet Union. Soviet intelligence told Stalin of this plan, and he drew back.

On this occasion as on others, Stalin demonstrated the basic traits of his policy, Pechatnov suggests:

> unconditional priority for the geopolitical tasks of extending the Soviet sphere of influence, stubbornness, toughness and tactical flexibility, the understanding of how to balance on the line between crisis and war, but also to give way to the pressure of superior force. This last feature indicated a sharp contrast between the Soviet leader as a strategist and Hitler who (in the words of Stalin in conversation with Eden) 'does not know where to stop'.[4]

While others have made comparisons between Stalin and Hitler, he himself appears to have thought most of his tsarist predecessors, especially Ivan the Terrible and Peter the Great. (As we have seen, these analogies occurred to Frank Roberts, too, while the Japanese in 1945 saw Stalin as more akin to Alexander III and Nicholas II than to Lenin.) His henchman Molotov is alleged to have said: 'It's good the Russian Tsars took so much land for us in war. This makes our struggle with capitalism easier.'[5] (Equally, of course, the struggle was made more difficult by the loss of Poland and the Baltic states following the Russian Revolution.)

While Stalin did not have a master plan in the estimation of Alfred J. Rieber, he nevertheless held the view (in Rieber's words) that 'war rather than revolution was the catalyst of social change'; between the wars he also had an 'obsession with the vulnerability of Soviet frontiers to foreign intervention in support of internal opposition.' After the Second World War, 'The main problem that Stalin faced in the borderlands ... was the resistance of local organised political groups and the population as a whole to the formal and informal arrangements agreed upon by the Big Three'. Beyond the borderlands, both recovered and assimilated, his concerns certainly included developments in the new divided Germany, to a lesser extent those to the West beyond.[6]

The observations of Koshkin, Pechatnov and Rieber may be profitably considered in the broader context set out by Theodore Von Laue. In the last decades of the nineteenth century, his argument runs, the peoples of Europe had been confronted with 'a fatal either-or': 'either to belong to a great empire with the capacity to shape the future of mankind, or to descend to political oblivion and ignominy'. With the survival of great empires at stake in the First World War, as millions of men went to their deaths, the individual counted for little or nothing. The experience of the war was 'traumatic beyond description' for the inhabitants of the Russian Empire, which caved in before the German onslaught. Von Laue comments: 'Stalin's generation of communists carried the blow in their bones for the rest of their lives, reinforcing it by the long-standing fear of weakness embedded in Russian relations with the West. The shock, aggravated by the intervention of the Western allies, the United States, and Japan, became one of the mainsprings of Stalinism.' Committed in both theory and practice to mass politics, they had to re-establish order in a dangerous, often hostile world situation, and thus sought to establish 'a "socialist" discipline far stricter than that imposed by the tsars'. In this process, 'The cost of precipitous industrialization by command had to be measured against the cost of foreign domination. The calculation was not the product of a paranoid mind, but of the First World War as interpreted by power-conscious patriots with long wills and long memories.' The broader context of the Five Year Plans, collectivization and the purges was 'revolution, defeat, civil war, and Russian history back to the Tatars'. While Von Laue readily condemns Stalinist excesses, he forcefully argues that they were not gratuitous, but conditioned by history.[7]

For his own part, publicly at least, Stalin paid continual tribute to Lenin. He was deeply committed to Marxism-Leninism, which could also be called Stalinism. His belief helped to sustain him. At the same time, he made a clear distinction between the private and the public. For example, he has been quoted as shouting at his son for exploiting his name: 'You're not Stalin and I'm not Stalin. Stalin IS Soviet power. Stalin is what he is in the newspaper and the portraits, not you, no not even me.'[8] In this sense, Stalin would no doubt want himself included among Great Men as described by Thomas Carlyle as 'the leaders ..., the modellers, patterns, and in a wide sense creators, of whatsoever the general mass of men contrived to do or attain'.

In this connection, Constantine Pleshakov's observation is appropriate:

Of course, there is a huge difference between a personal dictatorship (Stalin's) and the rule of oligarchy (under Khrushchev and Brezhnev), and in terms of the decision making process the contrast is striking indeed. But in the core *ideas* that went into decision making as a system, there was a very considerable continuity between 1945 and 1975, and perhaps even later.[9]

Even later, of course, with Gorbachev's failed attempt at comprehensive reform, the Soviet Union collapsed after years of trying to keep up with its fellow superpower, the United States. Nevertheless, although further continuity is apparent in the policies of Yeltsin and Putin, this is not the place to discuss it.

Was there a considerable continuity in the core ideas of the system of US decision making, too? Beginning with Roosevelt, we might first observe that his death in April 1945 may well have been untimely from the point of view of winning the war but, on the other hand, allowed his historical reputation to be a matter of unceasing speculation. Before then, of course, at least some of his fellow Americans had condemned him for what they saw as the socialist excesses of the New Deal as well as blaming him for the United States' entry into the Second World War. As far as his foreign policy in general is concerned, Roosevelt was an internationalist in the wake of Woodrow Wilson, although he dissociated himself from his predecessor's idealism. Much more apparently in 1945 than in 1919, the United States was taking an interest in every quarter of the globe, looking outward in a manner and to an extent that had previously been beyond the imagination. Thus, Roosevelt very much wanted the United Nations Organisation to succeed where the League of Nations had failed. Even on this point, however, his consistency of purpose has been questioned; critics from the right blaming him for his very internationalism, from the left for his extension of imperialism under the guise of internationalism. To take another example, his policy towards the Soviet Union has appeared inconsistent, compromising or rigid. To quote one of his more sympathetic critics, James MacGregor Burns:

> With his unconquerable optimism he felt that he could do both things –
> pursue global ideals and national *Realpolitik* – simultaneously. So he tried to
> win Soviet friendship and confidence at the same time he saved American
> lives by consenting to the delay in the cross-channel invasion, thus letting
> the Red Army bleed. He paid tribute to the brotherly spirit of global science
> just before he died even while he was withholding atomic information from
> his partners the Russians.[10]

Burns also touches here on the main reason for saying less about Roosevelt than his successor in the context of the onset of the Cold War, the fact that he died before the atomic bomb was used.

Two months after he became president, on 12 June 1945, Harry S. Truman wrote back home to his wife Bess from the White House: 'The floors pop and the drapes move back and forth – I can just imagine old Andy and Teddy having an argument over Franklin.'[11] No doubt, soon after he speculated about Presidents Andrew Jackson and Theodore Roosevelt discussing his immediate predecessor, Truman became conscious that some of the foundations for his own reputation would soon be laid at the forthcoming conference at Potsdam. In his memoirs, he classified himself as 'a Jefferson Democrat living in modern times', but he also said that he supported the program, both international and domestic, of Franklin Roosevelt, whom he deemed 'a man of vision and ideas'.[12] Little did he realize as the Cold War began that, just a few years after his death, 'nearly every Democratic or Republican candidate for president has claimed to be a latter-day Truman'.[13]

While a small minority of critics has branded Truman a war criminal, most of the academic discussion has been within a more conventional framework. Perhaps the most celebrated Western overview since the fall of the Soviet Union has been *We Now Know: Rethinking Cold War History* by John Lewis Gaddis. Gaddis blames Stalin and the Soviet system for the Cold War, as we have already observed, thus absolving Truman and the policy of containment. However, Arnold A. Offner in *Another Such Victory: President Truman and the Cold War, 1945–1953* has dubbed Truman a 'parochial nationalist who lacked the leadership to move the U.S. away from conflict and towards detente' and who claimed that 'Russia was at the root' of every problem in both Europe and Asia. In 1952, just before he left office, he entertained the thought of giving both the Soviet Union and the People's Republic of China ten days notice to leave Korea or face 'all out war'. Of course, no such ultimatum was ever delivered. Nevertheless, with his own reform programme 'dead' and McCarthyism 'rampant', Truman 'departed the presidency with extremely low public regard and the U.S. on Cold War footing at home and abroad for years to come'. Offner's title is itself critical, referring to the observation of King Pyrrhus on the heavy losses sustained in his victory over the Romans in 279 BC: 'Another such victory and we are undone.'[14]

On the other hand, Wilson D. Miscamble expresses the orthodox view, considering it 'undoubtedly a travesty that Truman and his administration have been subjected to ill-founded criticism by many American academic historians, historians who so easily shrug off the danger that Stalin and his system presented. He refers to Offner's book as 'but the latest exemplar of this genre'. For Miscamble:

> Regrettably, the Truman administration expended too much energy in 1945 negotiating with the Soviets and, in a way, attempting to reassure and placate them and to reach amicable settlements with them. It unfortunately took time for Truman and Byrnes to learn the essential lessons regarding Stalin and his ambitions.[15]

The debate will no doubt continue, with those who brand him a war criminal referring in particular to his decision to drop the bomb. Without doubt, as well as deeply affecting the nature of 'Great Men', this decision set atomic power off in the wrong direction. Even in the time of King Pyrrhus, it was difficult enough to beat swords into ploughshares. In our own time, to transform atomic bombs into power stations has been a task of far greater complexity, and much of the resistance to the process has been caused by the manner in which this awesome source of energy has been used in the past. Now, when even distinguished scientists are proclaiming the necessity of developing what they see as the only plausible alternative to contaminating fossil fuel, the legacy of Hiroshima and Nagasaki still makes it difficult for their arguments to gain general acceptance.

Back in 1945, a considerable number of those scientists in the know warned the president about the consequences of using the bomb, but neither he nor even they could have fully appreciated where the fateful decision was heading. In the circumstances of the time, when American lives were being lost every day in the Pacific War and much money was being expended, Truman would have found it difficult indeed not to use what he himself called 'the greatest thing in history', and the majority of those involved in the process of developing it agreed with him. One of them, J. Robert Oppenheimer, the manager of the project that produced the bomb, was reminded of the words of the Hindu God in the *Bhagavad Gita*: 'Now I become Death, the destroyer of worlds.'

Just as a minority of informed scientists were against dropping the bomb on Japan, there were few leading politicians advising the president to work with Stalin to control its use in the future. One of them was Secretary of War Henry L. Stimson, whose reaction to the news of the bomb was to jot down the following lines with his own italics:

In *size* and *character*
We don't think it *mere* new *weapon*
Revolutionary Discovery of Relation of man to universe
Great History Landmark like
    Gravitation
    Copernican Theory
But,
Bids fair [to be] *infinitely greater*, in *respect* to its *Effect*

on the ordinary affairs of man's life.
May *destroy* or *perfect* International *Civilization*:
May [be] *Frankenstein or* means for World Peace.[16]

While Stimson believed that it was necessary to use the bomb to bring the war with Japan to a swift end, he soon wrote to Truman on 11 September that if negotiations with the Soviet Union were conducted with 'this weapon rather ostentatiously on our hip, their suspicions and their distrust of our purposes and motives will increase'. He recommended

> a direct proposal after discussion with the British that we would be prepared in effect to enter an arrangement with the Russians, the general purpose of which would be to control and limit the use of the atomic bomb as an instrument of war and so far as possible to direct and encourage the development of atomic power for peaceful and humanitarian purposes.[17]

As we have seen, under pressure from the Senate, Truman was soon reluctant to discuss the bomb even with the British.

There remains a case for assessing the Truman presidency in a longer historical context stretching back to the early nineteenth century, as we suggested in the previous chapter. Yet we need to recognize also that a new age dawned in 1945. Stimson put the point well as he criticized those Americans who were 'anxious to hang on to exaggerated views of the Monroe Doctrine and at the same time butt into every question that comes up in Central Europe'. Stimson argued that, through bilateral (not trilateral nor multilateral) negotiations, each of the two future superpowers could have its own sphere of security.[18]

Towards the end of empire: Churchill and Attlee

One of the greatest writers on the British Empire, Rudyard Kipling, wrote in his 'Recessional' in 1897:

> The tumult and the shouting dies
> The Captains and the Kings depart....
> Lord God of Hosts, be with us yet,
> Lest we forget – lest we forget!

By the end of the Second World War, there were clear intimations that the Lord God of Hosts had deserted the British Empire for the United States. In August 1945, US Secretary of State James Byrnes declared 'To the extent that we are able to manage our domestic affairs successfully, we shall win converts to our creed in every land.' Historian Walter LaFeber comments: 'John Winthrop had not expressed it more clearly 300 years earlier at Massachusetts Bay. Only now the City Upon a Hill, as Winthrop called it, was industrialized, internationalized – and held the atomic bomb.'[19]

In July 1945, Winston Churchill, who preferred 'Onward Christian Soldiers' to 'Recessional', lost the general election, and some of his dream of empire went with him. Had he returned to power, he would probably have been forced to give up India, the jewel in the imperial crown, in 1947, but he would almost certainly have struggled vigorously to keep it. To what extent his policies on the Bengal famine in particular would have added to his reputation in India as a ruthless racist it is difficult to say.[20] Two observations may be made with more confidence: Whatever his reputation in the wider world, Churchill was seen as a bad man only by a minority of his fellow countrymen; and he would have made more of an effort to hold on to India than his successor.

'Who was he?' is a question sometimes asked. The short answer is that he chaired the British Cabinet in Churchill's frequent absence before replacing him as prime minister. There is no doubt that Churchill cut a greater figure on the world stage than Clement Attlee, not only because of his personal charisma but also because of the steep decline in the UK's influence, especially in Asia. In some works on the end of World War Two, Attlee's name is barely mentioned. For example, in Gar Alperovitz's big book, *The Decision to Use the Atomic Bomb*, he appears once and in brackets as 'Churchill's successor' even though he led the UK delegation in the significant later stages of the Potsdam Conference. [21] As far as the Far East was concerned, as early as 1942, following a statement from Roosevelt that Britain would not be able to revert to its previous position in Malaya after the war, a leading British official feared that the United States would decide then what should be done with the colonies without even consulting Great Britain. Regarding Hong Kong in particular, one of them was arguing that its handover would 'show the United States we are going to be liberal to their beloved Chinese.'[22] By 1945, the position was even clearer, and Attlee had to recognize it. The United States was assuming world leadership both in actual power and further aspiration.

The United States' superiority as a superpower had a threefold basis: military, economic and ideological. Attlee said later that he did not lay the blame for Great Britain being cut out of the atomic programme on Truman, who had seen the need for cooperation. The prime minister added: 'The trouble was they couldn't get it through the Senate. The Senate wanted to have everything for America.' By now, the manufacture of a British bomb was essential since, in his view, 'We had to hold up our position *vis-à-vis* the Americans. We couldn't allow ourselves to be wholly in their hands, and their position wasn't awfully clear always.' What did become awfully clear was that the UK lagged far behind the United States in the development of up-to-date weaponry.

A major reason for this was economic capability. At the end of the war and for some years afterwards, Great Britain could barely have survived without American loans. Three weeks after the end of the Potsdam Conference, the Lend-Lease programme was abruptly terminated as British officials were discussing with their American counterparts. Attlee later commented: 'It was a great shock. The tap was turned off at a moment's notice ... We had not a chance to reorganise ourselves on a peace-time basis'.[23] After difficult negotiations, further loans were agreed, but at a heavy price in bases as well as dollars, General Omar Bradley famously referring to the UK as an unsinkable aircraft carrier. For all the talk of the fundamental unity of the English-speaking peoples and the 'special relationship' of the UK with the United States, there could be no doubt of who was the senior partner, and by a long way.

For while the roots of American ideology stretched back to the Magna Carta of 1215, there were more indigenous developments from the new 'City Upon a Hill' in the early seventeenth century onwards, brought to a new level by Woodrow Wilson at the end of the First World War. By the end of the Second World War, with further updates from Roosevelt and Truman, the British world outlook appeared out of date because of the continuance of the British Empire, whose stoutest defender was Winston Churchill. Ernest Bevin, first foreign secretary in Attlee's Labour government, struggled manfully to develop a 'third force' between the two superpowers with democratic socialism as the foundation of an updated empire and Commonwealth, but with a limited degree of success. Centred on the Middle East, Bevin's strategy collapsed in 1947.[24]

This is no place to tell the story of British participation in the early years of the process that accompanied the end of empire and became known generally as decolonization. Suffice to say that for many patriots it compounded the unpopularity that Attlee and the Labour government had already incurred for its domestic policies at a time of great shortage and stringency; for some of them Attlee was a bad man, a traitor to his class and worse. However, a measure of the distance that had been travelled by the time of Attlee's departure from power in 1951 was that his successor Winston Churchill had gone a long way to accepting the end of empire. This is not to say that Churchill accepted Great Britain's inferior position in the world as a whole. Indeed, by seeking an end to the Cold War, or at least a pause in it, he believed that he would not only advance the cause of world peace but also help Great Britain to restore its strength, and thus enhance its status as a great power. Despite his reputation as one of the instigators of the Cold War in his Fulton speech of 1946, Churchill attempted after the death of Stalin to establish relations with the new Soviet government, explaining that the earlier spirit of wartime collaboration had been lost during the later meetings of the Potsdam Conference because he 'had not been in power', and his Labour successors led by Attlee, 'having no experience of relations with the Soviet Union', were unable 'to convince the Americans of the possibility and necessity of reaching agreement with the Soviet Union'. But neither the Soviet leaders nor the US President Eisenhower and his Secretary of State John Foster Dulles were in favour of fresh negotiations.[25]

The worsening state of his health, along with other circumstances, obliged Churchill to think, after all, about resigning and duly, in April 1955, he did step down. The 'grand old man' lived for another ten years, but in decline until his death in January 1965. Churchill in his dotage personified the collapse of nearly all that he had stood for. To use one of his own more hackneyed metaphors, he had been unable to turn back the tide of history.

Nevertheless, Churchill's name lived on as a byword for his country's greatness. Indeed, John Charnley has perceptively observed that 'as Britain's decline as a Great Power proceeded apace, so did the need for Churchill to grow'.[26]

The role of individuals in history: Conclusion

As well as posing questions concerning the morality and the power of Great Men, the Introduction to this book included a brief summary of the concept of the *longue durée* advanced by Fernand Braudel in 1946 and adopted here as a methodological framework.[27] This was followed by an account of some nineteenth-century writing on the individual beginning with Thomas Carlyle's *On Heroes, Hero-Worship and the Heroic in History* and continuing with the work of Tolstoy, Marx, Plekhanov and Weber, whose influence was felt throughout the twentieth century.

Concentrating on some new ideas from the Second World War onwards, let us begin with those of the American philosopher Sidney Hook who published *The Hero in History* in 1943. There is a distinct echo of Thomas Carlyle in his title, although Hook dismisses his nineteenth-century predecessor's ideas of historical causation as 'clearly false, and where not false, opaque and mystical'. He labels the Tolstoyan viewpoint with the inaccurate term of 'theological determinism' and does not consider the arguments about history set out at the end of *War and Peace*. He argues forcefully against the materialist determinism of Marx and Plekhanov, while barely mentioning Weber. Basically, he is in favour of broad participation in politics limiting the influence of any one individual. While making little specific mention of the war, Hook concludes with an optimistic recommendation for post-war development: 'As democrats, whatever planning we do must be planning for a free society in which every citizen can participate in the determination of collective policy.'[28]

Obviously, Hook would be against Napoleon, but nowhere near as much as the Dutch historian Pieter Geyl writing in 1944 in the Preface to his survey of previous writing on the subject in *Napoleon; For and Against*:

> When one sees the French licking the hand that chastised them; when one notices the errors and the crimes of the Hero, the trials of the people, the disasters and losses of the State, were forgotten in the glamour of military achievement, of power transitory though it was; when one notices the explanations and constructions, ingenious, imperative, grandiose, that were put up as much as a century later by historians – and such excellent

historians! – then one seems already to discern among later generations of
German historians the apologists and admirers of the man who was our
oppressor and who led them to their ruin.

However, Geyl also asserted that 'even when as in my case one had hated the
dictator in Napoleon long before the evil presence of Hitler began darkening
our lives, one almost feels as if one should ask the pardon of his shade by
mentioning his name in one breath with that of the other.'[29] No doubt, the fact
that he had done time in Buchenwald concentration camp influenced Geyl's
viewpoint. But his main message is that interpretation in history, in this case
of the individual, is fundamentally an evolutionary process, varying from
generation to generation against a changing background.

Thus, when Carlyle chose Napoleon as an example of Great Man in the
nineteenth century, industrial revolution was already beginning to transform
warfare beyond the experience of the French hero long before Pieter Geyl
attacked him. Nevertheless, Napoleon's shadow was apparent long after
the first appearance of Tolstoy's *War and Peace*, in which he played a major
role, in Vasily Grossman's novel *Life and Fate*. Tolstoy's masterpiece was the
only book that Grossman read while acting as correspondent during the
Second Great Fatherland War, and he read it twice. When he visited Yasnaya
Polyana, Tolstoy's estate, en route to the front, Grossman wrote: 'Everything
has combined to produce an entirely new image, the events that occurred
a century ago and those happening today....'[30] As he wrote his own novel,
Grossman replaced Borodino with Stalingrad as its centrepiece battle.
Possibly, the very title contrasts the lives of the characters with the fateful
circumstances in which they find themselves as well as echoing the antithesis
of its predecessor. Certainly, the novel makes further keen observations about
the role of the individual in history in the context of natural science.

While there is no philosophical Epilogue, as in *War and Peace*, one of the
major characters in *Life and Fate* is Viktor Shtrum, a physicist, who understands
that 'Science was progressing with ever increasing impetuousness in a world
liberated from the fetters of absolute time and space.'[31] Recognizing that 'The
century of Einstein and Planck was also the century of Hitler', Shtrum comes
to think that 'There is a terrible similarity between the principles of Fascism
and those of contemporary physics' for 'Fascism has rejected the concept
of a separate individuality, the concept of "a man", and operates only with

vast aggregates' while 'Contemporary physics speaks of the greater or lesser probability of occurrences within this or that aggregate of individual particles.' However, another character, Colonel Pyotr Novikov, believes that 'Human groupings have one main purpose: to assert everyone's right to be different, to be special, to think, feel and live in his or her own way' and that 'The only true and lasting meaning of the struggle for life lies in the individual, in his modest peculiarities and in his right to these peculiarities.'[32]

Thus, *Life and Fate* concerns the individual's struggle for the assertion of existence in the context of the Soviet bureaucracy, the all-enveloping war and the findings of contemporary science. Ironically, when Shtrum is shunned by his colleagues since his research appears to be challenging the dictates of the Soviet ideology of dialectical materialism, he receives a telephone call from Stalin himself who says 'I think you're working in a very interesting field' and 'I wish you success in your work.' It is clear to Shtrum that 'Stalin knew about the importance attributed to nuclear physics in other countries.' Of course, ostracism at work is immediately replaced by adulation.

Could it be that in the vast aggregate of Soviet society, Stalin acts as an individual particle? Later, after undergoing interrogation, another character sees Stalin as 'a slave of his time and circumstances, a dutiful, submissive servant of the present day, flinging open the doors before the new age.'[33] Could it be that not only Fascism but also Communism posed a threat to the concept of individuality in the light of the new physics? Indeed, given the added pressures of the Second World War, was not the concept of individuality under threat in all systems of government including democracy, as Sidney Hook had suggested?

Looking at an exhibition of war trophies taken from the Germans, Shtrum says 'By the time the next war comes, they'll seem as innocent as muskets and halberds.' He has an informed understanding of where nuclear physics is leading. As time progresses, not only the actions of the Second World War become clearer, so do the implications of a Third. Knowing this, Grossman cannot conclude *Life and Fate* on the optimistic note of Tolstoy's *War and Peace*. There is no hope of Shtrum or Novikov or any other character believing like Pierre Bezukhov that he was chosen to give a new direction to the whole Russian community and the world at large, rather the more modest expectation of 'the tears and laughter of children, with the hurried steps of a loved woman'.[34] The Great Patriotic War, 1941–5, against Nazi Germany was indeed categorically different to the Patriotic War of 1812 against Napoleonic France.

Just as Tolstoy's understanding of the structure of the atom dependent on Copernicus and Newton was transcended by Grossman's awareness of Einstein and Planck, so are we today confronted by a higher level of scientific explanation. And danger, too, since the Hiroshima and Nagasaki bombs were 'muskets and halberds' compared with the powers of destruction at our disposal now. Moreover, in 1960, when *Life and Fate* was first submitted for publication, there was little more awareness of climate change and other additional dangers than in 1869, when the publication of *War and Peace* was completed. Our perception of the role of the individual should change yet again as our acquaintance with subatomic particles and big data grows. Other questions far removed from those confronting the Big Three are pertinent now, too: are the few individuals charged with the decision on another world war that could end human life omnipotent, those on the possible receiving end impotent; to what extent do we all share responsibility for the no less mortal threat of ecological degradation in what we must learn to call the age of the Anthropocene?[35]

To return to the Big Three whose meetings from 1943 to 1945 have constituted our primary focus, a tentative conclusion could be that they were all Great Men with their 'great' moments in history. To paraphrase Shakespeare, Churchill and Roosevelt were born great, not only because of their privileged backgrounds but also because, respectively, they led a vast if declining empire and a rising superpower at critical moments. Churchill's finest hour was the earlier years of the Second World War in which the UK stood alone. Roosevelt's New Deal already qualified him for greatness before his drive as commander-in-chief and his vision of a new world order as a statesman were maintained from Pearl Harbor to his death. Stalin achieved greatness (although many would still want to deny this) through his contribution to the establishment of Soviet Power and the ensuing victory in the Great Patriotic War. Truman and Attlee had their greatness thrust upon them after their unexpected assumptions of high office in 1945, the former taking the United States into Cold War and mature superpower, the latter reconciling Great Britain to the beginning of the end of empire including decolonization. Jonathan Fenby suggests: 'Though Truman would rise to the occasion and Attlee would oversee fundamental changes in Britain, neither could have fulfilled the role [of Great Man] at an earlier stage.'[36] Arguably, they would have had even more greatness thrust upon them.

To continue counterfactually, all five individuals discussed here appear to have thought that they had a greater influence over the course of events than seems to be the case in retrospect. Had the Channel not existed, Churchill could not have been a great war leader; nor could Stalin had there been no vast Russian plain. Without the United States' long preparation for superpowerdom in the secure Western hemisphere, Roosevelt could not have stood out as he did. Truman probably would not have been so assertive with no atom bomb, nor Attlee had the end of empire and economic difficulties not pressed so heavily upon him.

To pursue counterfactuality further would be dangerous. To take just one example, what if Stalin had died instead of Roosevelt in April 1945? Subsequent events might have turned out better with the departure of a dictator, they could have been worse in the panic that would have ensued in the struggle for the succession.

To revert to the individuals constituting the Big Three as they were rather than as they might have been, let us recall that they were all creatures of the nineteenth century, imbued – albeit in different ways – with the idea of progress and the concepts of the 'Great Man' and the 'Great Power'. (As in so many other respects, Stalin was an exception, but his avowed creed Marxism shared the basic supposition of progress, while in his official view there was no greater hero than Lenin.) No doubt, their strong will was a consequence of the common beliefs of their time, sustaining Churchill, Roosevelt and Stalin through different levels of severe illness before healthier Truman and Attlee came to power.[37] No doubt, too, they were sustained by the high degree of public confidence that they enjoyed during the Second World War and just after. Had they been in office at a less critical time, had they been more exposed to the media, their popularity might not have been so great – let us recall that their deliberations were mostly kept from the press, radio and film, while television was completely absent. How would they have coped with the glare of 24/7 publicity? But again, we must resist the temptation to embrace counterfactuality, attempting to assess them according to what they actually said including some views which would certainly be seen as racist or otherwise non-politically correct today.

A final question needs to be posed, were the various members of the Big Three indeed 'Great Men'? Unfortunately or luckily, depending on how you look at it, there can be no final answer. While we have no certain explanation of the workings of the human brain, nor of the relative contributions to the development of individuals of nature and nurture, there can be no completely satisfying explanation of the thoughts and deeds of political leaders, let alone their interaction with those of their followers. Even a pandisciplinary approach involving the humanities, social and natural sciences might fall short of a full answer. However, some of us will want to agree with Plekhanov and Braudel that the truly great men are those who direct the tide a little at least as they swim with it. Moreover, many readers will want to accept the basis thesis set out in the Preface of Archie Brown's book, *The Myth of the Strong Leader; Political Leadership in the Modern Age*: 'the central misconception … is the notion that strong leaders who get their way, dominate their colleagues, and concentrate decision-making in their hands, are the most successful and admirable'.[38] The individuals who believed that they were in a position to solve the world's problems in 1945 have all been exposed to this misconception. Evidently, they all depended on reliable advisers: for example, among others, Roosevelt on Hopkins, Stalin on Molotov and Churchill on Eden, later Attlee on Bevin and Truman on Byrnes. Nevertheless, they all deserve inclusion in the top rank. Undoubtedly, as their discussions at Tehran, Yalta and Potsdam demonstrated, together they helped to win the Second World War even if their disagreements pointed towards an uneasy peace.

The dictum of Lord Acton cannot be neglected: 'Great men are nearly always bad men.' Were our great men all bad men? Certainly, some of the moral choices that they made were difficult. To consign hundreds of thousands of their fellow human beings, even millions of them, to their deaths is a *prima facie* infringement of the biblical commandment 'Thou shalt not kill' shared by Christians and Jews, not to mention the injunctions of other faiths, both religious and humanist. While those not faced with the necessity of such choices do not necessarily have the right to pass judgement, for most people in the West, nevertheless, demarcation has been easy: of the individuals mentioned above, Stalin was bad; the others were all good. Is the contrast indeed so stark? And is it evading the question to assert that it is not for historians to make such demarcations? No doubt they would all have been considered bad had the Allies lost the war and the Axis had instituted their own war crimes court.

Those who fought to achieve victory for the Big Three, especially the mostly anonymous Soviet, British and American victims of war, deserve at the very least enumeration. The Soviet Union was the only member of the Big Three to be invaded. Nearly half the total losses from the global conflict were Soviet: Their number has been estimated at twenty-seven million. Many died on the battlefield, in the Siege of Leningrad or less-well known deliberate Nazi extermination of the peasantry.[39]

Moreover, up to three million died in captivity. Consider the following eyewitness account from a British prisoner of war equating what he saw 'with the atrocities of Belsen and the other mass death camps which most people outside Germany only knew existed at the end of the war'. He continued:

> It was the stuff of nightmares. The compound seethed with masses of hooded skeletal figures, padded out with any rags of clothing available to keep themselves warm, so that their silhouettes assumed grotesquely weird shapes. Hardly any of them appeared to be wearing boots. Their feet were encased in filthy rags upon which they shuffled slowly around like animals insider their cage....
>
> How the Germans could inflict such inhuman treatment on one group of prisoners while showing concern for a few Britons suffering nothing more than mild blood poisoning it is difficult to comprehend. Unless we accept that the entire nation, with very few exceptions, had swallowed the Nazi creed in its entirety and thought the Russians truly sub-human and completely expendable.[40]

Jews, like Slavs, were considered subhuman by Hitler and his adherents. As is well known, up to six million Jews, many from the Soviet Union, but mostly from Poland and elsewhere in Eastern Europe, were annihilated in the notorious Holocaust.

And, in its turn, Soviet treatment of German prisoners of war was merciless at the start, Stalin himself declaring in November 1941: 'From now on it will be our task...to annihilate all Germans who have penetrated as occupiers, down to the last man'. However, in February 1942, Stalin countermanded his previous order: 'The Red Army takes German soldiers and officers prisoner when they surrender.' The leader was largely obeyed, with the Battle of

Stalingrad a major exception, while the NKVD and other police organs were a law unto themselves.[41] And then, even the prisoners of war returning to the Soviet Union after the war were harshly punished with many of them under suspicion of having fought against their motherland rather than for it.

The UK was never invaded, but was heavily bombed, during the Blitz of 1940–1 in particular, before its allies had entered the war. Approximately 400,000, military and civilian, were killed throughout. After Pearl Harbor, the United States itself was not attacked, but about 300,000, nearly all military, perished. Thus, the losses of the Western powers combined were in an approximate ratio to the Soviet losses of approximately 1:38. To indicate the difference in such a stark manner is by no means to denigrate the contributions of those killed in battles from Europe to the Pacific, nor the sufferings of those in prison camps, especially those run by the Japanese.

The novelist Evelyn Waugh aptly noted in his diary in October 1939: 'They are saying, "The generals learned their lessons in the last war. There are going to be no wholesale slaughters." I ask, how is victory possible except by wholesale slaughters?' The critic Paul Fussell, who quotes Waugh, wrote an outstanding book, *The Great War and Modern Memory*, in which he shows how concepts as of chivalry were largely erased in the first global conflict. However, in another fine work, he observes: 'It was not until the Second World War had enacted all its madness that one could realize how near Victorian social and ethical norms the First World War really was.' He illustrates the cynicism as well as the sufferings of the British Tommy and the American GI Joe in particular.[42] However, no matter how sceptical they were about the high-flown sentiments of their leaders, those of all ranks who served in all services deserve respect. We also have to understand how they welcomed the dropping of atomic bombs on Hiroshima and Nagasaki after what they had been through. Fussell quotes a compiler of an oral history of the war years: 'At that time virtually everyone was delighted that we dropped the bombs, not only because they shortened the war and saved thousands of American lives but also ... because the "Japs" deserved it'.[43]

Seventy years on, we can now recognize the losses of former enemies: more than four million Germans, more than two million Japanese. Those who died in Allied China are most difficult to calculate, with estimates up to fifteen million.[44]

Concluding with scriptural allusions from the materialist Plekhanov, I am sure that many would agree with his assertion that 'it is not only for "beginners", not only for "great" men that a broad field of activity is open. It is open for all those who have eyes to see, ears to hear and hearts to love their neighbours. The concept *great* is a relative concept. In the ethical sense every man is great who, to use the Biblical phrase, "lays down his life for his friend".[45] In this sense, there were millions of great men and women too during the years of the Second World War's Big Three, all making their individual contributions to a common cause.

Notes

Chapter 1

1. Sir J. E. E. Dalberg Acton, First Baron Acton, Letter of 1887 in *Life of Mandell Creighton*, London, 1904, vol. 1, p. 372; Geoffrey Roberts, *Stalin's Wars: From World War to Cold War*, London, 2006, p. 374 with his own italics.

2. Fernand Braudel, *The Mediterranean and the Mediterranean World in the Age of Philip II*, translated by Sian Reynolds, London, 1975, vol. 1, pp. 20–1.

3. Thomas Carlyle, *On Heroes, Hero-Worship and the Heroic in History*, ElecBook, 2001, pp. 5, 37, 278–9. Carlyle first gave *On Heroes* as a series of lectures in 1840. Napoleon was the last in the series, and, by implication, in history.

4. Leo Tolstoy, *War and Peace*, trans. Rosemary Edmonds, Harmondsworth, 1973, vol. 2, pp. 1400–1, 1408, 1419, 1425–6, 1432–44.

5. Karl Marx, 'The Eighteenth Brumaire of Louis Bonaparte', *Selected Works*, London, 1942, vol. 2, pp. 314–15. A comparable argument was put forward by, among others, Herbert Spencer.

6. G. V. Plekhanov, *The Role of the Individual in History*, as an appendix to his *Fundamental Problems of Marxism*, London, 1969, p. 176. The original publication was in 1898. Plekhanov used the term 'scientific' in a broader sense than would be customary in English.

7. David Beetham, *Max Weber and the Theory of Modern Politics*, Cambridge, 1985, pp. 227, 231, 242, 266.

8. Paul Kennedy, *The Rise and Fall of the Great Powers: Economic Change and Military Conflict from 1500 to 2000*, London, 1988, p. xxii, with Kennedy's own italics.

9. Simon Sebag Montefiore, *Stalin: The Court of the Red Tsar*, London, 2003, p. 21. Some might well think the longest night of the year appropriate for Stalin's birthday.

10. Harry's father and mother could not agree to honour his father Shipp or hers – Solomon. But the 'S' 'actually stood for nothing, a practice not unknown among the Scotch-Irish, even for first names'. David McCullough, *Truman*, New York, 1992, p. 37. Much later, when he was on the campaign trail in Washington State,

Truman was invited by a local Native American people, the Snohomish, to take their name as his. (Personal recollection supplemented by Wikipedia.)

11 Walter LaFeber, *The American Age: United States Foreign Policy at Home and Abroad since 1750*, New York, 1989, Chapter 6. LaFeber quotes David P. Crook, *Diplomacy during the American Civil War*, New York, 1975, p. 9 on the United States' 'headlong rush into superpowerdom'.

12 *Encyclopaedia Britannica*, Thirteenth Edition, London and New York, 1926, vol. I, pp. vii, xxxiv. A long, far from Olympian, and indeed passionate article on 'English-Speaking Peoples, relations' was included on pp. 1011–12.

13 McCullough, *Truman*, p. 213. Later, newly sworn in as vice-president early in 1945, Truman flew by military bomber to Kansas City to attend Pendergast's funeral even though the Boss had only recently completed a term in jail. Ibid., p. 336.

14 Brian Kassof, 'A Book of Socialism: Stalinist Culture and the First Edition of the Bolshaia sovetskaia entsiklopediia', *Kritika: Explorations in Russian and Eurasian History*, vol. 6, no. 1, Winter 2005 (New Series), pp. 87–95; J. V. Stalin, 'Talk with the German author Emil Ludwig', *Works*, Moscow, 1955, vol. 13, pp. 147–9. Ludwig wrote a biography of Napoleon among other works, beginning 'Talk' with the observation that he had been 'studying the lives and deeds of historical personages' for more than twenty years.

15 Stalin, *Works*, vol. 13, pp. 40–1.

16 Churchill, *The Second World* War, vol. 1, *The Gathering Storm*, London, 1948, p. 307.

17 L. Woodward, ed., *British Foreign Policy in the Second World War*, London, 1971, vol. 1, p. 161.

18 Churchill, *The Second World* War, vol. 1, p. 345; Warren Kimball, *Churchill and Roosevelt: The Complete Correspondence*, 3 vols., London, 1984, vol. 1, p. 24; David Reynolds, *In Command of History: Churchill Fighting and Writing the Second World War*, London, 2005, pp. 122–3.

19 Churchill, *The Second World War*, vol. 2, *Their Finest Hour*, London, 1942, pp. 21–2.

20 Walter LaFeber, *America, Russia, and the Cold War, 1945–1996*, New York, 1997, p. 6.

21 Gabriel Gorodetsky, *Stafford Cripps' Mission to Moscow, 1940–42*, Cambridge, 1994, p. x. On p. 70, Gorodetsky writes that already by August 1940, 'as recent experience had taught, little could be done to prevent the Foreign Office from making decisions in conformity with American policy, even if the two countries had in fact no common interest'.

22   Churchill, *The Second World War*, vol. 4, *The Hinge of Fate*, London, 1951,
     pp. 429–49; David Dilks, ed., *The Diaries of Sir Alexander Cadogan, O.M.,
     1938–1945*, London, 1971, p. 472;. M. Yu. Myagkov, 'The Seminar in London' [on
     'Churchill and Stalin'], Russian Association of the Second World War Historians,
     Information Bulletin, no. 7, 2002, pp. 8, 11, 12. Myagkov is reporting on the
     papers by P. V. Stegnii and O. A. Rzheshevsky; Warren Kimball, *Forged in War:
     Roosevelt, Churchill, and the Second World War*, New York, 1997, p. 158, quoting
     Churchill on 'valiant deeds'.

23   Churchill, *The Second World War*, vol. 4, pp. 604–22; Kimball, *Forged in War*,
     p. 182 on 'prior conferences'.

24   Kimball, *Forged in War*, pp. 201–12.

25   Churchill, *The Second World War*, vol. 5, *Closing the Ring*, London, 1952,
     pp. 72–84.

26   On the Cairo Conference, see Churchill, *The Second World War*, vol. 5, pp. 291–
     301. Kimball, *Forged in War*, pp. 234–7; Rana Mitter, *China's War with Japan,
     1937–1945: The Struggle for Survival*, London, 2013, pp. 308–13.

Chapter 2

1   Churchill, *The Second World War*, vol. 5, *Closing the Ring*,
     London, 1952, p. 303.

2   'Transcript of the Talk between J. V. Stalin and F. D. Roosevelt, November 28,
     1943', *International Affairs* (henceforth *IA*), 1961, no. 7, pp. 134–6, supplemented
     by SSMK, vol. 2, pp. 81–2, regarding the introduction of the Soviet system into
     India. Robert Beitzell, ed. and intro., *Tehran, Yalta, Potsdam: The Soviet Protocols*,
     Hattiesburg, MI, 1970, pp. iv–v, criticizes the protocols for omissions and
     distortions. Here, we have used a later, fuller Soviet version published in 1984
     supplemented by FRUS, Cairo and Tehran, on the first Roosevelt-Stalin meeting,
     pp. 482–6.

3   SSMK, vol. 2, pp. 91–2.

4   *The Tehran, Yalta and Potsdam Conferences: Documents* (henceforth *Tehran,
     Yalta, Potsdam*), Moscow, 1969, pp. 7–16; FRUS, Cairo and Yalta, pp. 488–
     90, 496.

5   FRUS, Cairo and Yalta, pp. 509–12.

6   'Transcript of the Talk between Stalin and Roosevelt, November 29, 1943', *IA*,
     1961, no. 7, pp. 143–5.

7   *Tehran*, pp. 25–37.

8   FRUS, Cairo and Tehran, pp. 553–5. This dinner conversation is unrecorded in SSMK, vol. 2.

9   'Transcript of the Talk between Stalin and Churchill, November 30, 1943', and 'Talk at the Luncheon', *IA*, 1961, no. 8, pp. 115–17; FRUS, Cairo and Tehran, pp. 565–8; SSMK, vol. 2, pp. 140–3.

10   *Tehran*, pp. 38–40. FRUS, Cairo and Tehran, p. 578 renders Churchill's observation: 'truth deserves a bodyguard of lies'.

11   FRUS, Cairo and Tehran, pp. 582–5. This meeting not included in SSMK, vol. 2.

12   *Tehran*, pp. 40–4; SSMK, vol. 2, pp. 137–50; FRUS, Cairo and Tehran, pp. 586–93.

13   FRUS, Cairo and Tehran, pp. 594–6; SSMK, vol. 2, pp. 168–70.

14   *Tehran*, pp. 44–50; SSMK, vol. 2, pp. 161–7.

15   FRUS, Cairo and Tehran, pp. 640–1. Tsuyoshi Hasegawa, *Racing the Enemy: Stalin, Truman, and the Surrender of Japan*, Cambridge, MA, 2005, p. 25 writes that Stalin promised to enter the war against Japan in return for the commitment by Churchill and Roosevelt to a Second Front in Europe. He adds: 'Although no record exists, it is likely that Roosevelt and Stalin discussed the reward for Soviet entry into the war'. He points out that, at a meeting of the Pacific War Council on 12 January 1944, Roosevelt revealed his agreement with Stalin at Tehran for the conditional grant of Dairen and the Manchurian railway to the Soviet Union, to which in addition southern Sakhalin would be returned and the Kuril Islands handed over.

16   Warren F. Kimball, *Forged in War: Roosevelt, Churchill, and the Second World War*, New York, 1997, pp. 260–1.

17   Daniel Yergin, *The Prize: The Epic Quest for Oil, Money and Power*, New York, p. 381; Paul Kennedy, *The Rise and Fall of the Great Powers: Economic Change and Military Conflict from 1500 to 2000*, London, 1988, pp. 357–8.

18   William T. R. Fox, *The Super-Powers: The United States, Britain and the Soviet Union – Their Responsibility for Peace*, London, 1944; 'The Super-Powers Then and Now', *International Journal*, vol. 15, 1979–80, pp. 417–30.

19   The widely agreed figure for Red Army prisoners killed through starvation or more violently during the whole war is 3.5 out of 5.7 millions. See Jonathan North, 'Soviet Prisoners of War: Forgotten Nazi Victims of World War II', *World War II*, January–February 2006. For a book-length study, see Christian Streit, *Keine Kameraden: Die Wehrmacht und die sowietischen Kriegsgefangen, 1941–1945*, Bonn, 1978.

Chapter 3

1   Quoted by Walter LaFeber, *The American Age: United States Foreign Policy at Home and Abroad since 1750*, New York, 1989, p. 436.

2   Warren F. Kimball, *Forged in War: Roosevelt, Churchill, and the Second World War*, Chicago, 1977, p. 261.

3   Churchill, *The Second World* War, vol. 6, *Triumph and Tragedy*, London, 1954, pp. 129–42. Churchill does not mention the Hyde Park Agreement, on which see Alperovitz, *The Decision to Use the Atomic Bomb and the Architecture of an American Myth*, London, 1995, p. 661; Michael B. Stoff, *Oil, War, and National Security: The Search for a National Policy on Foreign Oil, 1941–1947*, New Haven, 1980, p. 70.

4   Stoff, *Oil, War and National Security*, pp. 197–8.

5   Geoffrey Roberts, 'Beware Greek Gifts: The Churchill-Stalin "Percentages" Agreement of October 1944', *Mir istorii*, 1, 2003, pp. 1–7 (online).

6   Kimball, *Churchill and Roosevelt*, vol. 3, p. 365.

7   FRUS, *Malta and Yalta*, pp. 540–6.

8   Ibid., pp. 549–52, 558.

9   'The eagle suffers little birds to sing,/And is not careful what they mean thereby'. Shakespeare, *Titus Andronicus*, Act 4, Scene 4, 82.

10   FRUS, *Malta and Yalta*, pp. 570–91 on first plenary meeting. Bohlen's minutes, the fullest, will be followed throughout the conference with corroboration or disagreement from others.

11   *Tehran, Yalta, Potsdam*, p. 75.

12   Ibid., p. 80; FRUS, *Malta and Yalta*, pp. 611–33 on second plenary meeting.

13   SSMK, vol. 4, p. 87.

14   *Tehran, Yalta, Potsdam*, p. 85.

15   Ibid., p. 86.

16   Ibid., p. 90.

17   FRUS, *Malta and Yalta*, pp. 660–81, on third plenary meeting.

18   Ibid., pp. 708–28 on fourth plenary meeting.

19   Ibid., pp. 766–71.

20   SSMK, vol. 4, p. 143.

21   Ibid., p. 156.

22   FRUS, *Malta and Yalta*, pp. 771–91 on fifth plenary meeting.

23   Churchill, *The Second World War*, vol. 6, *Triumph and Tragedy*, London, 1954, p. 430.

Chapter 4

1   FRUS, *Malta and Yalta*, pp. 797–9.

2   Ibid., pp. 825–41.

3   Ibid., pp. 841–58 on sixth plenary meeting.

4   SSMK, vol. 4, pp. 207–12. Churchill, *The Second World War*, vol. 6, *Triumph and Tragedy*, London, 1954, p. 337 comments on the Polish problem: 'This was the best I could get'.

5   *Tehran, Yalta, Potsdam*, p. 128.

6   FRUS, *Malta and Yalta*, pp. 897–918 on the seventh plenary meeting.

7   Ibid., pp. 921–5.

8   Ibid., pp. 925–30 on the eighth plenary meeting and luncheon, supplemented by *Tehran, Yalta, Potsdam*, pp. 129–32; SSMK, vol. 4, pp. 220–3.

9   FRUS, *Malta and Yalta*, pp. 968–87. Tsuyoshi Hasegawa, *Racing the Enemy: Stalin, Truman, and the Surrender of Japan*, Cambridge, MA., pp. 34–7, points out that Stalin managed to insert the phrase 'handed over' rather than 'restored' as far as the Kuril Islands were concerned, and the word 'pre-eminent' in relation to the interests of the Soviet Union regarding the railroads. Soviet interests in China were recognized in infringement of the rights of China as a sovereign nation.

10 Diane Shaver Clemens, *Yalta*, New York, 1970, p. 290; E. R. Stettinius, *Roosevelt and the Russians: The Yalta Conference*, London, 1950, pp. 261–6, argues that the Russians made more concessions than they obtained at Yalta.

11 S. M. Plokhy, *Yalta: The Price of Peace*, London, 2010, p. 402.

12 Kimball, *Churchill and Roosevelt*, vol. 3, pp. 548–61, 565, 568, 572, 574.

13 Ibid., p. 605.

14 Churchill, vol. 6, pp. 391–8; Kimball, vol. 3, pp. 613–16.

15 Churchill, vol. 6, pp. 412–21.

16 Francis Williams, *A Prime Minister Remembers: The War and Post-War Memoirs of the Rt Hon Earl Attlee, K.G., P.C., O.M., C.H.: Based on His Private Papers and on a Series of Recorded Conversations*, London, 1961, p. 59. This was Attlee's recollection fifteen years later.

17 Churchill, vol. 6, pp. 480–94.

18 FRUS, *Berlin*, pp. 76–7.

19 Ibid., pp. 61–2.

20 Churchill, vol. 6, pp. 520–30.

Chapter 5

1   Adolf Hitler, *My Struggle*, London, 1937, p. 258.

2   Quoted by Geoffrey Roberts, *Stalin's Wars: From World War to Cold War, 1939–1953*, London, 2006, p. 243.

3   For example, O. A. Aleksandrov, 'Berlin: The Downfall, 1945', National Committee of Russian Historians: Russian Association of the Second World War Historians, *Information Bulletin*, no. 7, 2002, p. 32.

4   Klaus Lorres, *Churchill's Cold War: The Politics of Personal Diplomacy*, London, 2002, pp. 361–2; O. A. Rzheshevskii, 'Sekretnye voennye plany u Cherchillia protiv SSSR v mae 1945', *Novaia i noveishaia istoriia*, no. 3, 1999, pp. 98–123; D. Dilks, 'Cherchill i operatsiia "Nemyshlimoe", 1945g', *Novaia i noveishaia istoriia*, no. 3, 2002, pp. 126–42.

5   A. A. Fursenko, 'U. Cherchill: "sozdavat mosty, a ne vozdvigat bar'ery"?: neizvestnye stranitsy istorii "kholodnoi voiny" ', *Istoricheskie zapiski*, 2003, pp. 13–14.

6   DBPO, I, pp. 1–2.

7   Ibid., pp. 143, 145.

8   Ibid., pp. 181–7.

9   Ibid., pp. 187–91.

10 FRUS, *Berlin*, vol. 1, p. 255. The paper is dated 2 July 1945. Rudyard Kipling has often been considered to be the poet of the British Empire.

11 Ibid., vol. 1, pp. 265–6, 16 May; pp. 267–71, 2 June.

12 Tsuyoshi Hasegawa, *Racing the Enemy: Stalin, Truman, and the Surrender of Japan*, Cambridge, MA, 2005, pp. 128, 130–6.

13 Harrison to Troutbeck, DBPO, I, pp. 333–5.

14 Hasegawa, *Racing the Enemy*, pp. 136–40.

15 DBPO, I, pp. 340–5 on the first plenary meeting, supplemented by *Tehran, Yalta, Potsdam*, pp. 147–58.

16 Ibid., pp. 348–50.

17 Ibid., pp. 352–4.

18 Ibid., pp. 363–4.

19 Ibid., pp. 367–71.

20 Hasegawa, *Racing the Enemy*, p. 142. Hasegawa suggests that the two leaders had different reasons for surprising Japan: 'Stalin by crossing the Manchurian border, and Truman by dropping the atomic bomb'.

21 *Tehran, Yalta, Potsdam*, p. 159.

22 DBPO, I, pp. 377–86 on the second plenary meeting.

23 Ibid., pp. 386–90.

24 Ibid., pp. 418–33 on the third plenary meeting.

25 Ibid., pp. 458–70 on the fourth plenary meeting.

26 Ibid., pp. 499–512 on the fifth plenary meeting.

27 Ibid., pp. 530–9.

28 Ibid., pp. 530–47 on the sixth plenary meeting.

Chapter 6

1 DFPO, I, pp. 573–4.

2 Ibid., pp. 513, 549, 581–93, 599 on seventh plenary meeting and connected matters.

3 Ibid., pp. 642–56 on eighth plenary meeting.

4 Tsuyoshi Hasegawa, *Racing the Enemy: Stalin, Truman, and the Surrender of Japan*, Cambridge, MA, 2005, pp. 154–5.

5 DFPO, I, pp. 689–94 on ninth plenary meeting.

6 Ibid., pp. 709–10; FRUS, *Berlin*, vol. 2, pp. 1279, 1474, 1476, 1283; Harry S. Truman, *Year of Decisions, 1945*, London, 1955, p. 318; A. A. Offner, *Another Such Victory*, Stanford, 2002, pp. 76–7; Hasegawa, *Racing the Enemy*, pp. 155–63; Churchill, *The Second World War*, vol. 6, *Triumph and Tragedy*, p. 183. DBPO, I, p. 709, note 1 records that an undated, unsigned copy of the proclamation was given to the British delegation on 28 July 1945. As far as I have been able to discover, no immediate reference to the document was made by the British delegation. Hasegawa, *Racing the Enemy*, p. 336, note 60, observes: 'No original copy of the Proclamation was kept. The copy that was kept at the Byrnes Papers at Clemson University has Truman's signature, but Churchill's and Chiang Kai-shek's signatures were handwritten by Truman.'

7 David Dilks, ed., *The Diaries of Sir Alexander Cadogan, O.M., 1938–1945*, London, 1971, pp. 774, 778.

8 DFPO, I, pp. 956–7. Since there appeared to be no official British or American record of the Truman-Attlee meeting, DBPO quoted James F. Byrnes, *Speaking Frankly*, New York, 1947, p. 79.

9 Ibid., pp. 957–64 on tenth plenary meeting.

10 SSMK, vol. 6, pp. 220–8; FRUS, *Berlin*, vol. 2, pp. 471–6; Hasegawa, *Racing the Enemy*, pp. 163–5.

11 DFPO, I, pp. 1062–5.

12 There is no reference to Attlee's proposed statement in SSMK, vol. 6, p. 246.

13 DFPO, I, pp. 1072–90 on eleventh plenary meeting.

14 Ibid., pp. 1125–36 on twelfth plenary meeting.

15 Ibid., pp. 1143–4. Churchill's statement, printed in *The Times*, 7 August 1945, p. 4, makes much of Anglo-American collaboration in the making of the bomb. A statement on the same page by Truman also talks of scientists from the UK and United States collaborating in 'the harnessing of the basic power of the universe'.

16 Ibid., pp. 1146–51 for thirteenth plenary meeting and communications to Churchill and Eden.

17 David McCullough, *Truman*, New York, 1992, p. 452.

18 See, for example, *The Times*, 3 August 1945.

19 DFPO, I, pp. 1263–77 on Communiqué and Protocol; FRUS, *Berlin*, vol. 2, pp. 1478–98.

20 Truman, *Year of Decisions, 1945*, p. 322.

21 Cat Wilson, *Churchill on the Far East in the Second World War: Hiding the History of the 'Special Relationship'*, London, 2014, pp. 44, 51.

22 For this and other pertinent observations, see Arnold Toynbee and Veronica Wilson Toynbee, eds, *The Realignment of Europe: Survey of International Affairs, 1939–1946*, London, 1955, pp. 2–20.

23 Wilson, *Churchill on the Far East*, pp. 343–4.

24 DFPO, III, pp. xxiv, pp. 13–20, 55.

Chapter 7

1 DBPO, I, pp. 709–10.

2 Tsuyoshi Hasegawa, *Racing the Enemy: Stalin, Truman, and the Surrender of Japan*, Cambridge, MA, 2005, Chapters 5–7, and quotation, p. 298; Yukiko Koshiro, 'Eurasian Eclipse: Japan's End Game in World War II', *American Historical Review*, vol. 109, no. 2, 2004, pp. 417–44; David M. Glantz, *The Soviet Strategic Offensive in Manchuria: 'August Storm'*, London, 2003, p. xxv. See also Anatolii Koshkin, *Iaponskii front Marshala Stalina: Rossiia i Iaponiia: Ten Tsusimy dlinoiu v vek*, Moscow, 2004, pp. 270–98.

3 Richard B. Frank, *Downfall: The End of the Imperial Japanese Empire*, New York, 1999, p. 300.

4 L. Woodward, ed., *British Foreign Policy in the Second World War*, vol. 5, London, 1976, pp. 501, 505.

5   Ibid., pp. 505, 511–12, 514–15.

6   Ibid., pp. 526–7, 528.

7   Ibid., pp. 525–32; Glantz, *The Soviet Strategic Offensive*, 300.

8   Walter LaFeber, *The Origins of the Cold War, 1941–1947: A Historical Problem with Interpretations and Documents*, New York, 1971, pp. 69–72, 135–9; Walter LaFeber, *America, Russia, and the Cold War, 1945–1996*, New York, 1997, p. 39; Francis Williams, *A Prime Minister Remembers: The War and Post-War Memoirs of the Rt. Hon. Earl Attlee, K.G., P.C., O.M., C.H.: Based on the Private Papers and on a Series of Recorded Conversations*, London, 1961, pp. 102–17, 162.

9   Williams, *A Prime Minister Remembers*, pp. 96–119.

10   Kenneth M. Jensen, ed., *Origins of the Cold War: The Novikov, Kennan and Roberts 'Long Telegrams' of 1946*, Washington, DC, 1993, pp. 17–31.

11   Ibid., pp. 33–67.

12   Ibid., pp. 3–16. Earlier papers by Litvinov, Maisky and Gromyko had the common themes of (1) '*a primacy of Soviet security interests*'; (2) '*a unanimous acceptance of Big Three cooperation*' as the only effective basis for a peaceful and stable post-war world order protective of the Soviet interests at the same time; and (3) 'post-war cooperation in terms of *a great power concert based upon some kind of a division of the world into spheres of influence*'. See Vladimir O. Pechatnov (with his own italics), 'The Big Three after World War II: New Documents on Soviet Thinking about Post-War Relations with the United States and Great Britain', Working Paper No. 13, Cold War International History Project, Woodrow Wilson International Center for Scholars, Washington, DC, 1995, pp. 16–17.

13   Geoffrey Roberts, *Stalin's Wars: From World War to Cold War, 1939–1953*, London, 2006, p. 306.

14   Jensen, *Origins*, pp. 73–9.

15   Ibid., pp. 81–8.

16   Ibid., pp. 89–95.

17   Paul Dukes, *Russia under Catherine the Great*, vol. 1, Newtonville, 1978, p. 22.

18   Excerpts from the Monroe Doctrine and its context in Paul Dukes, *The Superpowers: A Short History*, London, 2000, pp. 15–16.

19   Walter LaFeber, *The American Age: United States Foreign Policy at Home and Abroad since 1750*, New York, 1989, p. 5.

20   On Wilsonism and Leninism and their sequel, see Dukes, *The Superpowers*, pp. 36–40.

21   Hughes and Sullivan quoted in Paul Dukes, *The USA in the Making of the USSR: The Washington Conference 1921–1922, and 'Uninvited Russia'*, London, 2004, p. 27.

22 Cat Wilson, *Churchill on the Far East in the Second World War: Hiding the History of the 'Special Relationship'*, London, 2014, p. 31.

23 Paul Kennedy, *The Rise and Fall of the Great Powers: Economic Change and Military Conflict from 1599 to 2000*, London, 1988, pp. 368, 425.

24 Warren F. Kimball, *Forged in War: Roosevelt, Churchill and the Second World War*, Chicago, 2003, pp. 281–2.

25 Howard K. Smith, *The State of Europe*, London, 1950, pp. 66–7.

26 Daniel Yergin, *The Prize: The Epic Quest for Oil, Money and Power*, New York, 1991, pp. 396, 407–8.

27 Quoted by Thomas G. Paterson, *Soviet-American Confrontation: Postwar Reconstruction and the Origins of the Cold War*, London, 1973, pp. 8–9.

28 Evan Mawdsley, *Thunder in the East: The Nazi-Soviet War, 1941–1945*, London, 2005, pp. 405–6.

Chapter 8

1 Fernand Braudel, *The Mediterranean and the Mediterranean World in the Age of Philip II*, trans. Sian Reynolds, vol. 2, London, 1975, p. 1244.

2 John Lewis Gaddis, *We Now Know: Rethinking Cold War History*, Oxford, 1997, p. 294.

3 Anatolii Koshkin, *Iaponskii front Marshala Stalina: Rossiia i Iaponiia: Ten' Tsusimy dlinoiu v vek*, Moscow, 2004, p. 5.

4 Vladimir Pechatnov, 'Ego imperiia/His empire' in series on fifty years without Stalin, *Rodina*, no. 2, 2003, pp. 19–25. The Joint Chiefs of Staff had completed 'Pincher', their first plan for global war against the Soviet Union, in April. 'Griddle', their plan for response to a Soviet attack on Europe with highest priority for Turkey and the Straits was completed by 15 August. A. A. Offner, *Another Such Victory: President Truman and the Cold War, 1945–1953*, Stanford, 2002, p. 169.

5 Quoted by Simon Sebag Montefiore *Stalin: The Court of the Red Tsar*, London, 2003, p. 454.

6 Alfred J. Reiber, *Stalin and the Struggle for Supremacy in Eurasia*, Cambridge, 2015, p. 283; 'Stalin as foreign policy-maker: avoiding war, 1927–1953', Sarah Davies and James Harris, eds., *Stalin: A New History*, Cambridge, 2005, pp. 140–1, 156.

7 Von Laue, 'Stalin among the Moral and Political Imperatives, or How to Judge Stalin?', *Soviet Union*, vol. 8, no. 1, 1981, pp. 5–13.

8   Quoted by Montefiore, *Stalin*, 4, p. 468.

9   Constantine Pleshakov, 'Studying Soviet Strategies and Decisionmaking in the Cold War Years', in Odd Arne Westad, ed., *Reviewing the Cold War: Approaches, Interpretations, Theory*, London, 2000, p. 235. Pleshakov's own italics.

10   James MacGregor Burns, *Roosevelt: The Soldier of Freedom, 1940–1945*, London, 1971, p. 608.

11   Quoted by David McCullough, *Truman*, New York, 1992, p. 398.

12   Harry S. Truman, *Year of Decisions, 1945*, London, 1955, pp. 12–13.

13   Offner, *Another Such Victory*, p. x.

14   Ibid., p. 470. See also James G. Hershberg, 'Where the Buck Stopped: Harry S. Truman and the Cold War' Feature Review in *Diplomatic History*, vol. 27, no. 5, 2003, pp. 735–9.

15   Wilson D. Miscamble, *From Roosevelt to Truman: Potsdam, Hiroshima, and the Cold War*, Cambridge, 2007, pp. 326, 331–2.

16   Oppenheimer and Stimson quoted by Richard Rhodes, *The Making of the Atomic Bomb*, London, 1988, pp. 642, 676.

17   Walter LaFeber, *The Origins of the Cold War, 1941–1947: A Historical Problem with Interpretations and Documents*, New York, 1971, pp. 67–8.

18   LaFeber, *The Origins*, p. 22.

19   Walter LaFeber, *America, Russia, and the Cold War, 1945–1996*, New York, 1997, pp. 26–7.

20   L. Collingham, *The Taste of War: World War Two and the Battle for Food*, London, 2011, pp. 145, 150–1. For a full consideration of Churchill's policy towards India, see C. Wilson, *Churchill on the Far East in the Second World War: hiding the history of the 'Special Relationship'*, London, 2014, Chapters 5 and 6, on Bengal famine in particular, pp. 110–14.

21   Gar Alperovitz, *The Decision to Use the Atomic Bomb and the Architecture of an American Myth*, London, 1995, p. 223.

22   John Kent, *British Imperial Strategy and the Origins of the Cold War, 1944–49*, Leicester, 1993, p. 3.

23   Francis Williams, *A Prime Minister Remembers: The War and Post-War Memoirs of the Rt Hon Earl Attlee, K.G., P.C., O.M., C.H.,: Based on His Private Papers and on a Series of Recorded Conversations*, London, 1961, pp. 118, 129.

24   See, for example, Kent, *British Imperial Strategy*.

25   A. A. Fursenko, 'U. Cherchill: "sozdavat mosty, a ne vozdvigat bar'ery"?': neizvestnye stranitsy istorii "kholodnoi voiny"', *Istoricheskie zapiski*, 2003, p. 7. And see Kevin Ruane, *Churchill and the Bomb in War and Cold War*, London, 2016.

26 Quoted by Wilson, *Churchill on the Far East*, p. 22.

27 Braudel, *The Mediterranean and the Mediterranean World*. First published in 1946.

28 Sidney Hook, *The Hero in History: A Study in Limitation and Possibility*, London, 1945, pp. 18, 101, 180–1. The book was first published in 1943.

29 Pieter Geyl, *Napoleon: For and Against*, Harmondsworth, 1965, pp. 7–10.

30 Vasily Grossman, *A Writer at War: With the Red Army, 1941–1945*, ed. and trans. Antony Beevor and Luba Vinogradova, London, 2005, xiii, pp. 54–5. Napoleon remained a byword for dictator, in, for example, *Animal Farm* where George Orwell gave the awesome name to the Stalin-like leader of the pigs.

31 Vasily Grossman, *Life and Fate*, trans. Robert Chandler, London, 1985, p. 79. Grossman completed the novel in 1960.

32 Ibid., pp. 94, 230.

33 Ibid., pp. 762–3, 766, 842.

34 Ibid., pp. 596, 870–1.

35 See, for example, Paul Dukes, *Minutes to Midnight: History and the Anthropocene Era since 1763*, London, 2011. And see Wikipedia on the Anthropocene.

36 Jonathan Fenby, *Alliance: The Inside Story of How Roosevelt, Stalin and Churchill Won One War and Began Another*, London, 2006, p. 30.

37 See, for example, H. L'Etang, *The Pathology of Leadership*, New York, 1970, pp. 86–101, 144–58, 200–3. And see David Owen, *In Sickness and in Power: Illness in Heads of Government during the Last 100 Years*, London, 2008, especially pp. 364–6 on hubris syndrome.

38 Archie Brown, *The Myth of the Strong Leader: Political Leadership in the Modern Age*, London, 2014, p. ix.

39 Chris Bellamy, *Absolute War: Soviet Russia in the Second World War: A Modern History*, 2008, p. 2; Evan Mawdsley, *Thunder in the East: The Nazi-Soviet War, 1941–1945*, London, 2005, p. 404.

40 A.E.V. Oliver, *Kriege*, Maidstone, 1998, pp. 107–9.

41 Bellamy, *Absolute War*, pp. 28–30.

42 Paul Fussell, *Wartime: Understanding and Behaviour in the Second World War*, Oxford, 1989, p. 132. Quote from Eveleyn Waugh on p. 4.

43 Ibid., p. 285.

44 Gerhard L. Weinberg, *A World at Arms: A Global History of World War II*, Cambridge, 2004, 894.

45 G. V. Plekhanov, *The Role of the Individual in History* as published with Plekhanov's own italics in his *Fundamental Problems of Marxism*, London, 1969, p. 177.

Further Study and Select Bibliography

Further study

An important development in the last decade or so has been the extended application of Wikipedia as an aid to research, first supplementing, later near to supplanting the still useful encyclopaedia as a source of information. Let us take an example the Wikipedia entry on the least known member of the later Big Three, Clement Attlee, Churchill's successor as the UK's prime minister, who is given a full treatment with no less than 148 notes and a considerable range of references. This may be supplemented by a freely accessible BBC programme entitled 'The Improbable Mr Attlee' by the authoritative David Reynolds (most recently accessed 27 May 2016). The other members of the Big Three may be examined even more extensively via YouTube as well as Wikipedia. Among subjects illuminated by Wikipedia, with appropriate maps, are the Curzon Line, the Montreux Convention, Kars and Ardahan.

However helpful, these new ways of advancing our understanding, they are not complete without books and articles, which provide essential content, shape and interpretation. The Select Bibliography lists the works which I have made most use of in this present endeavour.

Beyond history in Wikipedia and the Select Bibliography, we must take note of pertinent developments in other disciplines. Two years after Hiroshima and Nagasaki, in 1947, the Doomsday Clock was created by a group of atomic scientists to symbolize the perils facing humanity. Sixty years on, in 2007, it was set at five minutes before the final bell at midnight, the reasons given including for the first time new developments in the life sciences and technology, and the threat of climate change. Beginning with the Industrial Revolution from the late eighteenth century onwards, a new age, the Anthropocene, reached a key moment via the atomic bomb in 1945. To put the point mildly, the confluence of historical and geological time has underlined the significance of the fall of the Big Three in 1945, and needs to be taken into consideration in all further study.

Select bibliography

Primary sources (and abbreviations)

Beitzell, R., ed. and intro., *Tehran, Yalta, Potsdam: The Soviet Protocols*, Hattiesburg, 1970.

Correspondence between the Chairman of the Council of Ministers of the USSR and the Presidents of the USA and Prime Ministers of Great Britain during the Great Patriotic War of 1941–1945, Moscow, 1957.

Documents on British Foreign Policy Overseas, eds. Butler, Rohan and Pelly, M.E., Series I, vol. I, *The Conference at Potsdam, July–August 1945*, London, 1984. [DFPO, I]

Documents on British Foreign Policy Overseas, eds. Bullen, Roger and Pelly, M.E., Series I, vol. II, *Conferences and Conversations 1945: London, Washington and Moscow*, London, 1985. [DFPO, II]

Documents on British Foreign Policy, eds. Bullen, Roger and Pelly, M.E., Series I, vol. III, *Britain and America: Negotiation of the United States loan, 3 August–7 December 1945*, London, 1986. [DFPO, III]

Encyclopaedia Britannica, Twelfth Edition, 3 vols. Supplementing Eleventh Edition of 1910–11, Cambridge, 1921–2; Thirteenth Edition, Supplementing Eleventh and Twelfth Editions, London and New York, 1926.

Foreign Relations of the United States: Diplomatic Papers: The Conferences at Cairo and Tehran, 1943, Washington, DC, 1961. [FRUS, Tehran]

Foreign Relations of the United States: Diplomatic Papers: The Conferences at Malta and Yalta, Washington, DC, 1955. [FRUS, Yalta]

Foreign Relations of the United States: Diplomatic Papers: The Conference of Berlin (The Potsdam Conference), 2 vols., Washington, DC, 1960. [FRUS, Potsdam]

Jensen, K.M., *Origins of the Cold War: The Novikov, Kennan and Roberts 'Long Telegrams' of 1946: With Three New Commentaries*, Washington, DC, 1993. [Jensen]

Kimball, W., *Churchill and Roosevelt: The Complete Correspondence*, 3 vols., London, 1984. [Kimball]

Ross, G., ed. and intro., *The Foreign Office and the Kremlin: British Documents on Anglo-Soviet Relations, 1941–1945*, Cambridge, 1984.

Sovetskii Soiuz na mezhdunarodnykh konferentsiiakh perioda Velikoi Otechestvennoi Voiny, 1941–1945gg.

  tom II, *Tegeranskaia konferentsiia rukovoditelei trekh soiuznykh derzhav - SSSR, SSHA i Velikobritanii (28 noiabria – 1 dekabria 1943) sbornik dokumentov*, Moscow, 1978. [SSMK, vol. 2] tom IV, *Krymskaia konferentsiia … (4–11 fevralia 1945) sbornik dokumentov*, Moscow, 1979. [SSMK, vol. 4]

tom VI, *Berlinskaia (Potsdamskaia) konferentsiia … (17 iulia – 2 avgusta 1945g.): sbornik dokumentov*, Moscow, 1984. [SSMK, vol. 6]

Stalin, J.V., *Collected Works*, 13 vols., Moscow, 1953–4.

The Tehran, Yalta and Potsdam Conferences: Documents, Moscow, 1969. [*Tehran, Yalta, Potsdam*]

'Transcript of the Talk between J. V. Stalin and F. D. Roosevelt, November 28, 1943', *International Affairs* [Moscow], no. 7, 1961. [IA]

'Transcript of the Talk between Stalin and Roosevelt', November 29, 1943', *International Affairs*, no. 7, 1961. [IA]

'Transcript of the Talk between Stalin and Churchill, November 30, 1943' and 'Talk at the Luncheon', *International Affairs*, no. 8, 1961. [IA]

Woodward, Sir L., ed., *British Foreign Policy in the Second World War*, 5 vols., London, 1970–6.

Diaries and memoirs

Byrnes, J.F., *Speaking Frankly*, New York, 1947.

Byrnes, J.F., *All in One Lifetime*, New York, 1947.

Campbell, T.M. and Herring, G.C., eds., *The Diaries of Edward R. Stettinius, Jr., 1943–1946*, New York, 1975.

Churchill, W.S., *The Second World War*, 6 vols. vol. 1, *The Gathering Storm*, London, 1948; vol. 2, *Their Finest Hour*, London, 1949; vol. 3, *The Grand Alliance*, London, 1950; vol. 4, *The Hinge of Fate*, London, 1951; vol. 5, *Closing the Ring*, London, 1952; vol. 6, *Triumph and Tragedy*, London, 1954.

Deane, J.R., *The Strange Alliance: The Story of Our Efforts at Wartime Collaboration with Russia*, New York, 1947.

Dilks, D., ed., *The Diaries of Sir Alexander Cadogan, O.M., 1938–1945*, London, 1971.

Jensen, K.M., ed., *Origins of the Cold War: The Novikov, Kennan and Roberts 'Long Telegrams' of 1946*, Washington, DC, 1993.

Leahy, W.D., *I Was There*, New York, 1950.

Life and Letters of Mandell Creighton, by his wife, vol. 1, London, 1904.

Oliver, A.E.W., *Kriege*, Maidstone, 1988.

Stettinius, E.R. Jr., *Roosevelt and the Russians: The Yalta Conference*, ed. Johnson, W., London, 1950.

Truman, H.S., *Year of Decisions: 1945*, London, 1955.

Williams, F., *A Prime Minister Remembers: The War and Post-War Memoirs of the Rt Hon Earl Attlee, K.G., P.C., O.M., C.H.: Based on His Private Papers and on a Series of Recorded Conversations*, London, 1961.

Literature and philosophy

Carlyle, T., *On Heroes, Hero-Worship and the Hero in History*, ElecBook, 2001.

Geyl, P., *Napoleon: For and Against*, Harmondsworth, 1965.

Grossman, V., *A Writer at War: With the Red Army, 1941–1945*, ed. and trans. Beevor, A. and Vinogradova, London, 2008.

Grossman, V., *Life and Fate*, trans. Chandler, R., London, 1985.

Hook, S., *The Hero in History: A Study in Limitation and Possibility*, London, 1945.

Marx, K., *Selected Works*, vol. 2, London, 1942.

Plekhanov, G.V., *The Role of the Individual in History*, appendix to his *Fundamental Problems of Marxism*, London, 1969.

Tolstoy, L., *War and Peace*, trans. Edmonds, R., London, 1973.

Secondary sources

Aleksandrov, O.A., 'Berlin: The Downfall, 1945', National Committee of Russian Historians: Russian Association of the Second World War Historians, *Information Bulletin*, no. 7, 2002.

Alperovitz, G., *The Decision to Use the Atomic Bomb and the Architecture of an American Myth*, London, 1995.

Beetham, David, *Max Weber and the Theory of Modern Politics*, Cambridge, 1985.

Bellamy, C., *Absolute War: Soviet Russia in the Second World War*, London, 2008.

Braudel, F., *The Mediterranean and the Mediterranean World in the Age of Philip II*, 2 vols., London, 1975.

Brown, A., *The Myth of the Strong Leader: Political Leadership in the Modern Age*, London, 2015.

Bryant, A., *The Turn of the Tide and Triumph in the West: A History of the War Years Based on the Diaries of Field Marshal Lord Alanbrooke, Chief of the Imperial General Staff*, London, 1957, 1959.

Burns, J.M., *Roosevelt: The Soldier of Freedom, 1940–1945*, London, 1971.

Carlyle, T., *On Heroes, Hero-Worship and the Heroic in History*, London, no date.

Clemens, D.S., *Yalta*, Oxford, 1970.

Collingham, L., *The Taste of War: World War Two and the Battle for Food*, London, 2011.

Costiglia, Frank, 'After Roosevelt's Death: Dangerous Emotions, Divisive Discourses, and the Abandoned Alliance', *Diplomatic History*, vol. 34, no. 1, 2010.

Davies, S. and Harris, J., eds, *Stalin: A New History*, Cambridge, 2005.

Dilks, D., 'Cherchill i operatsiia 'Nemyshlimoe', 1945g., *Novaia i noveishaia istoriia*, no. 3, 2002.

Dilks, D., *The Conference at Potsdam, 1945*, Hull, 1995.

Dukes, P., *Minutes to Midnight: History and the Anthropocene Era since 1763*, London, 2011.

Dukes, P., 'The Rise and Fall of the Big Three', *History Review*, no. 52, 2005.

Dukes, P., *The Superpowers: A Short History*, London, 2000.

Dukes, P., *The USA in the Making of the USSR: The Washington Conference, 1921–1922, and 'Uninvited Russia'*, London, 2004.

Edmonds, R., *The Big Three: Churchill, Roosevelt and Stalin in Peace and War*, London, 1991.

Edmonds, R., *Setting the Mould: The United States and Britain, 1945–1950*, Oxford, 1986.

Feis, H., *Between War and Peace: The Potsdam Conference*, Princeton, 1960.

Feis, H., *Churchill, Roosevelt, Stalin: The War They Waged and the Peace They Sought*, Princeton, 1957.

Feis, H., *Japan Subdued: The Atomic Bomb and the End of the War in the Pacific*, Princeton, 1961.

Fenby, J., *Alliance: The Inside Story of How Roosevelt, Stalin and Churchill Won One War and Began Another*, London, 2006.

Fox, W.T.R., *The Super-Powers: The United States, Britain and the Soviet Union – Their Responsibility for the Peace*, London, 1944.

Fox, W.T.R., 'The Super-Powers: Then and Now', *International Journal*, vol. 15, 1979–80, pp. 417–430.

Frank, R.B., *Downfall: The End of the Imperial Japanese Empire*, New York, 1999.

Fursenko, A.A., 'U. Cherchill: "sozdavat mosty, a ne vozdvigat bar'ery"?: neizvestnye stranitsy istorii "kholodnoi voiny"', *Istoricheskie zapiski*, vol. 7, 2003.

Fussell, P., *Wartime: Understanding and Behaviour in the Second World War*, Oxford, 1989.

Gaddis, J.L., *We Now Know: Rethinking Cold War History*, Oxford, 1997.

Gallichio, M.S., *The Cold War Begins in Asia: American East Asian Policy and the Fall of the Japanese Empire*, New York, 1988.

Gardiner, P., ed. and intro., *Theories of History*, London, 1959.

Geyl, P. *Napoleon: For and Against*, London, 1949.

Glantz, D.M., *Soviet Operational and Tactical Combat in Manchuria, 1945: 'August Storm'*, London, 2003.

Glantz, D.M., *The Soviet Strategic Offensive in Manchuria, 1945: 'August Storm'*, London, 2003.

Gorlizki, Y., and Khlevniuk, O., *Cold Peace: Stalin and the Soviet Ruling Circle, 1945–1953*, Oxford, 2004.

Gorodetsky, G., *Stafford Cripps' Mission to Moscow, 1940–42*, Cambridge, 1984.

Hasegawa, T., *Racing the Enemy: Stalin, Truman, and the Surrender of Japan*, Cambridge, MA, 2005.

Hershberg, J.G., 'Where the Buck Stopped: Harry S. Truman and the Cold War', *Diplomatic History*, vol. 27, no. 5, 2003.

Holloway, D., *Stalin and the Bomb: The Soviet Union and Atomic Energy, 1939–1956*, London, 1994.

Kassof, B., 'A Book of Socialism: Stalinist Culture and the First Edition of the Bolshaia sovetskaia entsiklopedia', *Kritika: Explorations in Russian and Eurasian History*, vol. 6, no. 1, Winter 2005 (New Series), pp. 87–95.

Kennedy, P., *The Rise and Fall of the Great Powers: Economic Change and Military Conflict from 1500 to 1800*, London, 1988.

Kent, J., *British Imperial Strategy and the Origins of the Cold War, 1944–49*, Leicester, 1993.

Kimball, W.F., *Forged in War: Churchill, Roosevelt and the Second World War*, New York, 1997.

Kimball, W.F., ed. and intro., *Franklin D. Roosevelt and the World Crisis, 1937–1945*, London, 1973.

Kimball, W.F., 'Franklin D. Roosevelt and World War II', *Presidential Studies Quarterly*, vol. 34, no. 1, 2004.

Koshiro, Y., 'Eurasian Eclipse: Japan's End Game in World War II', *American Historical Review*, vol. 109, no. 2, 2004.

Koshkin, A., *Iaponskii Front Marshala Stalina: Ten' Tsusimy dlinoi v vek*, Moscow, 2004.

LaFeber, W., *America, Russia, and the Cold War, 1945–1996*, New York, 1997.

LaFeber, W., *The American Age: United States Foreign Policy at Home and Abroad since 1750*, New York, 1989.

LaFeber, W., *The Clash: U.S.-Japanese Relations throughout History*, New York, 1997.

LaFeber, W., *The Origins of the Cold War, 1941–1947: A Historical Problem with Interpretations and Documents*, New York, 1971.

Larres, K., *Churchill's Cold War: The Politics of Personal Diplomacy*, London, 2002.

Leffler, M.P., *For the Soul of Mankind: The United States, the Soviet Union, and the Cold War*, New York, 2007.

Leffler, M.P., 'The Cold War: What Do "We Know Now"', *American Historical Review*, vol. 104, no. 2, 1999.

Leffler, M.P., and Westad, O.A., *Cambridge History of the Cold War*, 3 vols., Cambridge, 2010.

L'Etang, H., *The Pathology of Leadership*, New York, 1970.

McCullough, D., *Truman*, New York, 1992.

Mawdsley, E., *Thunder in the East: The Nazi-Soviet War 1941–1945*, London, 2005.

Mikolajczyk, S., *The Pattern of Soviet Domination*, London, 1948.

Miscamble, W.D., *From Roosevelt to Truman: Potsdam, Hiroshima, and the Cold War*, Cambridge, 2008.

Mitter, R., *China's War with Japan, 1937–1945: The Struggle for Survival*, London, 2013.

Montefiore, S.S., *Stalin: The Court of the Red Tsar*, London, 2003.

Myagkov, M. Yu., 'The Seminar in London' [on 'Churchill and Stalin', London], *Information Bulletin*, National Committee of Russian Historians: Russian Association of the Second World Historians, no. 7, 2002.

North, J., 'Soviet Prisoners of War: Forgotten Nazi Victim of World War II', *World War II*, January–February, 2006.

Offner, A.A., *Another Such Victory: President Truman and the Cold War, 1945–1953*, Stanford, 2002.

Owen, David, *In Sickness and in Power: Illness in Heads of Government during the Last 100 Years*, London, 2008.

Pechatnov, V., 'Ego imperiia', in Series on 50 Years without Stalin, *Rodina*, no. 2, 2003.

Pechatnov, V., *Stalin, Ruzvel't, Trumen: SSSR i SSHA v 1940-kh gg.: dokumental'nye ocherki*, Moscow, 2006.

Pechatnov, V., 'The Big Three after World War II: New Documents on Soviet Thinking about Post-War Relations with the United States and Great Britain', Working Paper No. 13, Cold War International History Project, Woodrow Wilson International Center for Scholars, Washington, DC, 1995.

Plokhy, S.M., *Yalta: The Price of Peace*, London, 2011.

Reynolds, D., *In Command of History: Churchill Fighting and Writing the Second World War*, London, 2005.

Rieber, A.J., *Stalin and the Struggle for Supremacy in Asia*, Cambridge, 2015.

Roberts, G., 'A Chance for Peace? The Soviet Campaign to End the Cold War, 1953–1955', Working Paper No. 57, Cold War International History Project, Woodrow Wilson International Center for Scholars, Washington, DC, 2008.

Roberts, G., 'Beware Greek Gifts: The Churchill-Stalin "Percentages" Agreement of 1944', *Mir istorii*, no. 1, 2003 (online).

Roberts, G., *Stalin's Wars: From World War to Cold War, 1939–1953*, New Haven, 2007.

Ruane, K., *Churchill and the Bomb in War and Cold War*, London, 2016.

Rzheshevskii, O.A., 'Sekretnye voennye plany u Cherchilla protiv SSSR v mae 1945', *Novaia i noveishaia istoriia*, no. 3, 1999.

Rzheshevskii, O.A., *Stalin i Cherchill: Vstrechi, besedy, diskussii: Dokumenty, kommentarii, 1941–1945*, Moscow, 2004.

Smith, H.K., *The State of Europe*, London, 1950.

Stoff, M.B., *Oil, War, and American Security: The Search for a National Policy on Foreign Oil, 1941-1947*, New Haven, 1980.

Streit, C., *Keine Kameraden: Die Wehrmacht und die sowietischen Kriegsgefangen, 1941–1945*, Bonn, 1978.

Thorne, C., *Allies of a Kind: The United States, Britain and the War against Japan, 1941–1945*, Oxford, 1979.

Toye, Richard, *Churchill's Empire: The World That Made Him and the World He Made*, London, 2010.

Toynbee, A., and Toynbee, V.W., eds, *The Realignment of Europe: Survey of International Affairs, 1939–1946*, London, 1955.

Von Laue, T.H., 'Stalin among the Moral and Political Imperatives, or How to Judge Stalin?', *Soviet Union*, vol. 8, no. 1, 1981, with comments from A.G. Meyer, H.R. Alker, Jr and F.C. Barghorn.

Von Laue, T.H., 'Stalin in Focus', *Slavic Review*, vol. 42, no. 3, 1983.

Weinberg, G.L., *A World at Arms: A Global History of World War II*, Cambridge, 1994.

Westad, O.A., *Reviewing the Cold War: Approaches, Interpretations, Theory*, London, 2000.

Westad, O.A., *The Global Cold War: Third World Interventions and the Making of Our Times*, Cambridge, 2007.

Wilson, C., *Churchill on the Far East in the Second World War: Hiding the History of the 'Special Relationship'*, London, 2014.

Yegorova, N.I., and Chubarian, A.O., eds, *Kholodnaia voina, 1945–63: fakty, sobytiia*, Moscow, 2003.

Yergin, D., *The Prize: The Epic Quest for Oil, Money and Power*, New York, 1991.

Young, J., *Winston Churchill's Last Campaign: Britain and the Cold War, 1951–1955*, Oxford, 1996.

Index